Speaking Truth to Power

Two decades of analysis in the Department of Health

T0300271

Clive Smee

 **CRC Press**
Taylor & Francis Group
Boca Raton London New York

CRC Press is an imprint of the
Taylor & Francis Group, an **informa** business

First published 2005 by Radcliffe Publishing

Published 2018 by CRC Press
Taylor & Francis Group
6000 Broken Sound Parkway NW, Suite 300
Boca Raton, FL 33487-2742

ISBN-13: 978-1-85775-781-1 (pbk)

This book contains information obtained from authentic and highly regarded sources. While all reasonable efforts have been made to publish reliable data and information, neither the author[s] nor the publisher can accept any legal responsibility or liability for any errors or omissions that may be made. The publishers wish to make clear that any views or opinions expressed in this book by individual editors, authors or contributors are personal to them and do not necessarily reflect the views/opinions of the publishers. The information or guidance contained in this book is intended for use by medical, scientific or health-care professionals and is provided strictly as a supplement to the medical or other professional's own judgement, their knowledge of the patient's medical history, relevant manufacturer's instructions and the appropriate best practice guidelines. Because of the rapid advances in medical science, any information or advice on dosages, procedures or diagnoses should be independently verified. The reader is strongly urged to consult the relevant national drug formulary and the drug companies' and device or material manufacturers' printed instructions, and their websites, before administering or utilizing any of the drugs, devices or materials mentioned in this book. This book does not indicate whether a particular treatment is appropriate or suitable for a particular individual. Ultimately it is the sole responsibility of the medical professional to make his or her own professional judgements, so as to advise and treat patients appropriately. The authors and publishers have also attempted to trace the copyright holders of all material reproduced in this publication and apologize to copyright holders if permission to publish in this form has not been obtained. If any copyright material has not been acknowledged please write and let us know so we may rectify in any future reprint.

Visit the Taylor & Francis Web site at
http://www.taylorandfrancis.com

and the CRC Press Web site at
http://www.crcpress.com

British Library Cataloguing in Publication Data

A catalogue record for this book is available from the British Library.

Typeset by Anne Joshua & Associates, Oxford

Contents

Preface

The idea for this book came from John Wyn Owen, Secretary of the Nuffield Trust. I am grateful to him and to the Trust for funding its production through the offer of a Queen Elizabeth the Queen Mother Fellowship.

The book was written while I was living in New Zealand. Thanks are due to the New Zealand Treasury for allowing me to use their facilities to print out numerous drafts of each chapter, and to colleagues in the health section for listening patiently to several presentations. I am also grateful to the New Zealand Ministry of Health for providing a counterpoint from which I could appreciate more clearly the distinctive features of English health policy making and the role of analysis in that process. A very special thank you is due to Annette Evans who typed out the first drafts of 10 of the 12 chapters with great efficiency, speed and charm.

Although I take responsibility for the book's errors of omission and commission, in many ways it reflects a joint effort by past and present members of the Economics and Operational Research Division of the Department of Health. All contributed in some way, if only by providing subject matter. Those who contributed comments and materials for individual chapters include Robert Anderson, Keith Derbyshire, Peter Dick, Frances Dickinson, Richard Gibbs, Maria Goddard, Andre Hare, John Henderson, Leslie Hughes, Howard Malin, Barry McCormick, Richard Murray, Geoff Royston, Becky Sandhu and Nick York. I am grateful to them all.

Two former colleagues (and I hope friends) read and provided stimulating comments on early drafts of every single chapter. They are Jeremy Hurst and Mike Parsonage. If the book has any merits it is almost certainly due to their contributions. I cannot thank them enough for their patience and encouragement.

Drafts of Chapters 2 to 6 were discussed at a workshop organised by the Nuffield Trust in October 2003. I appreciate the comments of the Department of Health and academic colleagues who attended and commented at the time and/or subsequently in writing.

The book is built round my 18 years as Chief Economic Adviser in the Department of Health and, prior to 1989, in the Department of Health and Social Security. Many colleagues contributed to the experiences and opportunities that I enjoyed during those years. Among senior officials who opened doors for me I am particularly grateful to Sir Patrick Nairne, Sir Christopher France, Sir Graham Hart, Sir Alan Langlands and Sir Joe Pilling. It was also a privilege to work for eight Secretaries of State. Unsurprisingly, some were more interested in or supportive of the contribution of analysis than others. Three who were particularly receptive to, or tolerant of, the role of economics and operational research were Sir Norman Fowler, Virginia Bottomley and Alan Milburn. Their recognition of the virtues of a 'challenge' function – of the value of alternative evidence-based views – was essential for ensuring that analysts were able to 'speak truth to power' during this period.

Finally, I am grateful to my wife, Denise, and my children, Anna, David and Elizabeth, for their continued encouragement and support.

Clive Smee
July 2005

About the author

From 1984 to 2002 Clive Smee was Chief Economic Adviser and Head of Analytical Services in the UK Department of Health. During this period he served eight Secretaries of State. He has a particular interest in health reforms, both national and international. He led the NHS National Beds Inquiry and was part author of the 2000 NHS Plan. He has acted as a health economics consultant for a number of countries and from 1987 to 1990 he chaired the OECD's Social Policy Working Party. He has also been a long term member of the Commonwealth Fund's International Program in Health Policy and Practice Coordinating Committee. In 1997 he was made a Companion of the Order of the Bath (CB) for services to health.

Earlier in his career Clive worked as an economist for the UK Treasury, Cabinet Office, DHSS and Ministry of Overseas Development. From 2002 to 2004 he was principal adviser on social policy in the New Zealand Treasury. He has been a Visiting Professor of Economics at the University of Surrey since 1995.

This book was written when Clive was the Nuffield Trust Queen Elizabeth the Queen Mother Fellow.

The Nuffield Trust

FOR RESEARCH AND POLICY
STUDIES IN HEALTH SERVICES

The Nuffield Trust is one of the leading independent health policy charitable trusts in the UK. It was established as the Nuffield Provincial Hospitals Trust in 1940 by Viscount Nuffield (William Morris), the founder of Morris Motors. In 1998 the Trustees agreed that the official name of the trust should more fully reflect the Trust's purposes and, in consultation with the Charity Commission, adopted the name The Nuffield Trust for Research and Policy Studies in Health Services, retaining 'The Nuffield Trust' as its working name.

The Nuffield Trust's mission is to promote independent analysis and informed debate on UK healthcare policy. The Nuffield Trust's purpose is to communicate evidence and encourage an exchange around developed or developing knowledge in order to illuminate recognised and emerging issues.

It achieves this through its principal activities:

- bringing together a wide national and international network of people involved in UK healthcare through a series of meetings, workshops and seminars
- commissioning research through its publications and grants programme to inform policy debate
- encouraging inter-disciplinary exchange between clinicians, legislators, academics, healthcare professionals and management, policy makers, industrialists and consumer groups
- supporting evidence-based health policy and practice
- sharing its knowledge in the home countries and internationally through partnerships and alliances.

To find out more, please refer to our website or contact:

The Nuffield Trust
59 New Cavendish St
London
W1G 7LP
Website: www.nuffieldtrust.org.uk
Email: mail@nuffieldtrust.org.uk
Tel: +44 (0)20 7631 8458
Fax: +44 (0)20 7631 8451

Charity number: 209201

List of Trustees

Chapter 1

Introduction

Introduction

In his seminal work, *Speaking Truth to Power: the art and craft of policy analysis*, Aaron Wildavsky notes that:

> *Policy analysis must create problems that decision makers are able to handle with the variables under their control and in the time available.*[1]

This book is about how analysts in the UK Department of Health (DH) helped to find and define such problems and to suggest solutions over the period 1984–2002.

More precisely, the book has three main purposes:

1. to provide a history of selected analytical issues in healthcare over the last 20 years, and the role of Department of Health (DH) analysts in addressing those issues.*
2. to distil lessons from that history and experience in the hope that they may be of encouragement, interest or value to future health service analysts, particularly those thinking of working in the public sector
3. in passing, to provide a personal commentary on some of the more important analytical issues in healthcare.

The book adopts a selective and subjective approach to these aims. The next section of this introduction discusses the coverage of the book in terms of time period, analytical disciplines and issues. The following section provides a short history of the way in which analysts were organised in the Department of Health. There is then a discussion of the role of analysts in the Department, their formal and informal relationships with Civil Service colleagues, and their contribution to Departmental decision making.

Coverage

The focus of this book is the time period 1984–2002. The dates were chosen entirely for personal reasons. They cover the period for which I was first the Chief Economic Adviser to the Department of Health and Social Security (DHSS) and then, after the split of that Department, had a similar role in the Department of Health (DH). Of course, 1984 was not the beginning of a formal analytical function in the DHSS. I inherited the mantels of three distinguished Chief

---

*In this book, 'analysis' involves the examination and interpretation of data and other information, both qualitative and quantitative, in order to provide insights to improve the identification of problems, the formulation of policy and the delivery of services.

Economists, namely Leonard Nicholson, Andrew Roy and David Pole, and of the first Director of Operational Research, namely Alex McDonald. No more did 2002 represent the end of an analytical function in the DH. The post of which I was custodian is now in the safe hands of Professor Barry McCormick, and the number of internal economists and operational researchers continues to grow. So the two decades covered here are part of a much longer journey. Nevertheless, they were periods of dramatic and radical change for healthcare policy, including the Conservative internal market reforms announced in 1989 and the Labour 'investment and reform programme' from 1997 onwards. As this monograph attempts to illustrate, they were also years in which analysis, particularly in the form of economics and operational research, had an increasing influence on both the content of health policy and the process of decision making.

The terms 'analysis' and 'analyst' can be used to cover a wide range of disciplines and types of work. This book focuses almost entirely on the economics and operational research analysis carried out by the professional economists and operational research (OR) analysts who were employed by the Department and brigaded together in the command that became known as the 'Economics and Operational Research Division' (EOR). There were and are other groups in the Department who rightly call themselves 'analysts'. These include many of the professional statisticians in what was known as the Statistics Division, and the research officers in the Research and Development Division. Other members of the Department may have training in economics, operational research or statistics, even though their current roles are in management or policy admin- istration. Most administrative and policy colleagues have also of necessity developed skills in political and administrative analysis. Their contributions to policy analysis and development have often been vital in, for example, high- lighting considerations of administrative and political feasibility.* However, their role is not the subject of this book.

The two professional groups which during this period were brigaded together in the EOR share some analytical competencies in common (e.g. modelling), and have others in which they provide a diversity of skills and knowledge (e.g. economists' knowledge of markets and OR skills in analysing 'whole systems'). Consequently the different professions sometimes worked together in closely meshed inter-disciplinary teams. For example, the review of the Resource Allocation Working Party (RAWP) brought together economists, operational research analysts and statisticians.[2] On other occasions they worked separately, while remaining within a work programme for the whole division. For example, it was OR colleagues who led the command's work on risk communication, emergency planning and the innovative use of modern communication tech- nology to deliver faster and responsive services.[3] For reasons of manageability, and reflecting my own disciplinary background, this monograph focuses mainly on the contribution of economists.

A further dimension concerning which it has been necessary to be selective is the policy subjects covered. To avoid tedium I have focused on the policy issues in which analysts, particularly economists, have played a major role. Even within this limited domain there are some major exclusions. Virtually nothing is said

---

* I am grateful to Rudolf Klein for rightly insisting I make clear that policy analysis is not synonymous with economic analysis.

about personal social services. In this area, Departmental economists and operational researchers made major contributions to modelling future needs, to appraising alternative funding regimes and to developing a performance-monitoring framework. This contribution deserves a separate book on its own (perhaps one of my colleagues will endeavour to take it on). There are also some major omissions in the health field. There has already been reference to risk management and emergency planning. In addition, virtually nothing is said about work on equity, particularly in relation to resource allocation. The only legitimate excuse for this exclusion is that it is an area that has attracted considerable academic interest and work and has therefore been fairly extensively written up elsewhere.[4,5] There are also no chapters devoted specifically to the contribution of internal analysts to perhaps the two most seminal reforms of the period, namely Working for Patients (1989) and the NHS Plan (2000), although they receive many references. This reflects a decision to organise the book around more general themes, not the unimportance of the contribution of analysts to these reforms – in fact it was substantial for both of them.*

The history and organisation of analysts

The Department of Health and Social Security established an Economic Adviser's Office (EAO) in 1968 and an Operational Research Service (ORS) in 1970. The ORS initially focused on health issues while the EAO confined its attention to income distribution and social security questions. The first two health economists were appointed in 1970, and the ORS moved into social security in 1974. The two professional divisions grew steadily in the 1970s under their respective directors. On the retirement of the founding director of the ORS in 1982, the two groups were brought together under the leadership of the then Chief Economic Adviser, David Pole. However, there continued to be a separate professional Head of Operational Research Services.

The DHSS command that I inherited in 1984 was still known as the Economic Adviser's Office and Operational Research Service. The economists were divided into one branch of about 10 professionals working on health issues, and two branches with slightly larger total numbers working on income distribution and social security issues. The operational research analysts were divided into three branches with a rather greater relative weight on health issues. There was also a multi-disciplinary team of operational researchers, economists and statisticians (CARP), led by a senior operational research analyst. The staff of the command were distributed between several buildings north and south of the river in London.

* For both reforms the EOR provided members of the core teams that drafted the White Papers. In the review leading to *Working for Patients*, members of the Economic Adviser's Office (a precursor to EOR) laid out the main strategic options, analysed alternative financing options, reviewed the weaknesses in incentives already identified by Alain Enthoven and led the development of proposals for capital charges. They also contributed substantially to the subsequent Working Papers, particularly on self-governing hospitals, led the consultation with the NHS on the new pricing regime and developed evaluation frameworks for the key elements of the reforms.

For the NHS Plan, the EOR drafted the chapter on 'Options for Funding Healthcare', summarised the results of the consultation it had led on the National Beds Inquiry, added references to self-care and digital TV, estimated the requirements for additional hospital beds, staff and staff training, and provided most of the modelling and analysis underlying the Plan's other major policy initiatives.

In 1989, the Department of Health and Social Security (DHSS) was split into the Department of Health (DH) and the Department of Social Security (DSS). For a short time a single Chief Economist post supported the two largest government expenditure programmes, a situation that could not be allowed to continue. Reflecting the growing importance attached to economics and operational research analysis, the establishment of the two new departments was accompanied by the setting up of two separate analytical divisions of equal status to their progenitor. I remained Head of the Health Division, which was now renamed the Economics and Operational Research Division (EOR).* The EOR was divided into four branches (two of health economists and two of operational research analysts). The division now had about 30 professional members and 10 administrative and support staff.

The divide of the old DHSS into two departments of state had barely been managed before Ministers decided to underline the separate role of the NHS Management Executive by relocating its staff to a major new office, Quarry House, in Leeds. Following the principle that analysts should be located close to the staff whom they advise, the years 1991–92 saw roughly half of the complement of the EOR move to Leeds. Although the analytical staff in Leeds were on the budget of the Management Executive, that budget continued to be managed by the Chief Economic Adviser. I had offices in both Leeds and London and regularly commuted between the two. A number of attempts to split the division into two completely separate units were successfully rebuffed on the grounds that this would reduce flexibility and synergy. In order to maintain its corporate culture the division introduced several organisational innovations, including annual 'away-days' at locations roughly equidistant from Leeds and London. During the early and mid-1990s when there were severe strains in the relationships between the NHS Management Executive and the rest of the Department, the EOR was a major contributor to departmental 'glue'.

In 1993–94 the review of NHS management, *Managing the New NHS*, and the Banks *Review of the Wider Department of Health* presented further challenges to the EOR's role and organisation.[6,7] The EOR escaped relatively unscathed from the staff cuts of over 20% that were announced at the end of 1994. By 1995 there were 22 professional economists and a similar number of operational research analysts.

Around 1998, the budget for EOR staff in Leeds was reunited with the budget for the EOR in London, and the whole division became part of the Corporate Services Directorate. In 2000 the major programme of reform and investment announced in the NHS Plan strained the analytical resources of the Department to their limit. With the agreement of the then Permanent Secretary, a Working Group was set up to review analysis and modelling in the Department. This concluded that taking account of 'make or buy' options,† the number of analysts employed within the Department should increase by the order of 20–30%. Because of a further reorganisation of the Department, by 2002 this recommen-

---

* When I was offered a choice between the analytical divisions in health and social security, I initially chose social security, which was the area in which I had a stronger background. My choice was rejected by the new Secretary of State for Social Security on the grounds that I was thought to be too close to the Treasury.
† 'Make or buy' means choosing between 'making analysis in-house or buying it from an external agency such as a university or consultancy.

dation had been only partially implemented – at the beginning of 2003 there were 29 economists and 28 operational researchers in the EOR, plus around 10 administrative and support staff.

These numbers represented a rough doubling of the analytical resources devoted to health services compared with 1984. However, public expenditure on health was still left much more sparsely supported by analysts per £ million of expenditure than any other form of public spending, with the exception of transfer payments. In 2003 there was roughly one departmental analyst for every £500 million of expenditure on the NHS, compared with one analyst for every £200 million spent on education, one for every £150 million spent on areas covered by the Home Office and one for every £55 million spent on defence. Excluding the Department for Work and Pensions and its social security programmes, in 2003 the Department of Health employed 6% of government analysts (economists, operational researchers and statisticians) but was responsible for 30% of the government spending defined as 'final expenditure'. The significant contribution that analysts were able to make to health policy over these two decades was a reflection more of their quality than of their quantity.

Where did the EOR sit within the DHSS/DH? In the 1980s it was part of the Finance Directorate, and the Chief Adviser reported to the Director of Finance, (the latter reported in turn to the Permanent Secretary). For most of the 1990s, with the increasingly separate existence of the NHS Executive, the Leeds part of the EOR reported first to the Executive's Director of Corporate Affairs and later to the Planning Director. The London part of the EOR reported to the Deputy Secretary for Central Resource Services. Until 2001, the Chief Economic Adviser also had a personal reporting line direct to the NHS Chief Executive. After 1998, the EOR's reporting relationships were brought together as part of Departmental Resources and Services (DRS). From 2001, the EOR found a new home as a member of a conglomerate of divisions that included research and development, statistics and information technology.* These changes in formal reporting arrangements had little impact on the EOR's work programme or day-to-day relationships. For all of our period the whole of the Department were customers for the Division, and its effectiveness owed little to where it was parked for pay and rations purposes. Much more important was the quality of its relationships with the major policy divisions and with Ministers.

Role and contribution of analysts

As noted earlier, between 1970 and 2002 the number of economists and operational research analysts working on health issues in the Department increased from zero to well over 50. How was this role carved out? My long-term colleague Jeremy Hurst has pointed out that 'most if not all detailed policy formation in a government department is the result of multi-disciplinary team-work. Following the broad direction set by Ministers, the lead is usually taken by generalist administrators and managers, with professionals, such as economists, playing a supporting and mainly advisory role'.[8] Moreover, compared with other

---

*In 2004, after the end of our period, EOR was amalgamated with the statistics function to become ESOR. For line management purposes, economists, operational researchers and statisticians now report to the department's three business groups. For professional purposes they still report to the Chief Economic Adviser.

professional groups, such as doctors, nurses and statisticians, economics and operational research were relatively junior and new to the department. Because they came later to the party they had to work hard in order to gain influence.

At its most basic, economists and operational researchers brought into the Department ways of thinking and analytical and modelling capabilities aimed at maximising the production of health and healthcare from any given level of resources. Economists also contributed specific knowledge about the economic characteristics and behaviours of the health sector. From the beginning the challenge facing economists and operational researchers was to identify health policy issues where these tools and specific knowledge could add value. By the early 1980s, economists and operational researchers had carved out roles in relation to a good number of policy and management issues, including service planning, geographical equity and resource allocation, prioritisation of biomedical research, the appraisal of major capital projects, performance indicators, modelling of nurse supply, and the appraisal of new health technologies. They were also recognised as having a role in relation to the assessment of alternative financing mechanisms and to setting the level of funding for the NHS.[8]

As more policy questions proved amenable to insights and support from economics and operational research, the Division attempted to clarify its objectives, measures of success and distinctive contribution. The codifications went through various formulations. As an example, by the early 1990s the Division's objectives were being defined as to ensure that key policy and management decisions:

1 are supported by the best possible insight and analysis
2 use the best possible analytical tools.

From around the same date the Division saw the critical measures of its success as twofold:

1 the percentage of key Departmental policy issues to which it was contributing
2 the value that it added to each of those policy issues.

The first of these criteria was easier to assess than the second. Although value added was usually difficult to quantify, it could be classified in terms of a number of 'distinctive contributions'. One listing of these that was used in the EOR for some years referred to the following elements:

1 challenge role (identifying and appraising alternatives)
2 managing scarcity (via prioritisation)
3 reducing uncertainty (via anticipation and scanning)
4 managing complexity (through mapping and modelling)
5 building on experience (through evaluation)
6 developing core competencies (through coaching).

These classifications of the EOR's role may have been over-simplifications, but they did help the Division to market its services to the rest of the Department. Along with the objectives and success criteria, they also helped with the planning and prioritising of the EOR's work. Annual business plans were at the centre of the Department's process for prioritising work. The process was formally both top-down and bottom-up, with the balance between the two varying through time. Ministers and senior officials (generally known as Top of The Office or TOTO) agreed on the departmental priorities to which directorates, divisions and branches were expected to work. The EOR looked first to its section heads to identify with their policy customers how they could contribute to those priorities. The division and branch heads would then draw on their more senior contacts to add additional tasks and/or to rank the work identified at section level. In practice, many new priorities emerged between business planning rounds. Much emphasis was placed on developing a working style in which every member of the Division was encouraged to look out for these emerging priorities and to respond to the opportunities that they offered in a fast and flexible way.

Such was the effectiveness of the Divisions' collective antennae throughout the two decades that analysts often started work on an issue before policy and management leads had formally requested assistance, and in some cases before they had realised that analytical work was required. When requests from a senior level were unanticipated, the Division prided itself on the speed with which it flexed resources to support new priorities. From time to time there were proposals to establish a senior advisory or steering group to guide the EOR's work programme. However, they were never followed through. Instead there was reliance on less formal mechanisms for staying close to customers. These included at least annual meetings between the Chief Economic Adviser and the Permanent Secretary and the Chief Executive, frequent informal meetings between other senior officials and EOR managers, regular contacts between EOR managers and Ministerial Private Offices, regular meetings between the Chief Economic Adviser and political advisers to both the Secretary of State and the Prime Minister, ensuring that analysts attended meetings with Ministers on key policy issues, out-posting analysts to major policy customers, informal meetings between all analysts and their customers in policy and management divisions, and close contacts between EOR analysts and the health expenditure team in the Treasury.

These networks and communication channels assisted the Division in keeping abreast of shifting ministerial and government priorities. However, there is a large gap between being aware of an emerging issue and making a useful contribution to its solution. Most of this monograph is about how the Department's economists and operational researchers contributed to solutions. Those contributions can be classified in various ways.[8]

One distinction is between influencing the content of policies and influencing the process and language of decision making. Departmental analysts can point to significant achievements on both fronts. Examples of policies where the content was influenced include: listening to patients, self-care, equitable resource alloca-tion, NHS Direct, the rate of adoption of some medical technologies, development of regional pay, development of intermediate care, and the introduction of a ban on tobacco advertising. The impact on the process and language of decision making may have been more far-reaching. This included the introduction of economic criteria into decisions on the funding of pharmaceuticals and other new technologies; the introduction of economic criteria into health service guidelines and National Service Frameworks; the development of more hard-edged mea-sures of performance in the NHS; increased emphasis on output and outcome measurement; whole system approaches to modelling waiting-times targets and their staff and hospital bed implications; the development of a balanced scorecard approach to measuring the performance of the NHS; a disease-based, bottom-up approach to estimating public expenditure requirements; modelling the costs and impact on service responsiveness of different levels of hospital capacity utilisation; encouraging the adoption of international benchmarking; and stimulating the evaluation of a raft of recent policies. Many of these influences are discussed in more detail in later chapters.

A distinction can also be made between a direct impact on the content of policies or the process of policy making and an indirect impact, often with a lag, on the climate of knowledge and opinion in which policy makers operate. In practice it is often difficult to distinguish between the two. When an idea is raised by an economist or operational researcher at an early meeting it may be seen as innovative. However, by the time it reaches Ministers it may be presented by policy colleagues as a consensus view and only common sense. All good ideas in the public sector generate many claims to be their inventor. It was with a mixture of exasperation and pride that EOR colleagues regularly watched their ideas being claimed by others. Policy colleagues may have a similar response to some of the claims of this book!

Analysts are as inclined as any other group to want to exaggerate their achievements. In later chapters I have attempted to be realistic and not to exaggerate the EOR's influence. In most cases the claims are based on knowledge of the many papers and discussions that led to the particular policy or process decision. In some cases a catalytic paper or report was written by a member of the EOR. In others, official papers record that it was a member of the EOR who suggested the idea at a meeting with Ministers, political advisers or senior officials. However, in a significant proportion of cases I have had to rely on my memory or the memories of EOR colleagues who were present at the time. Unfortunately, those seeking chapter and verse on these claims will have to wait until official files are opened in (up to) 25 years' time. Even then the sources of some ideas will not be found in official records – not all ministerial meetings are minuted, and over the period meeting notes came (sensibly) to focus on actions that were decided, not on who said what.

There is no doubt in my mind that the two decades covered by this book saw a major increase in the contribution of economists and operational research analysts to both the content of health policies and the process of decision making. Why did the contribution increase? A number of factors can readily be identified. On the demand side, improved information threw up growing evidence of variations in healthcare access, efficiency and effectiveness, leading to pressure for more rigorous and systematic approaches to the geographical allocation of resources, the management of performance (including more effective incentives) and the prioritisation of public funds. There was also an increasing awareness among doctors, the chief professional advisers on health policy, that with constrained budgets, ethical decision making had to take account of opportunity costs as well as clinical effectiveness. The movement towards evidence-based policy making also increased the demand for analysis. There were always some Departmental doctors in favour of economic analysis, but the proportion grew remarkably over this period. A third important influence on demand was the growing awareness by Ministers and TOTO of the health economics literature. As the ideas of health economists and systems thinkers spread through the general population, Ministers came to take it for granted that Departmental submissions would take account of those ideas. A further influence was that of wider changes across the public sector in views on effective policy making and performance management. Most significantly these gave a larger role to evidence and analysis.

On the supply side, the EOR was hugely assisted by the rapid expansion of health economics both in the UK and throughout the world, and by the development of new quantitative and qualitative tools in operational research. External health economists generated methodologies for prioritising the funding of treatments and other interventions (e.g. cost per Quality Adjusted Life Year (QALY)) and for improving resource allocation (e.g. applications of small area analysis) that added greatly to the toolkits available to internal analysts. Operational researchers contributed both new quantitative instruments, like quicker and easier to use simulation tools for the modelling of waiting, and qualitative ones, like new approaches to scenario analysis and systems modelling. At the same time a growing literature on evaluations of new technologies and, to a lesser extent, of health service delivery arrangements provided the case study material that converted theoretical prioritisation techniques into practical tools of decision making. Improved measures of health service performance, particularly of clinical outcomes and patient experiences, also greatly strengthened the information available to internal analysts for monitoring and comparing performance. The expansion of international statistics and international research on health service funding, organisation, policies and performance further added to the knowledge resources available to internal analysts. Last, but by no means least, I inherited a particularly talented group of analysts, several of whom stayed in the department for two or more decades. The reputation of the Government Economic Service and the Government Operational Research Service and the appeal of the NHS and healthcare ensured that we were able to attract a steady stream of highly talented colleagues as the EOR expanded.

Organisation of the book

The heart of the book is organised around 10 issues, each with its own chapter. Chapters 2 to 4 look at the inputs to the health service and consider how the budget for the NHS has been set, the debates about how the money should be raised and the attempts to plan the medical workforce. Chapters 5 to 7 turn to how well the NHS has used its resources, how efficiency has been measured, how systems for allocating resources have been improved and how performance monitoring and management have evolved. Chapter 8 reviews the slow progress towards focusing the health service on the patient. Chapter 9 turns to organisational changes within the Department and how far they have (or rather have not) been based on rigorous analysis. Chapters 10 and 11 look at the Department as a learning organisation and ask how effective it has been in learning from its own policy experience and from health policies in other countries.

Each chapter follows a fairly similar form. It begins with a look at the broader policy context and then gives a brief history of NHS and/or DH developments. Later sections describe the role of Departmental analysts in these developments, and raise and attempt to address two or three interesting or important policy issues.

The final chapter (Chapter 12), draws on the experiences set out earlier to reflect on lessons that may be of interest to current and future decision makers and analysts. The reflections are of two kinds, namely on improving policy making and on optimising the contribution of policy analysts.

References

1 Wildavsky A (1979) *Speaking Truth to Power. The art and craft of policy analysis*. Little, Brown & Co., Boston, MA.

2 Royston GHD, Hurst JW, Lister EG and Stewart PA (1992) Modelling the use of health services by populations of small areas to inform the allocation of central resources to larger regions. *Socio-Econ Plan Sci*. **26**: 169–80.

3 Royston G, Halsall J, Halsall D and Braithwaite C (2003) Operational research for informed innovation: NHS Direct as a case study in design, implementation and evaluation of a new public service. *J Operat Res Soc*. **54**: 1022–8.

4 See, for example, Glenerster H, Hills J and Travers T (2000) *Paying for Health, Education and Housing: How does the centre pull the purse strings?* Oxford University Press, Oxford.

5 Smith P, Rice B and Carr-Hill R (2001) Capitation funding in the public sector. *J R Statist Soc Series A*. **164**: 217–41.

6 NHS Management Executive (1994) *Managing the New NHS*. NHS Management Executive, Leeds.

7 Department of Health (1994) *Review of the Wider Department of Health (the Banks Review)*. Department of Health, London.

8 Hurst J (1998) The impact of health economics on health policy in England, and the impact of health policy on health economics 1972–1997. *Health Econ*. **7(Suppl.1)**: S47–S62.

Chapter 2

Determining the NHS budget

Introduction

This chapter and the next look at the contribution of analysis to two key political issues – first, how much should be spent on the National Health Service (NHS), and secondly, how healthcare should be financed. Although the NHS was launched in 1948 with singularly little attention to the financial implications, these issues rapidly came to the fore. For the last 20 years they have rarely been out of the political headlines for any extended period.

Any discussion of the determinants of the NHS budget needs to recognise the broader economic and political context. The chapter therefore begins with a summary of the changing policy context. It then describes the search for objective factors to influence the political judgements that inevitably underlie all major public expenditure decisions. The changing contribution of analysis and analysts is the subject of the next section. The chapter ends with reflections on two questions. First, why did spending on the NHS lag behind healthcare spending in other countries for so long? Secondly, what role did analysis play in the dramatic increase in NHS funding in 2000 and 2002?

Policy context

At the beginning of the 1980s, the bulk of health service expenditure relating to hospital and community health services was governed by centrally determined global budgets. In the subsequent 20 years almost all of the initially 'non-cash-limited' services – essentially primary care services – were brought within cash limits. The discussion that follows therefore focuses on how the cash-limited budgets were determined. In line with the prioritisation of analytical effort, it also focuses on current expenditure. Capital expenditure is largely ignored.

Up to 1997, the cash-limited budgets of the NHS were set through annual negotiations between the Department of Health and the Treasury as part of the wider Public Expenditure Survey. From 1997, the negotiations became two-yearly and were renamed Spending Reviews. However cordial were relations at other times, the public expenditure negotiations were invariably adversarial. Finance officials in the DH measured their success by the size of the resource increase that was finally agreed. Health Secretaries of State used a similar criterion. Treasury officials, on the other hand, measured their effectiveness by how low was the resource increase finally conceded. When the Chancellor took a more generous view – as, for example, in 2000 and 2002 – it was usually to the deep regret of Treasury officials.

Over the last 20 years, public expenditure negotiations have been informed by a range of wider political and economic considerations. Two of these warrant attention, namely assumptions about the role and size of the public sector, and the extent to which budgets for the NHS have been seen as political judgements and not subject to objective assessment.

The broader debate about the role and size of the public sector as a whole and the appropriate share of aggregate public spending in national income has always been part of the backdrop to the annual negotiations. The new Conservative Government of 1979 believed that it inherited a public sector that had been allowed to become over-large given the economic costs of high and rising taxation and the inefficiencies of non-market organisations. It was determined to reduce public spending and taxation as a share of national income. It met with considerable success. Between 1980 and 1997, total public spending fell from 47.3% to 39.3% of national income, a larger fall than was seen in most other European countries. In the period up to 1997 the DH's attempts to increase the NHS budget were therefore constrained in large part because all public spending was constrained.

The Labour Government that came to power in 1997 was more sympathetic to public spending, provided that it was well managed. After 1999, the share of total public spending in national income again began to rise. In 2000, the Government concluded that 'The NHS has suffered from decades of under investment'.[1] It announced 'an historic commitment to a sustained increase in NHS spending', with the aim over time of bringing it up to the EU average.[1]

The second wider consideration has been changing views about the extent to which the NHS budget could be influenced or even determined by objective evidence. Throughout the 1980s and 1990s, the prevailing view under all governments was that budgets for the NHS were bound to be policy and political judgements and could not be determined by objective measures of 'adequacy'. This view was first put forward by the Guillebaud Committee in 1956.[2] In response to a remit to cost an 'adequate service', the Committee concluded that 'there is no objective and attainable standard of adequacy in the health field . . . we conclude that in the absence of an objective and attainable standard of adequacy, the aim must be . . . to provide the best service possible within the limits of the available resources'. The 1978–79 Royal Commission on the NHS reached a similar conclusion. It found that 'there is no objective or universally acceptable method of establishing what the "right" level of expenditure on the NHS should be'.[3]

This prevailing orthodoxy did not stop the search for objective factors that should influence government policy judgements. In one sense, the analytical history of NHS budget setting is the identification of more and more of these objective factors and the development of stronger evidence in support of each of them. The Wanless Report in 2002 can be seen as the culmination of this trend.[4]

Although not presented as such by its author, the Wanless Report can be interpreted as an overthrow of the post-Guillebaud orthodoxy. In line with Derek Wanless's interpretation of his remit from the Chancellor, his Final Report attempted to quantify 'the financial and other resources required to ensure that the NHS can provide a publicly funded, comprehensive, high-quality service available on the basis of clinical need and not ability to pay'.* While Guillebaud concluded that there was no way to objectively define a standard of 'adequacy' in the health service, Wanless concluded that it was possible to define a 'high-quality' service and, on various assumptions, to estimate the cost of achieving it. The new willingness both to define standards and, more particularly, to cost them is in large part a tribute to the development of analytical methodologies over the last two decades.

But if objective factors are now being given greater weight in judgements about the long-term resource requirements of the NHS, for the last 20 years judgements about short-term changes in budgets have been influenced as much or more by political considerations and broad swings in the economy and public finances as by objective health service pressures. The pattern of real NHS expenditure increases, with dramatic annual swings from near zero to 6% or more and back again (*see* Figure 2.1), cannot be attributed to changes in the main influences on the resources required for adequate or high-quality healthcare. As the diagram illustrates, there has also been a shift upwards in the expected long-term growth rate in health expenditure. The 3% per annum that was regarded as adequate in the 1980s and 1990s has been replaced by a planned average growth rate of over 7% per annum for the next five years, and an expectation in the Wanless Report that the annual increase will need to be between 4% and 5% a year for the next 20 years. This upward shift in expectations is again not a consequence of a seismic shift in the traditional pressures on health budgets. It flows from a government commitment to a new standard of care, described as a high-quality health service delivering clinical and service standards of world-class level.

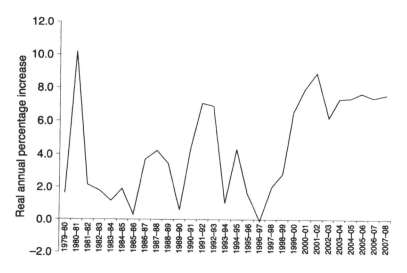

Figure 2.1 Patterns of NHS expenditure adjusted for the GDP deflator, 1980–2007.

*The terms of reference refer to 'identify[ing] the key factors which will determine the financial and other resources required . . .'. In the tradition of chairmen extending their briefs, Derek Wanless interpreted this as meaning 'to attempt to quantify "the resources, etc.".'

The search for objective factors to influence budget judgements

The perennial debates about the adequacy of NHS funding have generated a range of conceptual approaches or frameworks for judging the 'right' level of funding. One group of authors has identified seven different approaches or frameworks that they label as follows:

- the 'economic approach', where funding is increased until marginal costs equal marginal benefits
- the 'needs approach', where estimates are made of the funds required to meet the needs of demography, medical advance and changing expectations
- the 'rationing approach', which attempts to quantify the extent to which treatments and services are rationed
- the 'international perspective', which compares UK spending with that in other countries
- the 'public opinion approach', which looks at survey evidence on the public's willingness to spend more on the health service
- the 'affordability approach', which attempts to link health expenditure to the growth in national income
- the 'incremental approach', which uses rules of thumb to increase expenditure to fund demography, medical advance, efficiency, etc.[5]

This typology draws on the work of academic and other external commentators. However, Department of Health policy leads and analysts have not consciously approached discussions on NHS budgets with one of these frameworks consistently in mind. Instead, over the years they have drawn eclectically and opportunistically on the evidence and arguments suggested by all of these possible approaches. In retrospect, for most of the 1980s and 1990s, public expenditure discussions with the Treasury drew most strongly on the kinds of arguments highlighted by the needs approach and the incremental approach. Arguably, in the last five years much heavier weight has been placed on the arguments identified by the economic approach, the international perspective and the public opinion approach.

As no single analytical framework has been consistently used by the Department, the discussion that follows is structured in terms of the factors most frequently referred to by officials in discussions with the Treasury on future NHS budgets. These have been demographic pressures, public expectations, medical advance, service commitments and developments, relative price effects, new threats to public health, reform 'investments', and scope for efficiency savings. Brief comments follow on how the analysis of each of these possible expenditure pressures has evolved.

Demography

This factor has been studied over a longer time and more carefully than any of the other possible pressures on the NHS budget. Studies date back at least to work by Abel-Smith and Titmuss in the mid-1950s.[6] They all assume that each age group's past use of healthcare resources was efficient or at least unavoidable. Using gradually improving information and refined methodologies, estimates of the cost pressures from a growing population and changing age structure were a prominent feature of the Department's arguments for more resources well into the 1990s. The impact of demography then declined. Current estimates suggest that within the immediate future the changing age structure of the population is likely to have a much smaller impact on costs than it did, say, in the mid-1980s. The impact will also be smaller than tends to be believed by many politicians and clinicians (which is one of the reasons why this potential pressure was analysed so carefully by the Wanless Report).

Public expectations

All governments over the last 20 years have recognised that the population's demand for healthcare rises through time with increases in income and wealth (i.e. demand has a positive income elasticity). Some governments have been willing to acknowledge that the income elasticity of demand is greater than one (i.e. the public is willing to pay for health spending to take a rising share of national income). The problem for Departmental analysts has been to identify ways of trying to monitor and quantify changing patient and public expectations. Direct evidence of the public's spending priorities from the annual British Social Attitudes Survey was usually dismissed by the Treasury as failing to reflect real budget constraints. Another early approach was to look at the recent growth in health service volumes, sector by sector, and to assume that public expectations required recent trends to be at least maintained. For this purpose the Department has used a simple model (or more precisely a set of linked spreadsheets) since the 1980s. The model (or more accurately models) has become more disaggregated and sophisticated through time.* One weakness of the approach, of course, is that trends in services reflect the interaction of demand and supply, not the shift in demand alone. To try to make allowance for this, various supplementary analyses have been developed to cast light on unmet demands or expectations. These have included analyses of trends in hospital waiting times and the costs of reducing them; setting clinical and quality standards on the basis of consultation with clinicians and costing their achievement; and setting and costing wider service standards on the basis of survey evidence of what patients and the public expect both from the health sector and from other service providers.

The rising share of health spending in national income in other countries has also been presented as a relevant reflection of the public's willingness to pay for healthcare, particularly in those countries with open-ended financing systems, where it could be argued that the interdependence of supply and demand was not so marked as in the UK.

Medical advance

Although US economists have long seen new technologies and new drugs as the most important upward pressure on health service budgets, there was protracted

---

* An early version of the model is described in: Smee C (1995) Setting regional allocations and national budgets in the UK. In: F Schwarz, H Glennerster and R Saltman (eds) *Fixing Health Budgets: Experience from Europe and North America*. Wiley, Chichester.

resistance to this idea in the Treasury. It was noted that in most sectors new technologies reduced costs rather than increased them. It was argued that the same should be true in health. There is now broad agreement across government that although new technologies and new drugs can reduce unit costs, the net effect of medical advance in the last 30 or 40 years has been to increase pressures on health service expenditure by constantly expanding both the effectiveness of treatments and the range of treatable conditions. The pressure on expenditure is likely to continue unless and until the main impact of medical advance is on disease prevention rather than disease treatment.

Despite the gradual consensus on the role of medical advance, it has been difficult to find an objective way to calculate its impact on the NHS budget. For a period in the 1980s the Department argued that medical advance added 0.5% a year to the pressures on the NHS. However, this figure was dropped due to lack of supporting evidence. In the mid-1990s the Department's analysts developed a new approach based on the experience of two US federal agencies.* This took a bottom-up approach to estimating the impact of medical advance by looking for new technologies that were expected to diffuse rapidly over the next year or two, having already reached at least 5% of the target population. In practice, although this approach provided useful early warnings of some expenditure pressures and of technologies that should be subject to careful assessment of cost-effectiveness, it proved somewhat unwieldy. It also appeared to seriously underestimate expenditure pressures – there are too many technologies diffusing at any one time to enable individual studies to capture the effects of more than a small proportion of them.

Service commitments and developments

For all the public expenditure round discussions of the 1980s and 1990s, the Department produced long lists of existing service commitments that required funding, and of new policy initiatives that were said to warrant public financing. The latter emerged from numerous ad-hoc pressures on Ministers, the Department and the NHS. Nearly all of them could be justified as reflecting 'public expectations'. In practice, many of the new service initiatives were squeezed by tight resource constraints and a perceived need to convince the Treasury that they were relatively low cost. Partly as a consequence, costing was often poor, attention to implementation, particularly human resource implications, was even poorer, and the subsequent monitoring of delivery was often non-existent.

The development of National Service Frameworks (NSFs) gradually brought in a new and more robust approach to costing and implementing major service initiatives. Considerations of cost-effectiveness, human resource implications and a range of other implementation factors are now usually given proper attention. The Frameworks also provide a more holistic basis for assessing the costs of medical advance.

Relative price effects

Along with demography, perhaps the most persistent argument for year-on-year increases in real resources for healthcare has been that prices for health service

*The Prospective Payments Advisory Commission and the Physicians Payments Advisory Commission.

resources, including skilled staff, rise faster than the general level of inflation. This is true but unsurprising. It is also misleading. Input prices (such as wages) rise faster than output prices (such as the general level of inflation) more or less everywhere, with the latter rising more slowly because of increasing productivity. The real issue is whether there is less scope for productivity gains in the NHS than elsewhere, because of the face-to-face or handicraft nature of the services being produced. Nevertheless, in the 1980s Departmental analysts put a great deal of effort into developing and tracking a price index for non-labour hospital services. The index continues to be maintained, but in recent years with the return to low inflation its pattern has not been very different from that of the general price index.

Trends in health service pay are of much more importance. In the early 1990s, it was assumed that real improvements in wages should be 'earned' through improvements in productivity. For a few years rapid reductions in hospital lengths of stay and increases in the number of day cases did make this possible. However, more recently the 'handicraft service' nature of healthcare appears to have reasserted itself. It is now accepted that real improvements in wages cannot be rigidly tied to improvements in healthcare productivity. The analysis of pay pressures has been split into two components, namely pay awards and pay drift. For neither has it so far proved possible to produce a good predictive model.

New threats to public health

Evidence of changes in public health would seem to be the most obvious reason for changes in the NHS budget. In practice, with the exception of the AIDS epidemic, there have been no changes in public health in the last 20 years that have had a major short-term impact on the demand for health services (although for a time it was thought that CJD might). Modelling can be and has been undertaken of possible longer-term changes, such as different rates of change in mortality rates and the possible compression of morbidity.*

Investment in reform

Major health service reforms almost invariably require major investments in new infrastructure. The experience of the last 20 years suggests that this can be slow to be recognised. However, for the three years 1989–90 to 1991–92 the Department and the Treasury did agree that substantial additional resources should be made available for the information technology, training and other start-up costs associated with the introduction of the internal market. More recently, the Department was late in acknowledging that the huge expansion of the NHS begun by the 1998 Comprehensive Spending Review and continued by the 2000 NHS Plan required a major investment in human resources and physical infrastructure. Developing the analytical methodologies to properly cost the necessary human resource development programmes has proved particularly challenging. Good methodologies have still to be developed to estimate the implications of the NHS expansion, and the accompanying radical reforms, for

*The term 'compression of morbidity' is used to refer to a reduction in the average number of years of life spent in ill health or with disability.

the Department's administrative capacity and the capacity of Strategic Health Authorities and Primary Care Trusts. In their absence, capacity planning has relied on trial and error and management 'judgement'.

Efficiency savings

It has probably always been realised that there was scope for improving the efficiency of the NHS. However, it was only in the 1980s that formal allowance began to be made for an efficiency factor in the annual discussions over the health service budget. The discussions were facilitated by the development (by the Department's analysts) of a summary measure of trends in efficiency across the hospital sector. The development of this indicator is discussed more fully in Chapter 5 on efficiency in the NHS. Suffice it to say here that using this measure and other indicators, efficiency savings were claimed to add between 0.5% and 1.5% per annum to the resources available for hospital and community health services throughout the 1980s. In the late 1980s, the Department agreed with the Treasury on a formal efficiency target for the NHS. This was raised in steps from 1% per annum to a peak of 3% in 1995–96. More recently the annual target has been reduced, in response to both lower out-turns and greater understanding of the sources of cost savings. There have also been a series of major changes in the way in which efficiency is measured.

Changes in analysis over time

Standing back from the annual and more recently two-yearly negotiations of the NHS budget, it is possible to identify a number of general trends in the nature of the analytical arguments. First, the factors seen as the key drivers of expenditure have changed through time. Secondly, the quality of all of the analytical arguments has tended to improve due to better information, disaggregation and improved methodologies. Of particular importance has been the increased emphasis on outputs and outcomes, and the search for better measures of both. Thirdly, there has belatedly been greater transparency about the analytical models used, allowing the Department to tap into external expertise. Fourthly, there has been a shift, which still has further to go, from relying on simple extrapolations of past service trends to developing disaggregated estimates of resource requirements related to evidence-based standards of care. Fifthly, international comparisons have played an ever-increasing role in setting service standards and estimates of resource requirements.

These points can be briefly expanded.

Changing importance of different drivers

The period since 1980 can be divided into three broad periods. First, in the 1980s, demography, particularly the changing age structure, was seen as a major pressure on health expenditure, adding over 1% per annum to resource requirements in the peak year. In the same decade, relative price effects were also seen as very important, in part reflecting high and unpredictable inflation. Secondly, in the 1990s, as the importance of demography declined more weight was attached to the need to maintain service trends as a good proxy for public expectations. At the beginning of the decade, major additional resources were also obtained on the argument of 'investing in reform'. The potential scale of efficiency savings also became much more important, with the annual target peaking at 3% in 1995–96. In the third period, roughly since the NHS Plan in 2000, the dominant analytical argument has been around what is needed to 'catch-up' with public expectations of safe, high-quality treatment, fast access and clean and comfortable accommodation. Arguments about the costs of medical advance have also come to the fore with the establishment of the National Institute for Clinical Excellence (NICE). Expected trends in pay and relative prices and the assumed need to maintain activity trends across the major service areas are also still important, but are now built into the foundations of each negotiation under the heading 'baseline pressures'.

Turning to the future, looking over the 10 years leading up to 2013, the Wanless Report sees 'catch-up' in the quality of care, through the generalisation of National Service Frameworks to all areas, as far and away the biggest driver of additional expenditure, accounting for 50% or more of the forecast increase. Real pay and relative price effects are also important, accounting for around 20% of the increase. The cost of meeting public expectations with regard to reduced waiting times is expected to account for 10% of the total increase. Demography and the changing age structure are expected to contribute only around 6% of the additional cost pressures.

Greater disaggregation and sophistication

Major improvements in data and increased disaggregation and sophistication in modelling have improved the quality of the analysis used to quantify all of the major pressures on NHS budgets. Examples of particularly marked improvements in analysis include the costing of waiting-times initiatives and of National Service Frameworks. A further example is the use of more detailed information on hospital costs, case-mix-adjusted Health Resource Groups (HRGs), to produce reference costs and to permit better comparisons of both cost variations and trends over time.

Most notable of all has been the increasing switch in emphasis to outputs and outcomes. As measures of these types improve they can be used to throw direct light on whether clinical standards are keeping up with those in other countries and whether patient expectations are being met. They can also be used to adjust measures of efficiency for improvements in quality.

Greater transparency

With the exception of the methodology used to estimate the impact of demographic change, openness about analytical models was a long time coming. Proposals to share the baseline models or so-called 'Public Expenditure Survey model' with academics were made as early as 1993. A general description was published in 1994, but it was not until 2001 that the detailed assumptions were shared with selected academics and external experts. The obsession with secrecy delayed improvements to the model by several years.

From extrapolating service trends to standard-based estimates of future needs

For many years the Department relied on the argument that past service trends were the best guide to future needs. Policy and finance leads were led to do this by a belief that it was not possible either to agree standards of care with clinicians or to convince the Treasury that such standards were evidence based, effective and cost-effective. The Calman–Hine Cancer Report and work on mental health services foreshadowed the development of NSFs which increasingly showed that it was possible to set national standards based on the best evidence of clinical effectiveness and cost-effectiveness, and to cost them rigorously.

International comparisons

Although the Department's analysts made use of international comparisons throughout this period, the importance attached to them by Ministers grew enormously. With better-quality and more disaggregated international data there was increasing scope for identifying international benchmarks both for outcomes and for processes of care. Up to the mid 1990s, the international evidence still suggested that the NHS produced as good health outcomes as the average OECD or EEC health system. However, by the year 2000, UK health outcomes increasingly appeared to be in the bottom half of the distribution. Around the same time a growing media interest in comparative waiting times and other aspects of service responsiveness put a more intense spotlight on areas in which the NHS had always performed poorly.

The role of analysts

In any public policy area the use of analysis requires co-operation between policy customers and analytical advisers. The finance staff responsible for leading work on the regular reviews of the NHS budget have generally been more analytically minded and/or receptive to proposals for improved analysis than most parts of the Department. They must take a significant share of the credit for the improvements in budgetary analysis over the last 20 years.

However, it is possible to identify a large number of areas in which the Department's analysts (economists, operational researchers and statisticians) took the lead in developing a new analytical tool or in disseminating an existing tool more widely. Examples of such areas include the following:

- development of a hospital and community health service price index
- development of a forecasting model for the primary care drugs bill
- development of the Hospital and Community Health Service (HCHS) efficiency index and its many reformulations
- development of a bottom-up approach to costing medical advance
- the costing of service standards – both clinical standards (NSFs) and waiting times
- a range of analyses of international comparative data
- promoting the transparency of expenditure models through the 2001 Advisory Group on Modelling Demand for Health and Social Services (*see* Box 2.1).

- The promotion of measures of quality and outcome for both clinical and patient services
- tools to gauge and cost the ability of NHS hospitals to respond adequately to 'peak loads'
- 'whole-system' tools to link analysis of primary, secondary and social care.

Box 2.1 Opening demand modelling to external scrutiny

Departmental analysts argued for exposing PES models to external scrutiny from at least the early 1990s. Their hand was greatly strengthened by the recommendation of the 1999 Cabinet Office Report *Adding It Up* that all major departmental models were likely to be improved by opening them to academic scrutiny. The following year the Department's own Review of Analysis and Modelling Working Group concluded that this recommendation should particularly apply to the public expenditure-forecasting models. In consequence, an Advisory Group on Modelling Demand for Health and Social Services was established under the Chief Economic Adviser in the spring of 2001, with a view to improving the Department's models in time for the 2002 Spending Review.

The membership of the Group was drawn from academics, policy analysts and front-line managers. They were asked to comment on and suggest improvements to a range of papers setting out the methodologies used by the Department to model the demand for services and related supply issues. Suggestions for improvements that were adopted by the Department included the following.

1 Introduce joint modelling of the social care and NHS workforces.
2 Explore the value of modelling waiting times by specialty and test the predictive value of the waiting-times model by inserting historical data.
3 Develop a better understanding of the behavioural impact of modernisation work, particularly on demand management.
4 Review how greater efficiency has actually been achieved in the NHS and build trends in quality into the measurement of efficiency.
5 Improve forecasting of the demand for primary care and for community health services.
6 Review the modelling of hospital drug costs.
7 Disaggregate demand for inpatient hospital care in terms of the main specialties.

In addition to producing some important improvements in methodology, this exercise in transparency had other benefits. First, it reassured the Treasury that the Department's modelling could stand up to external scrutiny. Secondly, it alerted academics to the public expenditure modelling issues that required more research.

In retrospect, could more have been done? Could the quality of analysis and hence the Department's arguments for higher expenditure have been improved more rapidly? With hindsight the answer must be 'yes'. At the most obvious level more resources devoted to analytical support could have speeded up learning. However, learning was slower than it might have been for at least four other reasons. First, work on each public expenditure round was almost invariably concentrated into the three or four months before the settlement. As a consequence, only short-term pieces of analysis could be carried out. Attempts to develop longer-term work programmes extending across the periods between PES rounds usually disappeared into the ground either because of other priorities or because of staff changes. Secondly, the confidentiality that surrounded PES negotiations (usually encouraged by Ministers, but sometimes also played up by finance policy leads) ensured that most Departmental staff were not involved and did not learn how to contribute effectively. Thirdly, the same confidentiality arguments precluded opening the Department's analytical work to external scrutiny and challenge. As has already been noted, it was only in 2001 that the basic demand models were discussed with selected external experts. Up until then the growing cadre of university health economists was effectively excluded from any involvement in the analytical discussions on the NHS budget. Fourthly, in the absence of challenges from external experts, only Treasury analysts were in a position to scrutinise the Department's analytical work. However, although there were periods when they did this well, there were also periods, particularly towards the end of the 20 years, when small staff numbers and rapid turnover caused the Treasury challenge to be feeble in the extreme.

It remains to be seen how far these lessons have been learned, and in particular how far the Department will allow external analysts and externally funded research to play a more direct role in the arguments over funding requirements. The unwillingness of the Treasury to put the forecasting model developed for the Wanless Report into the public domain suggests that the public sector's willingness to be more transparent has important limits.

The big questions

Looking back at the history of NHS budget setting over the last 20 years, there are two big questions.

1 Why did spending on the NHS lag behind healthcare spending in other countries for so long? A related question is why the Department of Health's internal analysts did not highlight the apparent under-funding much earlier.
2 What role did analysis play in the dramatic increase in NHS funding in 2000 and 2002?

Why did spending on the NHS lag behind healthcare spending in other countries for so long?

Relative to national income, UK total health expenditure and public health expenditure both fell behind the trend increase in other Western countries from 1960 onwards. By 1980, the share of total health spending in GDP in the UK was 1.5% below the EU average, i.e. 5.6% compared to 7.1%. However, the new Conservative Government was committed to significantly reducing the share of total government expenditure and taxes in GDP. In these circumstances, arguing for the NHS budget to rise faster than the growth of national income was rather like trying to push water uphill. In practice, the health budget did relatively well. For example, between 1978–79 and 1994–95, expenditure on the NHS grew twice as fast as both national income and general government expenditure as a whole. Only expenditure on social security grew faster. The question therefore is not why health was not treated as a special case (it was), but why it was not treated as an exceptional case.

The short answer is that on the basis of the limited evidence then available, the nation's health status – taken as a proxy for health service outcomes – generally appeared to be comparable to that in other countries with more generously funded health systems. In the run-up to the annual Public Expenditure Survey, the Department's analysts would scour the OECD's latest database for evidence that UK outcomes were falling behind. However, on the basis of the health status indicators available, namely life expectancy, infant and perinatal mortality rates and premature mortality (potential years of life lost), the UK's performance remained solidly in the middle of the OECD road. There was recognition that these indicators might reflect living standards or broader social conditions, rather than the quality of healthcare. However, until the arrival of comparative cancer survival rates there were no real internationally comparable health outcome measures.

When Ministers asked (as they did) how this performance could be achieved given the low level of expenditure on the NHS, an answer was readily available both from the external analytical literature and from work within the Department. The answer was, in the words of the OECD, that the NHS was 'a remarkably cost-effective institution'.[7] There were a range of factors to hand to explain this cost-effectiveness, including low input prices, low administrative costs, high technical efficiency and high allocative efficiency. The evidence for some of these factors was stronger than that for others. For example, there was (and still is) much better evidence of high technical efficiency than of low administrative costs. But overall, throughout the 1980s and for most of the 1990s, there were few challenges to the view that the NHS was highly efficient relative to other health systems. It was therefore seen as unsurprising that it could achieve comparable outcomes at significantly lower costs.

The NHS did, of course, have one key visible weakness, namely very long waiting times for hospital care. However, somewhat strangely with hindsight, this was not generally attributed to under-funding. There was a widespread view among analysts that waiting times were inevitable given the supposedly almost 'infinite' demand generated by a service that was free at the point of delivery. There were even arguments that waiting times were preferable to other forms of rationing. It was late in the 1990s before it was widely noted that most other Western countries were able to offer free hospital services without requiring waiting times of the scale experienced in England. The debate continues as to how far these differences should be attributed to relative resources, to better hospital management or to superior clinician incentives.

While the NHS's greater efficiency was accepted as explaining how comparable outcomes could be obtained at a low relative cost, there appeared to be plenty of evidence that efficiency could be further improved. Within the UK, Ministers (and Prime Ministers) could point to large variations across the UK in average length of hospital stay, day-surgery rates, drug-prescribing costs and the rates at which patients were referred to hospital. Academics could also point to the lack of direct incentives for hospitals to search for better ways of doing things, and the perverse behaviours that were encouraged by fragmented budgets and the separation of clinical and financial responsibilities. In the face of this evidence it was very difficult for internal analysts and Department officials in general to argue that further improvements in outcomes, including reductions in waiting time, could only be obtained by increasing resources at rates well above those seen in the previous 30 years.

What role did analysis play in the dramatic increase in NHS funding in 2000 and 2002?

The dramatic increase in NHS funding foreshadowed in the Prime Minister's January 2000 commitment to match EU spending levels, and implemented in the 2000 and 2002 Spending Reviews, primarily reflected the political convictions (and conversion) of the Prime Minister and the Chancellor. Did hard analysis play any role? The answer is that it probably contributed little to the initial commitment (other than calculation of the rate of growth necessary to catch up with the European unweighted average; *see* Box 2.2). However, later it certainly became important in determining the size of the Spending Review settlements.

Box 2.2 The Prime Minister's commitment to match the average expenditure levels of the European Union, 16 January 2000

On the *Breakfast with Frost* programme on Sunday 16 January 2000, the Prime Minister said 'If we can carry on getting real-term rises of almost 5% then at the end of that 5 years we could bring our health service expenditure up to the average of the European Union.' In the ensuing weeks this conditional statement was variously presented as a commitment, an aim or an aspiration. At the time it was made the immediate concern of officials was to be in a position to explain the assumptions underlying the Prime Minister's statement, since it was clear that these were bound to be challenged.

Shortly after midday on 16 January I was asked to review the assumptions under which a 5% real growth rate for NHS expenditure would bring total health service expenditure (both public and private) up to the European Union average within 5 years. The illustrative calculations on which the Prime Minister had drawn in his remark had come from another government department (the Treasury), and it was thought prudent to check whether they were based on the latest available international data. On a Sunday no one else could be found with up-to-date OECD data to hand.

In the ensuing hours a large number of calculations were made using different assumptions about the base year, the growth in NHS expenditure between now and the base year, trends in private health expenditure and the growth in GDP. The levels and trends in health expenditure as a share of GDP in other EU countries were also reviewed. My daughter's boyfriend did most of the more complicated calculations, as he knew how to work the compound interest function on his calculator!

Drawing on these calculations the line to take was discussed with other departments at a conference call at around 2.00pm. It was agreed that the EU average referred to the latest year for which we had data, and included the UK. The 5-year growth path started from 2001–02, the start of the next Spending Review period. GDP was assumed to grow at 2.25% per annum, and private health expenditure was assumed to take a fixed percentage share of GDP. On the basis of these and other assumptions, a growth rate of 5% per annum in NHS expenditure would take UK total health expenditure to 8% of GDP by 2006–07. A press notice was subsequently issued setting out these assumptions.

The press generally correctly interpreted the message agreed at the conference call. However, a surprising number of policy analysts later chose to question the Prime Minister's conclusion that over 5 years real-term rises of 5% per annum would take total UK health expenditure to the average of the EU. They did so either by ignoring the assumptions set out in the press notice (which was not referenced by any of the critics) or by basing their own calculations on a different set of assumptions. Virtually all of these alternative assumptions had been considered and rejected in the discussions on 16 January. The major one which was not was that 'average of the EU' might mean average weighted by national income, not the simple arithmetic average. The former had not been considered because OECD and EU comparisons normally use arithmetic averages in order to give equal weight to the decisions made by all of the individual member countries.

At the time of the Prime Minister's EU announcement, the OECD Secretariat was just concluding a study of UK healthcare. It came to radically different conclusions to the 1994 review that had called the NHS 'a remarkably cost-effective institution'. The new study[8] highlighted recent information on the poor cancer survival rates in the UK, suggested that other disease-specific outcomes were also poor, and noted the limited progress on waiting times and the apparent under-investment in both doctors and buildings. Instead of drawing attention to the efficiency of the NHS, it drew the conclusion that the latter was under-funded. The poor survival rates for cancer were recognised by Departmental officials and Ministers as a serious challenge to the longstanding argument that the NHS achieved health outcomes comparable to those of other countries. At roughly the same time, work commissioned by the Department from external consultants on the public's expectations of service levels in other sectors and other countries reinforced Ministerial views that long waiting times should not be seen as inevitable, but as simply unacceptable in a modern public service.* In short, there was a range of evidence that health service outcomes were slipping either in relation to other countries or in relation to public expectations.

At the same time, internal analysts produced evidence that there was diminishing scope for efficiency gains. The major technical sources of the large efficiency gains in the NHS in the late 1980s and early 1990s appeared to have

---

*The media's increasing use of the term 'Third World Medicine' also undoubtedly affected Ministerial thinking, however inaccurate it was as a description of the NHS.

run their course – the decline in hospital length of stay slowed and then stopped (at least temporarily), and the increase in day-surgery rates also slowed. More sophisticated studies of variations in whole hospital performance across the country suggested that these were much smaller than had previously been estimated, implying either that the differences had earlier been exaggerated or that they had now narrowed. New calculations showed that the cost savings achieved by bringing all parts of the country up to the efficiency levels of the best would be relatively small. The clear message was that if outcomes were to be improved there would need to be more reliance on additional funding and less on improved efficiency than in the recent past.

Ministers recognised that measurable and observable improvements in the quality of care would require major injections of new resources. They saw the commitment of substantial extra resources to the NHS as a major part of their political programme of public service improvement. Given this political steer, the Department's internal analysts could focus on what levels of resources would be necessary to deliver the standards of care set out in the NHS Plan. This Plan and the Wanless Report effectively redefined and raised the standard of care being used as a yardstick. Matching the OECD or EU spending average was replaced by aspiring to international best practice in quality of care. The National Service Frameworks were the critical and most costly element in this raising of the bar. Departmental analysts convinced the Wanless Review team that its assessment of resources required to deliver a high-quality health service should rest heavily on the costings of National Service Frameworks, and that the costings produced from the five most advanced frameworks could reasonably be extrapolated to other disease areas (*see* Box 2.3). The Wanless estimates of future resource requirements were in turn used as the basis for the Chancellor's April 2002 Budget commitment to increase NHS funding by an average real growth rate of 7.4% in each of the next five years. Had the Department's analysts been unable to provide Wanless with relatively robust disease-based costings, supported by evidence of cost-effectiveness, it is doubtful whether such high levels of funding could have been recommended. A speculative guesstimate is that the work of the Department's analysts on the National Service Frameworks may have justified increasing the required medium-term growth in NHS resources by between 0.5% and 2% per annum.

Box 2.3 The Wanless Report expenditure projections

There are two common approaches to long-term forecasts of health expenditure – first, aggregate projections (often extrapolations) of pressures such as demography and medical advance, and secondly, disaggregated projections of expenditures on diseases or types of care, often tied to specific care standards. In meetings with Derek Wanless and his team, the Department's analysts argued strongly for attaching most weight to the latter approach. They generally had a sympathetic audience.

To help to ensure that this sympathy was reflected in action, the Department's analysts:

1   developed detailed costings of the clinically effective and cost-effective interventions that would be required in five NSF areas if standards were

to be brought up to world class over the next 10 years. The costings were converted into expenditure growth rates for disease areas accounting for about 15% of total NHS expenditure

2 collected evidence on current standards of care and world-class standards in a sample of the major disease areas not yet covered by NSFs. They produced rough estimates of the increase in expenditure that would be required to bridge the gap. They used this evidence to convince the Wanless team that the NSF costings were representative of the expenditure growth rates that would be required across all disease areas if NHS standards were to catch up with world standards

3 highlighted the aspects of public and patient expectations that were not captured in the costings of NSFs (e.g. the increasing concern about the clinical quality of care and public pressure for faster access to health services of all kinds). They provided estimates of the costs of these additional pressures (e.g. the net costs of a major expansion of clinical governance).

By providing the detailed building blocks for estimating what expenditure was required if the NHS was to catch up with world standards, the Department's analysts made it possible for Wanless to come up with higher rates of growth in required resources than would have come out of any broad analysis of aggregate trends. The roll-out of NSFs across all disease alone accounted for at least half of the forecast growth in expenditure in the 10 years to 2013.

References

1 Department of Health (2000) *The NHS Plan.* The Stationery Office, London.
2 Parliament (1956) *Report of the Committee of Enquiry into the Cost of the National Health Service.* HMSO, London.
3 Parliament (1979) *Report of the Royal Commission on the National Health Service.* HMSO, London.
4 Wanless D (2002) *Securing our Future Health: taking a long-term view. Final report.* HM Treasury, London.
5 Dixon J, Harrison A, New B (1997) Is the NHS under-funded? *BMJ.* **314:** 58–61.
6 Abel-Smith B and Titmuss RN (1956) *The Cost of the National Health Service in England and Wales.* National Institute of Economic and Social Research, Cambridge.
7 Organisation for Economic Co-operation and Development (OECD) (1994) *OECD Economic Surveys 1993–94: United Kingdom.* OECD, Paris.
8 Organisation for Economic Co-operation and Development (OECD) (2000) *OECD Economic Surveys 2000: United Kingdom.* OECD, Paris.

Chapter 3

Alternative funding mechanisms

Policy context

From an international perspective, at the beginning of the 1980s the funding of healthcare in the UK had three distinguishing characteristics:

1 relative to national income, a low level of total expenditure. The UK healthcare share of 5.6% of GDP compared with an average of 6.9% across the OECD
2 a high level of dependence on public finances. Public expenditure accounted for 89% of total healthcare expenditure, compared with an average of 76% for the countries of the OECD
3 a reliance on general taxation as the predominant source of public funding. General taxation provided nearly 90% of funding, and the NHS element of National Insurance contributions was (and is) essentially an accounting convention.

Although there was some increase in the share of private funding, these characteristics remained distinguishing features of UK healthcare for the next 20 years (*see* Tables 3.1 to 3.3).

The three features go a long way towards explaining why these years saw regular reviews of the mechanisms used to fund health services in general and the NHS in particular. For most of this period the reviews were concerned with trying to identify additional funding streams that could narrow the gap between public expectations for healthcare and public willingness to pay. The reviews fell into two groups, namely those that focused on ways of encouraging greater private contributions to healthcare and those that searched for ways of escaping the 'chains of public expenditure control' by identifying tax bases that people would pay more willingly than general taxation. After 2000, when the 'chains' on healthcare were effectively unshackled, reviews of funding mechanisms continued, but the focus shifted towards establishing and demonstrating that tax-funded health systems were (or could be) as equitable, efficient and responsive as systems based on alternative financing mechanisms.

All of the reviews were constrained by the unwillingness of any government to seriously question the basic principles of the NHS (i.e. a universal system providing a fairly comprehensive range of services on the basis of need, not ability to pay). This reflected the perceived political costs of dismantling a system to which the public was – and is – strongly attached. Its main consequence was to severely limit the range of options for change, and in particular to rule out any serious consideration of a major shift to private insurance or charging.

Another constraint on change, at least in the eyes of the Treasury concerned the possible implications of health financing reform for the wider economy,

Table 3.1 Three distinguishing characteristics: low level of total expenditure

	Total Health Expenditure as a Percentage of GDP		
	1980	1990	1998
UK	5.6	6.0	6.8
New Zealand	6.0	7.0	8.1
Australia	7.0	7.9	8.6
France	7.4	8.6	9.4
Germany	8.8	8.7	10.3
OECD average	6.9	7.6	8.2

Source: OECD.

Table 3.2 Three distinguishing characteristics: high dependence on public finances

	Public funding as a percentage of health expenditure, 1980–98		
	1980	1990	1998
UK	89	84	83
New Zealand	88	82	77
Australia	63	67	70
France	79	78	78
Germany	79	76	76
OECD average	76	76	75

Source: OECD.

Table 3.3 Three distinguishing characteristics: reliance on general taxation

	NHS Sources of Finance (%)			
	General taxation	NHS contributions	Charges	Land sales and miscellaneous
1980	88.6	8.9	2.7	—
1990–91	78.8	15.7	4.5	1.1
1997–98	81.7	12.2	2.2	3.9

Source: DH.

particularly the labour market. For example, a drawback of social insurance is that it would almost certainly entail a shift in the burden of taxation towards taxes on labour, with consequences for employment and competitiveness. For much of the period in question, major efforts were being made (with some success) to reform the labour market and reduce labour costs. A switch to social insurance would in some sense have been going against the grain of wider policy. Comparisons of economic performance between the UK and countries like France and Germany tended to reinforce this argument, with persistent high unemployment in the latter countries being increasingly seen as due in part at least to very high non-wage labour costs.

This chapter provides a short description of the main Department of Health reviews of financing mechanisms, and notes the evolving contribution of analysis and analysts. It ends with some reflections on two big questions. First, why did the reviews bring about so little change in the mix of funding streams for UK health services over this period? Secondly, why does the search for alternative means of financing healthcare continue to attract so much attention both within government and more particularly outside it?

History of reviews

Since 1980 the reviews of financing methods that looked across all healthcare or at least the whole NHS can be divided into four groups, namely the review of 1981–82, the 1988 review, a series of mini-reviews in 1991, 1993 and 1997, and a period of almost continuous review between 2000 and 2002. These will each be discussed in turn below.

There were also a number of reviews of financing mechanisms for particular health services, notably dental and ophthalmic services and long-term care. These are not specifically covered, but it is worth noting that they shared a common theme with the more general reviews. The theme was whether it was possible to identify a core set of services to be funded out of general taxation, with non-core services being hived off to private funding. There have been small movements in the public/private boundaries from time to time. However, more radical proposals have foundered on the equity and political costs of drawing a dividing line which has more than relatively trivial implications for the overall balance of funding.

The 1981–82 working party on alternative means of financing healthcare

In 1981, Ministers asked for 'a quick survey of the possibilities for developing alternative means of financing and providing healthcare in order to improve standards, increase efficiency and consumer choice, and respond to increasing demands for health services while keeping public spending down'. This was the first major review of the financing of health services since 1948, as the 1978–79 Royal Commission on the NHS had only looked superficially at the possibility of insurance finance. Arguably this was also the first, and so far the last, true inter-departmental review. The main motivation appears to have been the expectation of the new Conservative Government that it would be possible to find ways of injecting greater private finance and private service delivery into healthcare while maintaining the basic principles of the NHS. In some right-of-centre think tanks there was also a belief that introducing the disciplines of the market would make health services more patient oriented, efficient and responsive.

In its 'quick survey', the Working Party considered a wider range of alternatives than any subsequent study. The options were grouped into three strategies, namely a tax-based strategy (but with a greater role for patient charging and the possible privatisation of dental, ophthalmic and pharmaceutical services), a social-insurance-based strategy with scope for contracting out, and a private-insurance-based system with services for the elderly and the non-employed continuing to be financed via general taxation. Officials concluded that there were major problems with the two insurance strategies. Either of these would be uncertain in benefit and extremely complex and costly to introduce on a large scale in the UK, given the existing health service arrangements and the Government's commitment to the principles of access to adequate care for all, regardless of cost. Officials also saw an inherent conflict between developing a more consumer-oriented, demand-led system and holding back costs. They therefore advised that further work might be concentrated on the proposals for the tax-based strategy. This was seen as offering some limited scope for increasing private finance and the private-sector supply of services.

In the event, Ministers decided not to embark on a second stage of the review or to publish the results of the initial quick assessment.* However, later that year (1982), Treasury Ministers asked the Central Policy Review Staff (CPRS) (who had been members of the inter-departmental review) to consider radical options for reducing pressures for public spending. The political furore caused by the leaking of subsequent CPRS proposals,[1] including the replacement of the NHS with a system of private insurance as one way to cut public expenditure, effectively stopped all work on radical funding alternatives for six years. Some of the ideas raised by the 1981–82 Working Party did later come about – for example, the partial privatisation of dental and ophthalmic services, paying hospitals by work done, and the (partial) abolition of the upper earnings limit on National Insurance contributions. However, these developments were largely coincidental. In most cases, all memory of the Working Party had been lost long before they were implemented.

The 1988 NHS Review leading to Working for Patients

The next major study of alternative funding methods came as part of the wide-ranging review of the NHS announced by Mrs Thatcher in January 1988. The announcement of a review was forced by a series of reports of clinical disasters, big ward closures and nursing crises, all of which were generally attributed by the media and the public to chronic under-funding. Before the announcement on the TV programme *Panorama*, officials had already begun to consider alternative models for both the financing and provision of healthcare. Afterwards, work on alternative financing mechanisms continued for some months with a particular focus on ways of broadening the private contribution to healthcare. There was recognition that this was an area in which the UK was an OECD outlier. There was also interest in whether alternative financing methods might help to distance government from operational issues (and the opprobrium that they sometimes brought) and might increase efficiency and choice. The options considered were

---

* Sir Norman Fowler, the Secretary of State, subsequently gave as his reason that 'There was no inherent cost advantage in moving over to an entirely new financing system and . . . that whatever system was chosen, taxation would still have to finance a giant share of the service.' *Source*: Fowler N (1991) *Ministers Decide*. Chapmans, London.

similar to those in the 1981 review, and included augmenting the tax-base system with greater charging and private-sector capital and a social insurance system based on the French or German model. There was a particular focus on providing incentives to contract out by increasing identifiable National Insurance contributions to fund new NHS expenditure and offering rebates to those willing to take out private insurance.

In practice, almost none of this work survived to the White Paper, *Working for Patients*, which was published in early 1989.[2] The general conclusion was that a National Insurance rebate scheme would involve a substantial 'dead weight' (i.e. payment to those who would have insured themselves privately anyway), and the pattern of healthcare would become unbalanced because low-risk contributors would contract out, leaving higher-risk people, notably the very young and the elderly, still within the NHS. The market for private health insurance was in any case already growing rapidly, weakening the case for giving it a further boost through National Insurance rebates or tax relief. The Chancellor also argued that without improvements in supply, tax concessions to the private sector would simply inflate prices.[3] There was also a change in Secretary of State in the middle of the review, with Kenneth Clarke showing much more sensitivity to the political risks of financing reform than his predecessor John Moore. For these various reasons the only glimmer of this debate that found its way into *Working for Patients* was a proposal to give income tax relief on insurance premiums for those aged 60 years or over.

The smaller reviews of 1991, 1993 and 1997

In 1991, 1993 and 1997, Ministers or senior officials commissioned short studies of the advantages and disadvantages of hypothecated health taxes. The commissions were partly preparations for public expenditure round discussions with the Treasury and partly responses to the continuing interest of think tanks and policy analysts in alternative means of finance.* All three reviews noted that there were two possible major objectives for a hypothecated health tax. The first objective was that the health tax would make it more evident (or transparent) to the tax payer what he or she was contributing towards the NHS, and would thus provide the base for a more rational debate about health expenditure. Secondly, a hypothecated tax might lower resistance to tax increases, thereby releasing health expenditure from the constraints of general public expenditure control. Unsurprisingly, the second of these objectives was particularly attractive to the Department of Health. A wide range of tax options was examined in order to determine whether they might contribute to this objective.

In the event, none of these reviews was pursued far with the Treasury or other government departments. It was concluded that the Treasury was unlikely to be receptive to ideas that would reduce its flexibility and, at least during the period of the Conservative Government, would undermine the arguments for lower taxes and lower spending and the pursuit of a wider tax base.

The 1997 review of hypothecation was an initial element of the Department of Health's Comprehensive Spending Review. One project in this review was a study of alternative sources of funding. In practice the focus was rapidly narrowed

* For example, 'Reconnecting taxation', DEMOS, 1993.

down to user charges and private-sector sponsorship of capital investment. The project was the only across-the-board review of user charges in the NHS during these 20 years. The introduction of new charges was ruled out on two main grounds – either they would deter needy patients from seeking treatment (e.g. charges for GP consultations) or collection difficulties would limit the potential revenue (e.g. hotel charges for inpatients). On both of these criteria a revision of prescription charges looked more promising. However, political considerations stopped further work. The only proposal to be pursued was the recovery of the costs of treating road accidents from insurance sources.

2000–02: comparing the sustainability of different healthcare-funding systems

Once the Prime Minister had made a commitment to raise UK healthcare expenditure to the average level in the European Union, policy interest switched from whether alternative methods of financing could add to the buoyancy of healthcare expenditure to what methods of financing were most likely to be sustainable in the longer term. In the Government's view, sustainability was linked to the perceived fairness and efficiency of different financing mechanisms. A paper was commissioned to review the evidence. Originally intended for stand-alone publication, it was decided at the last minute to incorporate it into the NHS Plan. The chapter in the Plan on 'Options for Funding Healthcare' assessed the main alternatives to general tax funding (i.e. private insurance, patient charges and social insurance) in terms of efficiency and equity criteria. All three alternatives were judged to be deficient in one or both of these criteria relative to general taxation. Predictably, the Plan announced no changes to the way in which healthcare was to be financed.

Although it was widely welcomed, the NHS Plan did not silence the critics of the NHS who saw the popularity of the French and German healthcare systems and the absence of long waiting times in both countries as evidence of the innate superiority of social-insurance-based funding. In 2001, Ministers commissioned a more detailed internal review of the relative strengths and weaknesses of tax and social insurance funding. This reached the following conclusions.

- Few if any of the commonly claimed advantages (and disadvantages) of social insurance systems were inherent to that method of funding. Most of the supposed advantages, notably responsiveness and choice, were due to other specific features of the French and/or German healthcare systems. With adequate funding they could be replicated in an NHS based on general taxation.
- Within OECD countries there was little or no evidence that methods of public funding were an important determinant either of public satisfaction with healthcare or of health outcomes.
- As the arguments both for and against social insurance funding were generally overdrawn, the two strongest arguments against a radical change from general taxation to social insurance funding were first the large transitional costs involved, and secondly the high opportunity costs of diverting Ministers, officials and health service managers from the more important task of reforming health service delivery.

In 2002, the Wanless Report raised the prospect that it would not be possible to increase NHS spending at the rate it recommended relying only on existing taxes and tax rates. Both the Department of Health and the Treasury therefore undertook work to identify new sources of revenue. Both reached similar conclusions, namely that an increase in National Insurance contributions through a partial lifting of the upper earnings limit looked to score well in terms of both equity and efficiency relative to the obvious tax alternatives. In the 2002 Budget the Chancellor announced that the huge increase in NHS expenditure required to meet Derek Wanless's recommendations would be funded in part through changes in both the rates and structure of National Insurance contributions, to take effect in 2003.[4]

Summary comments

Three conclusions stand out from this short history of the Department of Health's reviews of alternative means of financing health services.

1 Far more attention has been given to the alternative offered by hypothecated taxes in general, and social insurance in particular, than to the alternative of private insurance. User charges have been the least explored option, except in the important areas of long-term care and dentistry.*
2 In terms of their overall impact on the mix of funding streams, all of the reviews have broadly maintained the status quo.
3 Nevertheless, there have been some smaller shifts. Under the Conservative Government there was an increase in the share of private finance in total healthcare funding. And with the earmarking of additional tobacco tax revenues and the presentational linking of the 2003 National Insurance contribution increase to the expansion of the NHS budget, a loose form of hypothecation has come to play a larger part in the public financing of health services under the Labour Government.

Changing role of analysis and analysts

Looking back at this 20-year history, two other interesting features stand out – first, how regularly the issue of alternative financing has been raised, and secondly, how relatively little has been learned. The limited learning in part reflects how few of the reviews have gone beyond the stage of quick overviews of the major options. However, another factor has been the absence of any follow-up research programme. The secrecy accompanying nearly all of the reviews has also not encouraged learning. In general, once Ministers concluded that the dominant role of tax-based funding should remain untouched, there was no further work on financing issues until the next review several years later. The fact that each subsequent review did not start entirely from scratch in terms of its understanding of the issues was due largely to the longevity of service of several Departmental economists. For example, one of the economist members of the

---

* It has usually been recognised that in most areas user charges could not be taken far without needing the underpinning of some form of insurance.

1981 inter-departmental Working Party contributed to all of the succeeding reviews up until 1997.

However, over the 20-year period there was some building up of evidence and some learning. Areas of learning included the following.

1   *Appraisal criteria.* As was common in much analytical work at the time, the 1981–82 Working Party Report was not transparent about the criteria used to assess the very wide range of options that were reviewed. However, the Working Party based its appraisal on three sets of criteria, namely sufficiency (including public expenditure and capacity for control), efficiency (including choice and administrative costs) and equity (including distribution between individuals and geographical areas). Similar criteria appear in most of the later reviews, although they were usually reported more clearly. Different reviews attached different weights to the various criteria, but there was a tendency for the number of assessment criteria to grow through time and for the analysis against the criteria to become more evidence based. For example, the review of hypothecated taxes in 1997 compared various forms of hypothecation with general taxation in terms of ten criteria (adequacy and stability, control of spending, fiscal flexibility, fairness, willingness to pay, neutrality, maximising healthcare behaviour, economy of administration, transparency, and cost-consciousness).

2   *International evidence.* International evidence played a role in all of the reviews. In the 1981–82 review it was particularly important. In anticipation of the review study, tours to North America and Europe were undertaken by two members of the Working Party.[5] Foreign countries provided plenty of examples of other ways of financing health services, but without detailed research (which was generally not undertaken) it was difficult to separate out the advantages and disadvantages of an alternative form of finance from the other characteristics of a particular foreign healthcare system. It was not until around 2000 that the Department undertook detailed work attempting to separate out, for example, the core features of social health insurance from the accompanying structural and delivery characteristics of health services in countries such as France and Germany. However, if Departmental analysts were slow to separate out the effects of particular funding mechanisms from other national features, they were not alone. Throughout this period much of the output from think tanks and pressure groups advocating alternative funding models completely failed to distinguish between the effects of different financing mechanisms and the effects of the organisational and delivery structures to which those funding mechanisms were attached.

3   *Distributional effects.* Few of the reviews got as far as simulating the impact on income distribution of different funding options. The main exception was the 1988 review. This showed that shifting the funding of the NHS from general taxation to National Insurance contributions would produce several million significant gainers and losers. While these first-round effects could probably be ameliorated by other tax changes, the modelling well illustrated the range and scale of the transitional effects that would need to be managed if there was to be a major change in financing methods.

4   *Transition costs.* Across all of the reviews it was recognised that transition costs would be large if there was a radical shift of financing mechanisms. Awareness

of how large these costs would be grew with the more refined distributional modelling referred to above. It was also informed by awareness of the difficulties encountered by the Central and Eastern European countries that shifted from tax to social insurance financing in the 1990s.[6]

There remain a number of important unanswered questions about the effects of different financing regimes. Examples include the following.

- *On the demand for healthcare*, does a shift from general taxation to earmarking or hypothecating taxes for health services reduce or increase pressures for greater health expenditure? At different times and in different places policy analysts and politicians have taken radically different views on this question, presumably drawing on divergent assumptions about whether people under- or overestimate the current costs of health services. They may also have made different assumptions about whether it is consumers or providers who drive health service expectations. Perhaps the question needs to be reformulated along the lines of 'in what circumstances will a shift to hypothecation lead to reductions (or increases) in pressure for more health spending?'.
- *On the willingness to pay for healthcare*, do social insurance and other forms of hypothecation enable or facilitate more buoyant funding of health services? Attitude surveys suggest that people are more willing to pay taxes linked to specific services that they feel are under-funded.[7] At the inter-country level few econometric studies have (apparently) tested for this relationship, but one that indirectly did so found no positive relationship.[8]
- *On increasing transparency*, is hypothecation an effective way of increasing transparency, of enabling people to see where their taxes are going and hence being better able to judge whether particular services are over- or under-funded? Are there more effective ways of improving transparency (e.g. annual reports to taxpayers on what different services cost the average user, or user reports that include the average cost each time a service is used)?

The Department's analysts, particularly economists, can take most of the credit for what analysis was undertaken in this area. Except in the 1981–82 review and in the 1988 review, work on alternative financing mechanisms was left to the Department's economists. The confidentiality that surrounded nearly all of the reviews meant that few other parts of the Department developed any relevant expertise. Although internal analysts did not substantially push out the frontiers of knowledge on funding mechanisms, they did make a number of important contributions to the regular Departmental and Government debates. In particular, they drew attention both to the range of alternative funding and tax mechanisms and to the lack of evidence that those alternatives had significant advantages over the NHS's traditional funding system. They consistently argued that funding mechanisms have limited impact on the effectiveness of service delivery, although they may have important consequences for equity of service access. They also drew attention to the evidence that all countries are unhappy to some extent with their system of healthcare funding, and nearly all think that the grass looks greener elsewhere in the world.

The big questions

In retrospect, this history raises two major questions.

1 Why did the reviews bring about so little change in the way in which heathcare was financed in England?
2 Why does the search for alternative financing mechanisms continue to attract so much attention from think tanks and politicians?

Why was there so little change in the way in which health services were financed in England?

Expenditure on health services has grown enormously over the last 20 years, but the relative importance of the different sources of funding has changed very little. As Table 3.2 shows, there was some increase in the share of private funding in the 1980s, but over the last 10 years the contribution of general taxation has remained stable. With a promised real annual growth rate of over 7% per annum for the five years to 2007–8, tax-funded services are likely to increase their share of total expenditure to over 85%, a share of public funding currently surpassed in only two other OECD countries.

There are perhaps five main reasons why the various reviews of alternative financing mechanisms brought no major shift away from reliance on general taxation.

1 The reviews found little or no evidence that alternative means of financing would produce better health or healthcare outcomes. Looking across the world, there is no clear relationship between financing mechanisms and public and patient satisfaction, the quality of care (to the extent that it can be measured) or health outcomes.

   Prima facie there is an association between responsiveness and choice and either the share of private funding or the presence of competitive social insurance schemes. However, judged by their actions, until relatively recently governments in the UK did not attach great weight to expanding choice and responsiveness within the NHS. Although seen as desirable, they were not ends for which cost control should be put at risk. These attributes are now much more prominent in political thinking. Indeed many commentators and politicians see their relative absence as the key weakness of the NHS. The current Government believes that with adequate resourcing and a change in the way in which providers are funded, it should be possible to deliver both choice and responsiveness within a health system funded through general taxation. Most Scandinavian countries appear to share this view.

2 There is considerable evidence that some alternative financing mechanisms are associated with poorer performance, when judged by the basic fairness values of the NHS.[9] For example, there are clear limits on how far user charges can be expanded before access to care is adversely affected. There is also no doubt that heavy reliance on private insurance will reduce the progressivity of health system finance and encourage the expansion of two-tier access to healthcare.[10]

3 As already noted, the Treasury was concerned about the implications of reform

for wider economic and fiscal policy. For most of the period a shift to social insurance was seen as both a challenge to attempts to reform the labour market and a potential threat to the Treasury's grip on public spending.

4 The reviews consistently drew attention to the high transition costs involved in moving from general tax funding to a social-insurance-based system, the most commonly favoured alternative. If the benefits appeared to be small and relatively uncertain, it was easy to conclude that they would be swamped by the costs of moving from one funding base to another.

5 Probably most importantly, no government was willing to face the political costs of departing from the basic principles of the NHS or, until recently, to contemplate the kind of increase in resources that would make new funding streams essential. While the Department of Health regularly floated arguments about the greater acceptability of taxes that were earmarked for popular causes such as health, these arguments only found favour with the Chancellor and the Treasury when there was government-wide agreement that health should be given an exceptional expenditure boost. Even then they only found favour in the softest form of earmarking, as a way of making tax increases more palatable. By referring to ring-fencing tobacco tax increases for healthcare and by linking the expansion in the NHS budget to a change in the rate and structure of National Insurance contributions, the Treasury was endeavouring to make both taxes more palatable.

Why does the search for alternative means of financing continue to attract such attention from politicians and policy analysts?

Internal and external pressures for reviews of funding mechanisms have increased in frequency and intensity over the last 20 years. In the UK this can be largely explained by a combination of two factors. On the one hand, there was a growing recognition that the NHS was falling behind both public expectations and other healthcare systems, and on the other there was a belief that meeting those expectations from general taxation was impossible because it would require a politically unacceptable increase in the level of general taxes. However, the interest in alternative financing mechanisms has not been confined to the UK. Moreover, proposals to change the mix of funding have barely abated in the UK, even though the Government has committed itself to a huge increase in general tax-based funding for the next five years.

There are probably two main reasons why shifts in financing mechanisms continue to hold such fascination, and indeed are pursued at times with all the zeal of a Holy Grail.

The first reason is the tendency everywhere for patient and public expectations, medical advance and provider ambitions to put pressure on existing funding mechanisms. Shifting the pattern of funding can be presented as a way of easing the pressures either from the supply side, by increasing the willingness to pay taxes or to make private payments, or from the demand side, by reducing the public demand for additional spending. Viewed from the supply side it is understandable that politicians in general tax-based systems may see the answer as lying either in special forms of taxes that generate less resistance than general taxes, or in increased 'voluntary' payments through private insurance contributions or user charges. Similarly, in systems with a heavy reliance on private insurance and user charges, an expansion of tax funding may be seen as a way of spreading the pain or broadening access to 'necessary' services.

From the demand side, a change in funding mechanisms may be seen as a way of reducing those pressures, rather than of meeting them less painfully. Public and private insurance mechanisms hide the cost of services at the point of use. Most public mechanisms also hide the cost at the point of contribution or taxation. Some advocates of greater transparency in public funding through hypothecated or earmarked taxes see this as a way of sensitising the public to the costs of healthcare and hopefully abating pressures for more expenditure. The possibility that there are more effective ways of improving transparency and the absence of evidence that cost transparency does curtail the pressures for improved health services (see, for example, the situation in France and Germany) have not ended the interest in using hypothecation or earmarking as a way of dampening enthusiasm for greater health expenditure.* It is indicative of the absence of a good evidence base that the same reform, namely hypothecation, can be advocated by those wishing both to accelerate and to reduce the growth of public spending on health.

A second major reason for the continuing interest in alternative funding streams is because the debate about funding mechanisms is linked to wider philosophical and theoretical debates about the desirable role of government. Fiscal orthodoxy favouring flexibility in tax raising comes under attack from believers in both the minimalist state and the active state. On the one hand, earmarked taxes are favoured by 'public choice' theorists who advocate the 'benefit principle' and wish to minimise the role of the state. On the other hand, earmarked taxes are also supported by those who want a strong state and who believe that earmarked taxes are a way of legitimising expenditure by enabling citizens to see more clearly what they are paying for.[7] An even more fundamental source of destabilisation is the perennial argument between those who favour private user charging and those who favour public funding.

Debates about optimal funding systems are unlikely to go away, but unless they are accompanied by rigorous research they seem destined to continue to generate more heat than light.

References

1 (1982) *Economist*. 18 September. p. 25.
2 Department of Health (1989) *Working for Patients*. Department of Health, London.
3 Lawson N (1992) *The View from No. 11: memoirs of a Tory Radical*. Bantam Press, London.
4 Chancellor of the Exchequer's Budget Statement. 17 April 2002.
5 The results of one of the study tours were subsequently published in Hurst J (1985) *Financing Health Services in the United States, Canada and Britain*. The King's Fund, London.
6 Saltman R and Figueras J (1997) *European Health Care Reform: analysis of current strategies*. World Health Organization, Geneva.
7 Fabian Society (2000) *The Commission on Taxation and Citizenship. Paying for progress*. Fabian Society, London.

* New Zealand illustrated such interest in 2002–03.

8 Organisation for Economic Co-operation and Development (OECD) (1995) *New Directions in Health Care Policy*. Health Policy Studies No. 7. OECD, Paris.
9 Wagstaff A, van Doorslaer E, van der Burg H *et al.* (1999) Equity in the finance of health care: some further international comparisons. *J Health Econ*. 18: 263–90.
10 *See*, for example, Evans RG (2002) Financing health care: taxation and the alternatives. In: E Mossialos *et al.* (eds) *Funding Health Care: options for Europe*. Open University Press, Buckingham.

Chapter 4

Planning human resources

Introduction

The National Health Service has around one million workers, including 100 000 doctors. The planning of doctor numbers has arguably been one of the most enduring examples of detailed (Soviet-style) central planning in recent UK history. On the other hand, the management of these workers has been relatively neglected. It is therefore all the more remarkable that the NHS has provided an effective health service with a smaller number of doctors per head of population than in any other comparable OECD country.

Over the last 20 years the contribution of Departmental analysts (particularly economists and operational researchers) to human resource planning has tended to wax and wane in line with the attention given to the area by the Department as a whole. For example, the decentralising of labour market responsibilities in the 1990s led to severe cutbacks in central analytical support which had to be rapidly reversed at the end of the 1990s when it was realised that human resources were the main constraint on the Labour Government's new service ambitions. The contribution of analysts has also been affected by the silos that long constrained policy work on human resource planning issues, namely the compartmentalisation of the planning of hospital doctors, GPs and nurses and an even sharper divide between quantitative planning and pricing decisions. In a fragmented policy-making world, the contribution of analysts has tended to focus on a limited number of areas, with occasional forays into a wider range of human resource questions.

This chapter focuses on medical workforce planning. It begins with a discussion of the policy context, including the radical changes in the importance attached to human resource planning and to the integration of such planning both across skills and with services. A short history of medical workforce planning is followed by a more detailed examination of the major criticisms of such planning and how the Department has tried to address them. This is followed by a consideration of the role of internal and external analysts in improving workforce planning in the NHS. The chapter ends with reflections on one big issue, namely how the effectiveness of medical workforce planning can be improved.

Policy context

Throughout the last 20 years the Government has sought to forecast the demand for and supply of the medical workforce, and to adjust the supply in order to ensure 'equilibrium' in the labour market. Over this period the scale of the supply adjustments has increased dramatically. At the beginning of the period, demand forecasts rested heavily on broad assumptions about the affordable growth in NHS expenditure, and were held down by Treasury concerns about costs and medical profession concerns about the dangers of unemployment. As late as 1985, the British Medical Association Council was pushing for a reduction in medical school intake.[1] Twenty years later, forecasts of service demand were much higher, more visible and more disaggregated and the supply of doctors was seen as the key constraint on the delivery of the government's service priorities. One indicator of the change in the importance attached to doctor numbers is provided by the contrast between the additional consultant numbers announced in the Conservative Government's *Working for Patients* reforms in 1989 and in the Labour government's 'NHS Plan' in 2000. In 1989, it was announced that 250 additional consultant posts would be funded over the next three years. In 2000, it was announced that 7500 more consultants would be in post within four years.

Other changes ran alongside this huge shift in the importance attached to the medical workforce. One of these was a cyclical movement – stronger (so far) in rhetoric than in reality – between a highly centralised mechanical and quantity-based approach to planning and a more decentralised approach that allowed for market-based behavioural adjustments and for prices as an equilibrating mechanism. The cycle is now arguably well into its second oscillation. The 'internal market' that was introduced in 1991 saw a determined attempt to decentralise human resource planning responsibilities. However, medical school numbers continued to be set centrally, and there was much less use of pay flexibilities as a price-equilibrating mechanism than had been expected. The 1997 Labour Government rapidly recentralised the planning function once the size of the expected shortfalls was clear. However, the desperate need to increase the supply of all kinds of skilled health workers also led to much greater use of price signals than at the time of the formal 'internal market'. Now in line with the Government's stated intention to decentralise NHS management there is the beginning of a new cycle of decentralising human resource planning.

A second change has been in the integration of planning. For much of the last 20 years there was separate forecasting and planning of doctors, nurses and the various other healthcare professions. In addition, service developments were planned with little attention to their human resource implications. In the last five years serious attempts have been made to incorporate human resource planning into service planning. Driven by severe staff shortages, a more holistic approach has also been adopted to human resource planning. These are trends that still have further to go.

Another dramatic shift in context has been around the roles and expectations of both doctors and nurses. Hospital doctors have seen a move from a consultant-led to a consultant-based service, major changes in training to bring it more in line with European practice, determined attempts to reduce junior doctors' working hours, a proliferation of sub-specialties, and a transformation in the way in which doctors are managed and measured. The shift in roles of GPs has been as large if not larger. Nursing, too, has witnessed huge changes, including the replacement of an apprenticeship-based training system by full-time degree-level training and the development of a whole raft of new posts (from practice nurse through nurse practitioner to nurse consultant) that were barely thought of 20 years ago.

Medical workforce planning

A short history

Governments have attempted to forecast the demand for and supply of the medical workforce for 60 years. To bring supply and demand into balance, the focus has been on adjustments in supply and particularly on medical school intake. In 1968, the Royal Commission on Medical Education,[2] under the chairmanship of Lord Todd, recommended a near doubling of medical school intake to 4230 to be achieved by 1980. This programme of expansion broadly determined policy throughout the 1970s and 1980s, although the Todd target was not exceeded until 1991. The Todd Report used a change in the doctor-to-population ratio as the basis of its estimates of future demand. A series of reviews of medical manpower policy and manpower needs from 1978 to 1989 did not seek to change the direction of policy, although they based estimates of the required growth in doctor numbers on assumptions about growth in health expenditure rather than about population growth.* All of these reports made assumptions about the growth in NHS resources that proved pessimistic. For example, the two reports by the Advisory Committee for Medical Manpower Planning both based their estimates on a 1983 Health Circular which stated:

> For longer-term planning purposes should assume that resources for Hospital and Community Health Services . . . could grow at about half a per cent per year over the next 10 years. This does not imply a commitment to such growth.

A new standing committee on medical manpower that was announced in 1991, namely the Medical Manpower Standing Advisory Committee (MMSAC),† was the first advisory group to recommend an increase in medical school intake above the level proposed by Todd. MMSAC's first report in 1992 recommended an increase of 240 in medical school intake. The second report in 1995 recommended a further increase in intake of 250, to be achieved over five years. The third report in 1998 proposed an additional and much more substantial increase in intake of 1000 students. Hard on the heels of this report, the NHS Plan which was launched in 2000 announced that the government would seek yet another increase in the number of medical school places of up to 1000. This series of expansions is expected to increase the medical school intake to a total of around 7500 in 2005 and 8000 by 2008.

In retrospect it can be seen that within a short period of four to five years the Department and its advisers went through a 'Damascan' conversion over future doctor requirements. One factor that contributed to this change was a review by the Department's economists in 1995 of the past record for forecasting the growth in doctor numbers. This found that every one of the six advisory committee reports, from the 1968 Todd Report onwards, had underestimated the subsequent actual growth in doctor numbers. The Treasury's concern to avoid expenditure

---

*The reports included the Green Paper, *Medical Manpower: the Next 20 Years* in 1978, the *Medical Manpower Steering Group Report* in 1980, and two reports by the Advisory Committee for Medical Manpower Planning in 1985 and 1989.

† The Committee's name was later changed to the Medical Workforce Standing Advisory Committee (MWSAC).

blowouts had combined with the medical profession's concern to avoid un-employment, to produce 'pessimism bias'. The Treasury's insistence on using low-health-expenditure assumptions was supported by the view, common among health economists, that increasing the supply of doctors would inflate service demand and threaten cost inflation. The worries of the medical profession about unemployment went virtually unchallenged because of the dominant position that they were given in all of the medical workforce reviews.

The implication of the pessimism bias was that if the future was like the past, there would be a need for faster growth in doctor numbers than recent reports had assumed. Within a year there were two good reasons for believing that the future would not be like the past, and that the requirement would be even greater. First, it became clear that hospital patient services were growing more rapidly than during the 1980s, a trend that public expectations and waiting-time targets could be expected to continue. Secondly, it became evident that recent changes in human resource policies on the training of hospital doctors (the Calman Report)[3] and on reducing trainee doctors' working hours had not been properly assessed for their implications for medical staff numbers. By mid-1996 the NHS Board recognised that there might be a significant gap between demand for and supply of the medical workforce in the next five to ten years. The Labour Government's announcement of successively larger expansions in health services in 1998, 2000 and 2002 turned the projected gaps into gaping chasms.

Medical workforce planning: a critique

The practice of medical workforce planning in England has been criticised by academic economists since the 1960s.[4] In more recent years the best-known critic has been Alan Maynard.[5] The major criticisms have continued up to the present, and have been extended to human resource planning in many other countries.[6] The Department's advisory committees, policy leads and analysts have generally been aware of these criticisms. It may therefore be of interest to briefly discuss the Department's evolving response to the external criticisms as well as to one or two weaknesses that have been given more prominence internally than externally.

The main areas for improvement perennially identified by external critics reflect a view that human resource planning has been both too mechanistic and based on an assumption that the current ways of delivering healthcare are efficient and should continue into the future. Criticisms have included the following.

1 The planning of different categories of medical human resources, most notably doctors and nurses, has been kept in different silos, ignoring substitution possibilities.
2 Current levels of efficiency with regard to the use of human resources have been assumed to be optimal, with little or no exploration of the scope for improving efficiency through better human resource management.
3 There has been slow recognition of the changing characteristics, expectations and behaviours of the sources of medical workforce supply, particularly women and overseas doctors.
4 The difficulties in all of these areas have been exacerbated by a poor information and evidence base.

5   The role of pay and incentives as mechanisms to bring medical labour markets into equilibrium has been systematically ignored.

As well as attempting to grapple with these problems, Departmental analysts have been aware of three other challenges:

1   failure to quantitatively assess the human resource implications of changes in service policies and plans including, ironically, changes in human resources policies
2   a tendency for human resource planning decisions to oscillate between pessimism bias when estimating future demands during periods of low-expenditure growth, and optimism bias when estimating future workforce supply in periods of high-expenditure growth
3   difficulty in establishing an efficient balance between decentralised and centralised human resource planning responsibilities, particularly given the shortage of human resource planning capabilities at all levels in the NHS.

The sections that follow comment on each of these challenges in turn.

Skill mix and scope for skill substitution

Although committees advising on future workforce numbers tended to assume either no or very slow changes in skill mix, the Department did occasionally review the scope for improving the efficiency or quality of care by changing the mix of skills. The issue was approached from a range of directions. In the earlier part of the period, the focus tended be on the scope for changing the mix of nursing skills (e.g. the 1985 study 'Mix and match: a review of nursing skill mix') and the latitude for changing the mix of medical staff (e.g. 'Achieving a balance' aimed to move hospital care from being consultant led to being consultant based[7]). In the later part of the period the focus shifted more to the opportunity for substituting nursing and other skilled staff for doctors (e.g. the Greenhalgh Report published in 1994 and the various pilot projects funded to examine the role of nurse practitioners in general practice). All such reviews tended to encounter resistance from the powerful professional groups affected. While skill markets remained in rough balance, internal analysts were limited to highlighting the (rather limited) international evidence on skill mix changes in other countries, and to advocating the establishment of pilot projects to test the feasibility and cost-effectiveness of more innovative ways of delivering patient services.

The few rapid changes that did take place before the late 1990s were driven primarily by scarcity. For example, the growth in the number of practice nurses in GP surgeries in the late 1980s and early 1990s can be seen as a response to a rapid growth in demand for primary care services, the right incentives on GPs to respond to those demands, and very slow growth in the supply of GPs. The acute labour market shortages that became apparent from 1998 onwards look likely to do more to change the health service skill mix than all of the reviews over the previous 20 years. Issues that were previously quickly shunted into the 'too politically difficult' basket are now being actively explored. An example is the use of non-medical staff in the delivery of anaesthesia services. Skill shortages also seem to be driving a more determined effort to integrate planning across the professions, including designing new types of worker (e.g. part occupational therapist, part nurse) to help to fill particular skill gaps. However, it is too early to judge how successful this will be.

Ignoring inefficiency in the use of the current human resource stock

Most reviews of the clinical workforces have assumed that current staff are efficiently deployed. They have also chosen to project forward recent trends in productivity. In earlier reviews there may not have been the information base to justify different assumptions. By the early 1990s, there was clear evidence of large variations in labour productivity for both nurses and doctors in hospitals and for GPs in primary care. In the Department's 1994 Fundamental Review of Expenditure, a key conclusion was that labour productivity was the largest measured cause of variations in unit costs in the NHS, and therefore potentially the largest source of future efficiency savings. However, attempts to follow through on this understanding with any vigour were seen as incompatible with the new policy emphases on promoting quality of care and on improving staff retention rates and reducing sickness rates. Members of the NHS Executive Board also doubted that there were enough good managers in hospital trusts to tackle the variations. However, one legacy of these findings was a stronger resolve to strengthen the management of hospital doctors through more rigorous work plans. In the 1998 Comprehensive Spending Review, Ministers also agreed to the production and distribution of data on the comparative workloads of hospital doctors by specialty and hospital. This was finally implemented in December 2002. Data difficulties prohibited any similar centrally led attempts to follow up on variations in the productivity of nurses.

In the mid-1990s, Departmental analysts also undertook work on time trends in the productivity of doctors and nurses. The work was quite crude,* but it suggested that over the previous 15 years nurse productivity had increased quite significantly, GP productivity on some measures had improved by around 1% per annum, and hospital doctor productivity had remained unchanged. When combined with the data showing significant variations in productivity across the country, officials concluded that it should be possible to continue or better these trends in the immediate future. Subsequent experience suggested that this view was too optimistic. With the slowdown and more recently the (possibly temporary) reversal in the decline in average hospital length of stay, the improvement in nurse productivity as currently measured has also slowed right down. Hospital doctor productivity has remained unchanged, and at the time of writing (2004) is falling in the majority of specialties. From an international perspective, assumptions about improving on these trends would appear to be optimistic. A unique if now somewhat dated attempt to compare hospital doctor 'productivity' across countries found a strong inverse relationship between measured productivity and hospital specialists per capita. At the time of the comparison (1988–89), hospital doctors in the UK were the least numerous (per capita) and appeared to be the most productive of those in the 12 European countries for which data were available. Now that the number of medical staff in the UK is increasing rapidly, it would be timely to expand and update such international comparisons, not least in order to identify international bench-

---

* As with other Departmental work on productivity and efficiency up to 2002, it was unable to allow for changes in the quality of care. It also made little or no allowance for changes in case mix.

marks. However, to be credible any future work on productivity must build in a measure of the quality of care.

Changes in the supply of hospital doctors

The Department and its advisory committees have been criticised for being slow to recognise the implications of two supply trends – first, the increasing proportion of women in medical school intakes, and secondly, the increasing dependence on foreign doctors. Criticism on the first count is probably unwarranted. There was quite early acknowledgement that women doctors might expect different work patterns to their male colleagues. The problem was to foresee how different their expectations might be and what types of policies might best address them.

There is more basis for the argument that the Department was slow to adjust its policies to take account of the increasing reliance on doctors trained overseas. In the early to mid-1990s, ignoring the opportunities for recruiting more overseas doctors could be excused by the aspiration to move towards 'self-sufficiency'. However, as this aspiration became increasingly unrealistic, the Department was slow to build up its capacity to attract recruits from overseas. The need to explore such options was recognised as early as 1996, but as late as 2000 Ministers had to be told that the Department had very little understanding of what might be possible in terms of the recruitment of hospital specialists from abroad.

In defence of the Department, it is worth noting that recognition of the major skill shortages in the NHS came at the same time as the headquarters head count was being slimmed by 20%, a reduction that fell particularly on policy and analytical staff working in the human resources area.

Inadequate information base

A major contributor to all of these weaknesses was the poor information base. In the early years of this period there was very little timely information on either the stocks of different types of human resources employed by the NHS or the annual flows in and out. These basic data only gradually improved, and arguably still remain poor in important respects. For example, it is not possible to track flows of nurses into and out of the NHS workforce. We only know the total numbers working for the NHS and the total numbers registered. For many categories of therapist and scientific officer we do not even know the total numbers qualified. Information on variations in the productivity levels of doctors, nurses and other types of staff has also remained poor. To identify and manage variations requires better risk adjustment systems and improved performance indicators. It also requires the development of measures of healthcare quality that can be linked to individual clinicians. It is to be hoped that the Department will overcome its fear of the medical profession and decide to collaborate with and/or emulate the innovatory work of the British United Provident Association (BUPA), which is using a health-related quality of life measure (the SF36) to monitor improvements in health between hospital admission and three months after discharge for selected surgical interventions.[8]

Pay and incentives

Perhaps the most long standing and most justified criticism of health workforce planning has been its failure to look at price (wage) adjustment and quantity adjustment together. The various official committees that were established to advise on the supply and demand of the medical labour force were either confined by their terms of reference to focusing on quantities or chose to largely ignore the role of prices and wages. A major reason for this one-eyed approach was that wages and salaries of staff had been fixed on an annual basis by pay review bodies. Pay review bodies for doctors had been established in 1960, and a Pay Review Committee had been set up for nurses and professions allied to medicine in 1984. The quantity/price split in responsibilities between external bodies was mirrored within the Department by a similar split in responsibilities between policy branches. The work of internal analysts followed this bifurcation. For example, for many years modelling of the supply of nurses took no account of wages at all.

The rigidities caused by the failure of quantitative planning to consider prices were exacerbated by the nature of the pay systems for both GPs and hospital doctors. Capitation payments and salaries meant that there was little incentive for doctors to respond to unmet demand by increasing their activity. However, for hospital consultants the private sector offered a fee-for-service escape route, and this route grew rapidly in the 1980s. Arguably Japan exemplifies a more appropriate combination of quantity and pay policies. There, controls on doctor numbers have been almost as tight as in the UK but they are matched with fee-for-service payment systems.*

The relationships between quantities and pay were not ignored altogether. While quantitative planning tended to ignore pay, pay policies did give some attention to quantitative issues. For example, in preparing evidence for pay review bodies, the Department gave consideration to the implications of pay for recruitment, retention and turnover.

The organisational barriers to reviewing prices and quantities together were supported by deep-seated beliefs in much of the Department and the NHS. On the demand side it was held that the mix of labour inputs could be little affected by relative pay. On the supply side there were some who appeared to believe that wage levels had little impact on the decision to join, participate in or leave the workforce. The same group tended to be much more concerned about the perceived inequalities that might be caused if remuneration was allowed to vary in line with labour market supply and demand or productivity. This reluctance to accept that financial incentives mattered, except as an equity issue, may also help explain the unwillingness to face up to and tackle the perverse incentives caused by the rapid growth in consultant private practice in the 1980s. It almost certainly contributed to the longstanding (and in some parts of the Department continuing) resistance to the introduction of adequate variations in local and regional pay. It may also help to explain why there was so little attempt to research the wage elasticities of supply of nurses and other health service professions.[9]

As a consequence of this neglect, Departmental policy officials and analysts found themselves poorly placed when from 1999 onwards Ministers sought advice both on pay modernisation and on the means and scope for using financial incentives to improve recruitment and retention and to promote productivity. For their advice analysts had to rely on the theoretical labour economics literature or

*I am grateful to Jeremy Hurst for making this point.

the evidence from other sectors, such as education and the limited health evidence from overseas, notably from the USA. In some cases Ministerial time-tables allowed for piloting of new approaches to remuneration. For example, there was a modest attempt to pilot team bonuses in various parts of the NHS.[10] However, in many other areas ranging from nurse recruitment schemes to the new consultant contract, changes in remuneration were developed and announced with inevitably limited understanding of what their impact might be on labour market behaviour and productivity.

The limited evidence meant that it was difficult to challenge the beliefs of many Departmental and NHS human resource specialists that flexing pay to reflect supply and demand or performance was more likely to provoke claims of inequity than to improve efficiency. This helps to explain the reliance of the new consultant contract on performance regulation (via mandatory job planning and appraisal) rather than on financial incentives (e.g. fees for service). In this respect there is a contrast with the new GP contract; but then NHS remuneration policies have long implicitly assumed that GPs are more sensitive to financial incentives than are hospital doctors.* As others have noted,[11] stronger systems of job planning and appraisal will severely test NHS information systems and management processes. Judging by past experience they will also test the courage or 'bottle' of many local managers.

Integrating human resource and service planning

For the bulk of the period up to 2000 the expansion of most health services was so gradual that arguably it was not necessary to analyse the human resource implications of individual new policies. This may help to explain, if not to justify, why the Department found it so difficult to integrate service and human resource planning when the expansion of health services accelerated at the end of the 1990s. However, it is harder to explain why the workforce implications of new human resource policies were underestimated from the early 1990s onwards. The explanation was probably a combination of faith in continuing to muddle through on doctor numbers and an unwillingness to confront the Treasury with the full costs of new Departmental policies.

The specialist medical training reforms (Calman) and the New Deal (reducing junior doctors' hours) were the most significant examples of human resource policies in the early 1990s that were initially inadequately assessed for their workforce implications. Later the Department was very slow to react to the implications of the EU Working Times Directive which was first assessed by analysts in 1998. Policy staff responsible for medical workforce planning were not unaware of these problems. As early as 1996 they proposed the introduction of a 'workforce compliance statement' requiring all new policy initiatives to assess their effects on the demand or supply of staff and their impact on morale and motivation. Like many other attempts to improve and formalise Departmental policy appraisal processes, the idea was not followed through.

It was at about the same time (1996) that one of the Department's senior economists wrote a paper headed 'Are current service and medical staffing

---

*In some other countries the distinction is even sharper. In New Zealand, for instance, the majority of GPs are paid entirely by fee for service, but doctors employed by public hospitals depend on salaries with no distinction, merit or other performance-related payments.

policies consistent?'. The conclusion he drew was that they were not consistent. Service development, including the rapid development of hospital elective and emergency activity and movement towards a 'primary care-led NHS', required an annual increase of about 3% per annum in total doctor numbers. However, the stock of UK doctors was expected to grow at only 1.7% per annum over the next five to ten years. At the time the policy responses by the NHS Board were fairly limited. However, lessons were being learnt.

Two years later, when the much more ambitious service development plans of the Comprehensive Spending Review were under consideration, the EOR was commissioned to provide a detailed analysis of the number of qualified staff (and beds) likely to be required in the acute sector over the next four years in order to meet the Government's objectives on waiting lists and other acute pressures. From then on it became a regular practice to analyse the human resource implications of the Government's waiting times and emergency care objectives. The policy leads in other parts of the Department were also gradually persuaded of the importance of estimating the human resource implications of their policy proposals. However, some areas were more conservative than others. At times primary care policy leads were particularly slow to acknowledge that new responsibilities and new performance targets would have significant workload implications that should be rigorously assessed.

Through 2002 most policy divisions continued to find it difficult to estimate the impact of new policies on the demand for and supply of the relevant categories of staff. Detailed estimation was left to statisticians, operational researchers and economists. In retrospect, these difficulties raise interesting questions about the level of accuracy of the costing of policies over the previous decades when the Department's analysts had not been regularly involved in such work.

From pessimism bias about demand to optimism bias about supply

Future NHS historians may conclude that at the end of the twentieth century a long period of over-pessimism about the demand for medical personnel was replaced by a period of over-optimism about the ability to rapidly expand supply. As has already been noted, Treasury caution, the medical profession's fear of weakening its bargaining position and the conservatism of Departmental officials together go a long way towards explaining the earlier pessimism. In contrast, the recent optimism in relation to supply stems from Ministerial enthusiasm for improving the level of services, and the unwillingness of officials to be seen to be unhelpful. Analysts found themselves acting as moderators with regard to both forms of bias. In the early to mid-1990s they drew attention to the persistent under-forecasting of demand and the growing imbalance between the assumptions of service planning and those of human resource planning. At the end of the decade they drew attention to the lack of realism of forecasts that combined historically very high productivity growth with exceptionally rapid workforce expansion. In the past the two have shown a strong inverse relationship. An insistence on more realistic assumptions helped to force the exploration of options that had previously been confined to the 'too hard' basket, notably skill substitution and the more active use of pay and other financial incentives.

Balancing centralised and decentralised human resource planning responsibilities

Over this period, responsibilities for human resource planning shifted back and forth between the Department and local organisations (whether regions, districts or providers). When decentralisation has been in vogue, local organisations have been brought together in consortia or, more recently, Workforce Planning Confederations.[12] The arguments for decentralising demand forecasting to local organisations are in theory very strong. They should have access to better and more up-to-date information, and they should have stronger incentives to develop such information and to use it carefully. If there are major regional differences in the balance between supply and demand, as there frequently are in the NHS, there may also be strong arguments for decentralising supply planning and policies.

However, the experience with decentralised planning between 1991 and 1997 points to a number of potential limitations. These include the following.

- The disjunction between the relatively short business planning periods of local organisations and the long times required to train new medical staff. As the UK record with regard to medical workforce planning shows, this is a significant if lesser problem for the centre, and will remain so even with expenditure commitments of five years into the future.
- Limited modelling and analytical skills, resulting in what has been described as 'crude capacity planning and simple-minded interpretations of national targets'.[13] Yet here there is an obvious chicken-and-egg problem, as unless local organisations are required to undertake workforce planning they will never develop the capacity to do it well.
- Lack of knowledge of wider labour market developments, both national and international. Without a model of the labour market it is difficult to predict changes in retention rates and recruitment, but for each local organisation to develop such models would involve considerable duplication of effort.
- When it is accompanied by devolved budgets, there is a risk of money leaking away from investment in the future workforce towards today's service priorities. This appears to have happened to nurse training monies that were devolved to regional health authorities in 1992.

These risks of local planning support the need for a balance between central and local responsibilities for human resource planning. The balance needs to take account of the relative strengths and weaknesses of local and national planners. Some of the most obvious strengths and weaknesses are summarised in Box 4.1.

Box 4.1 Local and national workforce planning: relative strengths and weaknesses*

Local workforce planning

Strengths

- Knowledge of current local service and workforce
- Planning responsive to local circumstances

- Able to engage local stakeholders and gain ownership
- Counterweight to centralist 'priors'.

Weaknesses

- Lack of resources and expertise
- Problem of cross-border flows and free-riding
- Duplication of effort across health authorities
- Risk of resources being diverted away from training workforce.

National workforce planning

Strengths

- Support and influence national service planning (e.g. NSFs)
- High level of expertise and greater knowledge of wider labour market developments due to economies of scale
- Earlier recognition of need for new support policies (e.g. overseas recruitment)
- Able to adopt longer planning timescale.

Weaknesses

- Lack of ownership by NHS and other stakeholders
- Insufficient attention to mechanisms to deliver at local level
- Risk of undue influence by politicians and the Treasury
- Innovation stifled (e.g. in skill mix).

* I am grateful to Keith Derbyshire for the idea and much of the contents of this box.

Achieving a good balance is clearly challenging, and is likely to be the subject of considerable experimentation for the foreseeable future.

The role of analysts

A number of academic economists, led by Alan Maynard, have for many years been consistent critics of the Department's approach to medical workforce planning. Some of the criticisms have been overstated, and their method of presentation has sometimes weakened their influence. Nevertheless, they have provided a continuing series of valuable challenges to the thinking of internal analysts and their policy colleagues.

As was noted earlier, the role of internal analysts has waxed and waned in line with the priority accorded to human resource planning by Ministers and the Department. Internal analysts can take some credit for alerting the Department to the following:

- the advisory committees' record of persistently underestimating the demand for doctors
- the growing imbalance between service plans and human resource plans in the mid- to late 1990s
- the chronic failure of service and human resource policies and plans to

properly assess their implications for workforce requirements of all types (not just doctors)

- the flat time profile of medical productivity (as currently measured without allowance for quality) and hence the lack of realism of expecting large improvements in productivity in the absence of identifying new ways in which this might be achieved
- the apparent high average level of UK doctor productivity (again without adjusting for quality), particularly of hospital doctors, relative to peers in other countries
- the growing dependence of consultants on private-sector earnings in the 1980s, and the importance of continuing to monitor the size and source of consultants' incomes via a special Inland Revenue survey
- the unexplained variation in hospital specialist productivity, the scope for using routinely collected administrative data (Hospital Episode Statistics) for monitoring the variations, and the potential value of such data to hospital managers
- for nurses, the need for regional pay premiums for London and the South East if labour markets were to be brought into better balance.

As most of the chapter focuses on medical staff, this last contribution may warrant a little expansion. Departmental economists can point to a long history of drawing attention to the need for NHS policies to take account of geographical differences in wage and salary costs. In 1980, work that they initiated led to the addition of a *market forces factor* (*MFF*) to the formula used for the geographical allocation of NHS resources. The MFF has been revised on a number of occasions, but by 2000 it was apparent that it was not being adequately passed through into higher wages in those areas (London and the South East) with the highest local pay levels. As a consequence, those areas with the highest general wages (as represented by the staff MFF) continued to experience the highest nurse vacancy rates and the lowest nurse participation rates. The existing London allowances were insufficient in size and imperfectly targeted.

As the Labour Government had abolished the previous administration's policy of local wage flexibility, analysts argued that 'an alternative and more effective method [of taking account of local labour market conditions] might be for the centre to set local differentials based on external labour market pressures'. The Agenda for Change agreements introduced in the NHS from 2003 to 2004 effectively employed such a system by building local and regional flexibilities into national pay arrangements.[14] The agreements exemplify the Treasury's belief that 'meeting the objectives for local pay is likely to be best achieved through national bargaining arrangements, rather than devolving responsibilities for bargaining down to the local level'.[15]

In retrospect, a major failing of the management of internal analytical work was the run-down of resources devoted to it in the mid-1990s, leaving the Department without the analytical capacity to respond rapidly to the huge service expansion required by Ministers from 2000 onwards. A stronger analytical capacity would not, of course, have conjured more doctors or nurses into the labour force overnight, but it might have helped to provide earlier warning of the need for increased recruitment and training. It could also have brought forward the identification of effective policies to accelerate the expansion of supply. It would certainly have produced a better assessment of the realism and feasibility of the service plans and targets discussed in the 1998 Comprehensive Spending Review, the 2000 National Plan and the 2002 Spending Review. The run-down of analytical capacity was the direct consequence of decisions first to decentralise human resource planning under the 'Internal Market' and secondly to reduce overall staff numbers in the Department by 20%. With greater prescience I could have maintained or even built up the Department's analytical capacity in this area, but it would have meant taking analysts away from areas where there was strong customer demand and redeploying them on work which at that time had virtually no customer support.

How can the effectiveness of medical workforce planning be improved?

Viewed from the early years of the twenty-first century, medical workforce planning has been one of the least successful aspects of the NHS's history over the last 20 years. But how does the performance look in comparative rather than absolute terms? For example, did other countries get human resource planning as badly wrong as we now appear to have done, or are we an outlier? Measures of the success or failure of health human resource planning are rather limited. However, there is evidence that many countries struggle to keep supply and demand in balance and to avoid cycles of 'shortages' and 'surpluses'.[13] Elsewhere the most prevalent imbalance currently relates to nurses rather than to doctors. However, it would be reasonable to conclude that human resource planning in health is very difficult, most obviously because of the long lead times in changing supply and the difficulties in predicting demand.

With hindsight, the major error in England in the 1980s and much of the 1990s was hubris. No one could have predicted that decades of expanding real NHS expenditure at around 3% per annum would suddenly be replaced by spending increases of 7% a year, for year after year. However, it was insolent at worst and wishful thinking at best to believe that the NHS could continue to deliver a high-quality universal and comprehensive health service with doctor numbers that were dropping further and further behind those in other countries with similar incomes and public expectations. Within the Department the warning flags were raised well before 1998.

For the future, how can the effectiveness of medical workforce planning be improved? Most of the lessons from the recent past probably overlap with those found in other countries (e.g. by the Organisation for Economic Co-operation and Development and the World Health Organization),[16] but they may still be worth repeating. An initial list would include the following:

- the importance of regular monitoring and evaluation of human resource forecasts and plans
- the need to integrate workforce planning with health service plans and policies (including new human resource policies!)
- the importance of addressing price and quantity adjustment mechanisms together
- the critical role of personal incentives, particularly financial incentives, in determining recruitment, retention, geographical location and performance

- the importance of 'whole-system' approaches to human resource planning, or at least of explicitly considering substitution possibilities
- the importance of timely and appropriate data
- the importance of high-quality senior administrative leadership (a large proportion of the EOR's most useful work in the mid-1990s appears to have been commissioned directly or indirectly by one human resources director)
- the obvious value of having strong political interest and involvement
- the contribution of international comparisons to raising questions, if not to answering them
- acceptance that medical workforce planning is too important to be mainly determined by the medical profession.

References

1 (1985) Reductions in medical school intake – a matter of urgency (from the Council). *BMJ.* **290**: 1445.

2 Parliament (1968) *Report to the Royal Commission on Medical Education (Chairman, Lord Todd).* HMSO, London.

3 Department of Health (1993) *Hospital Doctors Training for the Future: the Report of the Working Group on Specialist Medical Training (Chairman, Kenneth Calman).* Department of Health, London.

4 *See,* for example, Jewkes J (1960) *Memorandum of Dissent to Royal Commission on Doctors' and Dentists' Remuneration.* HMSO, London.

5 *See,* for example, Maynard A and Walker A (1995) Managing the medical workforce: time for improvements? *Health Policy.* **31**: 1–16.

6 *See,* for example, Bloor K and Maynard A (2003) *Planning Human Resources in Health Care: towards an economic approach. An international comparative review.* Canadian Health Services Research Foundation, Ottawa.

7 Department of Health and Social Security (1987) *Hospital Medical Staffing. Achieving a Balance: plan for action.* Department of Health and Social Security, London.

8 Valance-Owen A and Cubbin S (2002) Monitoring national clinical outcomes: a challenging programme. *Br J Health Care Manag.* **8**: 412–17.

9 Antonazzo E, Scott A, Skatun D and Elliott RF (2003) The labour market for nursing: a review of the labour supply literature. *Health Econ.* **12**: 465–78.

10 Smith P and York N (2003) *Contracting and incentives for quality and efficiency: the UK experience.* Paper prepared for a Commonwealth Fund/Nuffield Trust Conference at Pennyhill Park, Bagshot, England, July 2003.

11 Bloor K and Maynard A (2004) *Managing Variations in Clinical Activity in England.* University of York, York.

12 Department of Health (2000) *A Health Service for All the Talents: developing the NHS workforce.* Department of Health, London.

13 Bloor K and Maynard A (2003) *Planning Human Resources in Health Care: towards an economic approach. An international comparative review.* Canadian Health Services Research Foundation, Ottawa.

14 Department of Health (2003) *The New NHS Pay System: an overview.* Department of Health, London.

15 HM Treasury (2003) *Government Guidance Note on Progressing Local Pay.* HM Treasury, London.

16 *See,* for example, Egger D, Lipson D and Adams O (2000) *Achieving the Right Balance: the role of policy-making processes in managing human resources for health problems.* Issues in Health Service Delivery. Discussion Paper No. 2. World Health Organization, Geneva.

Chapter 5

How efficient is the NHS?

Introduction

All governments have an interest in better meeting the public's needs by maximising the value for money of public expenditure on health services. Economists distinguish two ways of improving value for money, namely allocative efficiency or 'doing the right things' and technical efficiency or 'doing things right' (i.e. at the lowest cost for a given quality and quantity of output). This chapter reviews the contribution of analysis to improving the measurement and monitoring of technical efficiency in the NHS. A subsequent chapter considers allocative efficiency.

To measure technical efficiency properly requires measures of the quality of outputs as well as their quantity. For most of the period covered here, the absence of measures of the effectiveness of care meant that measures of efficiency – whether through time or between organisations – implicitly assumed that the quality of care was constant and unchanged. Steps were taken to adjust for this problem, initially by excluding quality-enhancing expenditures on the inputs side, and later by complementing the efficiency index with measures of quality and effectiveness. However, neither approach was really successful. As in other countries, the best measures of trends in overall technical efficiency almost certainly understate the improvements in health service performance, both in absolute terms and relative to other sectors that make a better job of capturing improvements in the quality of their products.

The distinction between technical and allocative efficiency is not just an artefact of economics. It has been reflected in the way in whch policy and management initiatives have been organised in the Department of Health over the last 20 years. With perhaps one major exception, all of the significant formal reviews of 'efficiency' and all of the attempts to develop new indicators of 'efficiency' have focused on improving or measuring the health service production process. In short, they have been concerned with technical efficiency. The only review to look at both technical and allocative efficiency was the 1997–98 Comprehensive Spending Review. One of the projects for that review was entitled 'Maximising efficiency and effectiveness in the National Health Service'. Box 5.1 summarises the coverage and illustrates what became of some of its recommendations.

To indicate why there has been so much interest in measuring and improving technical efficiency (hereafter referred to simply as 'efficiency'), this chapter begins with a reminder of the policy context. Then it briefly sets out the different measures of efficiency over the last 20 years, their purposes and the problems associated with them. The development of efficiency targets and the policy issues that they have generated are the subject of the next section. This is followed by a summary of the contribution of analysis and analysts. The chapter ends with reflections on two important policy issues. First, how efficient is the NHS? And secondly, have efficiency targets improved the efficiency of the NHS? The contribution of other policies to improving NHS efficiency is covered in Chapter 7 on performance management.

Box 5.1 1998 Comprehensive Spending Review project on maximising efficiency and effectiveness in the NHS

This project was led by a senior Departmental economist. From a huge potential agenda, an interim report in September 1997 identified six areas for further work:

1 identifying opportunities for improving technical efficiency
2 comparative information and benchmarking
3 effective performance management
4 clinical effectiveness
5 new drugs and technology
6 promoting clinician performance.

Some of the earlier recommendations of this project were incorporated in the 1997 White Paper, *The New NHS: Modern, Dependable*. Recommendations from later reports (produced up until the summer of 1998) were taken forward in the implementation of the 1998 Comprehensive Spending Review (CSR) over the following five years. (A few that were accepted by Ministers were subsequently lost from sight because of the overloading of the Department.) Examples of the outcome from this work include the following.

1   *Identifying opportunities for improving technical efficiency.* A new and more sophisticated analysis of variations in hospital unit costs suggested that there was considerable scope for 'catch-up' improvements in technical efficiency. Partly as a consequence, the CSR set an annual efficiency target for the next three years at 3% per annum.

2   *Comparative information and benchmarking.* A 'framework' was proposed for developing benchmarking across the NHS. Particular priority was given to developing adequate measures of efficiency in the acute sector, in part through the development of a system of reference costs.

3   *Effective performance management.* The White Paper announced a new performance management framework, subsequently known as the Performance Assessment Framework, and an illustrative set of high-level indicators was produced.

4 + 5 *Clinical effectiveness and new drugs and technology.* Proposals for 'nationally coordinated and led approaches to assessing effectiveness and cost-effectiveness' of clinical guidelines were reflected in the White Paper's proposals for a new National Institute of Clinical Excellence (NICE). Later work focused on developing systematic and comprehensive procedures for assessing the cost-effectiveness of new drugs and other new technologies. This area of work was subsequently added to NICE's agenda.

6   *Promoting clinical performance.* The Project put forward recommendations on measuring hospital consultants' performance, developing workload standards for consultants and improving the consultant contract. As of 2004 some of these proposals were still being implemented.

Policy context

In the 1980s and 1990s a series of political and policy developments strengthened the general interest of government in ensuring that public resources were used efficiently. First, changes in the measurement of public expenditure that had begun in the late 1970s caused a shift from volume planning to cash limits and then to cash planning. This stimulated interest in the costs of inputs, including relative price effects,* and in what outputs were being delivered by these inputs. Secondly, the new Conservative Government of 1979 was determined to reduce public spending and taxation as a share of national income. If public spending on the NHS was to escape from the downward pressures, it had to demonstrate that it was not marked by the inefficiencies that the new government normally associated with non-market organisations. Thirdly, the introduction of the NHS to the business management approaches exemplified by the Roy Griffiths 1983 management review reinforced a shift in management from inputs alone to both inputs and outputs and the relationship between the two.[1] Fourthly, the Conservative Government promoted new mechanisms specifically to improve efficiency in the NHS, notably competitive tendering in the early 1980s and the 'internal market' after 1989. Monitoring the impact of these innovations required better measures of efficiency. Fifthly, the new information systems that were developed in response to these pressures in turn further strengthened interest in the NHS's efficiency, by facilitating comparisons of performance both over time and between organisational units within the NHS.

Arguably Departmental interest in (technical) efficiency reached a peak in 1994–95, when the NHS Executive commissioned *A Strategic Framework for Efficiency Gain in the NHS*. Interestingly, however, the framework was never implemented. Within a year the NHS Executive had widened its interest to *Improving Performance in the NHS*, which was defined as covering not only (technical) efficiency but also quality and effectiveness. Acceptance of the importance of looking beyond efficiency to other aspects of performance, such as effectiveness, quality and equity, never subsequently went away.

However, the measurement and management of efficiency continued to generate a distinct stream of work in the Department. From 1990 onwards the immediate cause of this work was Treasury insistence that agreement on additional resources for healthcare should be tied to a Departmental commitment to the achievement of specific efficiency targets. The argument was that it was only possible to quantify the new resources required to deliver on Ministerial

---

* It has been claimed that health and some other (public) services suffer from 'relative price effects' or rates of inflation above those in other sectors, because the personal nature of the service that they provide limits the scope for productivity gains through the substitution of capital for labour.

objectives once allowance had been made for the resources that could be freed up by improving the efficiency of current services. The Treasury insistence on efficiency targets was not unique to health, but the history of formal efficiency targets goes back as far as or further in health than in any other major public service programme.

Measuring efficiency

There has been concern about the efficiency of the NHS almost since it was established.[2] Initially, poor information precluded comparison of efficiency either between hospitals or over time. However, by the 1960s detailed hospital activity and cost information meant that 'efficiency became a watchword'.[3] At least as early as 1968 there were claims that national services were growing faster than expenditure because of improvements in efficiency.[4] However, it was another 14 years before an attempt was made to produce an overall index of trends in the efficiency of hospital and related services.

At the national level the first trials to systematically and regularly relate changes in health service activities to changes in expenditure can be traced back to 1982 (*see* Box 5.2).[5] A composite index of activity was put together using measures of activity in eight areas, namely inpatients, outpatients, Accident and Emergency, day cases, day patients, community health services, ambulances and blood transfusions.* Each area of activity was weighted by its share of total expenditure. The resulting hospital and community health services (HCHS) cost-weighed activity index (CWAI) was extended back to 1975. Although it was subject to considerable modification and development, it was calculated and publicly reported annually up to 2003, providing a rough if increasingly unreliable indicator of the growth of health service activity outside primary care. When related to the change in the volume of inputs (total expenditure on hospital and community health services, adjusted for input prices), it could be used to produce an aggregate efficiency indicator. This indicator has been variously known as the HCHS efficiency indicator, the purchaser efficiency indicator and the CWAI efficiency index. Like the CWAI, it continued to be calculated into the new century.

Box 5.2 Origins of the HCHS efficiency index

A cost-weighted activity index was used by Jeremy Hurst in 1981 to compare the levels of efficiency of the US, Canadian and UK healthcare systems. However, the first recorded sighting of a time-series cost-weighted activity indicator and associated efficiency index was in a paper written by the then outposted Economic Adviser in Finance Division, Michael Parsonage. As noted earlier, the introduction of cash planning led to much interest in the relative price effect (RPE), and in early 1982 Mike was commissioned to do a think piece in order to clarify the Department's approach. This resulted in two papers. The first emphasised that as

---

* Primary care was deliberately excluded because at the time these services were not cash limited. The Department did not therefore need to make bids for the relative price effect in this sector.

conventionally measured the RPE was based on a comparison of input prices in the NHS with output prices in the rest of the economy. This was a valid procedure only if one assumed that productivity in the NHS was constant, so that input and output prices changed together.

The second paper challenged this assumption and sought to put it to the test. It noted that usable measures of final output for health were not available, so it suggested instead a composite index of activity in the hospital and community health services. The index was constructed for the period 1975–76 to 1980–81. Further analysis in the paper showed that the true RPE in this period was effectively zero (i.e. NHS input prices rose by about 2% per annum in real terms, but so did productivity), implying that 'output' prices were more or less constant relative to general inflation.

The paper noted various possible qualifications concerning the activity index, including its implicit assumption that the quality of care is constant. Nevertheless, it argued that it was a significant improvement on the previous convention of constant productivity, which implied that the volume of output could only rise if there was a corresponding increase in the volume of inputs.

The cost-weighted activity index fairly rapidly became an accepted tool of analysis in the Department, and first saw the light of day publicly the following year in a DHSS publication.

The national trends in hospital and community health service activity, inputs and efficiency over the period 1974–75 to 1999–2000, as calculated for these indicators, are shown in Figure 5.1. Given the political, policy and management

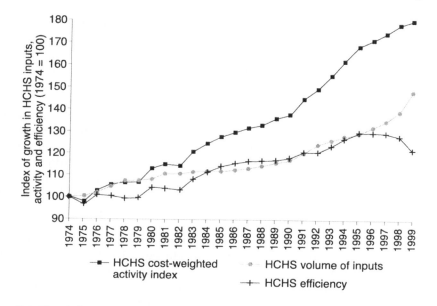

Figure 5.1 Hospital and community health service (HCHS) activity, expenditure and efficiency for the period 1974–75 to 1999–2000.

weight that has been given to the cost-weighted activity indicator and the related HCHS efficiency indicator, it would be a useful research project to set out a full history of the indicators and assess their comparability over time. This is not attempted here. Suffice it to say that, for reasons that will be discussed later, there must be serious doubts about the long-term consistency and comparability of the indicators.

In the second decade of their history, the national HCHS activity and efficiency indicators were disaggregated to sub-national units. Indicators were first developed for regions (in 1992–93), then for districts (in 1994–95) and then for individual hospitals or trusts (from around 1998–99). As is discussed further below, this disaggregation to smaller provider units was largely driven by the conversion of the efficiency indicator from a retrospective analytical exercise into a management tool associated with rewards and sanctions. In 1990 the Treasury required the Department to take powers to set efficiency targets for regions, and the first such targets were agreed with each region from 1991–92.

Although the hospital and community health service efficiency indicator was the longest-standing continuing guide to efficiency trends in the NHS, it was for many years complemented by a labour productivity index. This related cost-weighted activity to labour inputs (measured in terms of full-time labour equivalents) rather than to total expenditure. Although taken back to 1975–76, it too was probably first calculated in 1982. It has been used intermittently both to monitor changes in hospital and community health service labour productivity over time and to compare NHS labour productivity performance with that of the whole economy and with other service sectors. In 1994, a Departmental review of efficiency recommended that a labour productivity index should be calculated for each NHS provider, with the results fed back both to providers and to purchasers. It was expected that this would encourage local benchmarking. There was no follow-up monitoring to ascertain whether it did so.

Alongside the attempts to develop overall measures of efficiency in the NHS by aggregating activity, expenditure and labour inputs, there were a raft of measures of single aspects of efficiency or productivity. The roots of most of these indicators date back to the Performance Indicators Initiative of 1981. By the mid-1980s, the 192 health authorities had each been issued with a package that compared performance across more than 400 indicators. Expert systems showing known (or at least plausible) causal links allowed their diagnostic use both centrally and locally, and facilitated the linking of them to improvement action. Most of these indicators related to activity, but a number of them threw light on aspects of efficiency. Those that were focused on by the NHS Management Board included bed-throughput rates, day-case rates, costs per acute patient, and nurses per occupied bed. On all of these indicators the variation between districts was huge (e.g. in 1985 general surgical day-case rates ranged from 2% to 42%).

The Department used the evidence of variation to inform the annual Ministerial review of regional performance that was introduced in 1982. The reviews were part of the Conservative Government's drive to shift the emphasis of Departmental regulation from 'planning' to 'performance'. Indicators of efficiency on single aspects of performance have continued to be used up to the present both by the Department (for public accountability and performance management) and by regions, districts and providers (for internal management and for benchmarking).

Compared with aggregate efficiency indicators, single-aspect indicators such as day-surgery rates are easier for managers (and politicians) to understand, easier to attribute to the behaviour of particular individuals and, as a consequence, easier to influence. The most widely used of these indicators have probably been average hospital length of stay and day-surgery rates. They can be relatively easily monitored and compared over time and space within the NHS, and they can also be compared with the position in other countries to allow international comparisons. Although only partial indicators of efficiency, these two particular indicators have together tracked (and in retrospect predicted) the main trends in the aggregate HCHS efficiency indicator over the last 20 years.

However, single-aspect indicators can also be misleading and encourage perverse behaviours. Hospital bed occupancy rates are an example of one such indicator. For most of the period under consideration, the rise in occupancy, to an average of around 83% at the end of the 1990s, was seen as both desirable and illustrative of the efficiency of resource use in the NHS. However, work by Departmental operational researchers for the Emergency Services Action Team in 1996–97 showed that hospital bed occupancy rates over 85% were associated with rapidly growing problems both in handling emergency admissions and in the quality of patient care. The major hospital investment programme announced in the NHS Plan in 2000 was partly predicated on the view that average occupancy rates should be allowed to fall in order to reduce the incidence of these problems.

This brief history of efficiency measures would not be complete without recognition of some of the problems that have hindered the development of a good understanding of levels of and trends in efficiency in the NHS. Perhaps the most important problems have been data quality and definitions, service coverage, and the inability to capture improvements in quality and outcomes. All three problems make it difficult to draw robust conclusions about changes in long-term trends in efficiency and (sometimes) about changes in efficiency improvements from year to year.

For its basic building blocks the efficiency index has always relied on activity data collected for other purposes. Thse data have been criticised for being too aggregate (e.g. until recently there has been no way of allowing for case mix), for being based on non-standardised definitions (e.g. finished consultant episodes) and for using inappropriate measures of output (e.g. finished consultant episodes rather than bed days for long-stay services). Addressing these criticisms improved the quality of the efficiency measure but undermined its reliability as a guide to long-term trends. Changes in activity measures that have been introduced for other reasons (e.g. the substitution of finished consultant episodes for deaths and discharges) have also increased the problem of long-term comparability. The inflation of finished consultant episodes for emergency care in the late 1990s led the Department to abandon the use of this measure for some purposes (e.g. as a guide to average length of hospital stay), but it continued to be used for calculating the HCHS activity and efficiency indices. Over the years there have also been changes in the definition of HCHS expenditure used as the denominator in the calculation of the efficiency index. These changes have included making various allowances for capital expenditure and for expenditure aimed at improving quality.

A second problem with the efficiency index, which was recognised from its beginning, was its partial coverage. It never purported to cover primary care,* and it also failed to capture varying amounts of hospital and community health service expenditure. For example, in 2003 it still did not capture non-consultant-led outpatient activity, such as clinics run by nurses and physiotherapists, nor did it capture outreach clinics. Activities that were appropriately and efficiently moved out of hospital and into primary care could not be picked up as an improvement in efficiency. On the other hand, the indicator overestimated the system-wide efficiency gains from reductions in hospital lengths of stay that were facilitated by the development of post-acute services funded from local authority or primary care budgets.

The third and probably greatest weakness of the efficiency index was that it measured only the quantity of services, and made no allowance for changes in service quality or health outcomes. As a consequence, an increase in quality which results from increased expenditure would register as a reduction in efficiency, and vice versa. This problem has long been recognised, but it is only now being properly addressed.† The main difficulties are well known – neither in this country nor elsewhere is there yet an adequate range of indicators of the quality of health services or of health outcomes.

In recognition of these problems the Department has pursued three strategies:

1 Providing a more rounded view of performance by developing indicators of other aspects, particularly of clinical quality and of patient experience to set alongside trends in cost efficiency. This was the major approach up to 2000.
2 Using the growing coverage of reference costs‡ to disaggregate and expand the measurement of outputs. Replacing 12 categories of activity with 1700 categories allows a much better account of changing case mix. Coverage is also being expanded by adding in primary care activities and the activities of NHS Direct and Walk-in Centres. This broader measure of outputs was to be used to calculate a new cost-efficiency growth measure for monitoring progress against the 2002 public-sector agreement on value for money.
3 Attempting to directly build quality into the efficiency indicator or a broader value-for-money indicator. One way of doing this, which has been much used in setting past efficiency targets, is to subtract expenditure on quality improvement programmes from the expenditure denominator. However, this assumes that it is possible *ex ante* to identify the expenditures that will contribute to quality. A second approach is to build recorded quality improvements directly into the measures of output. In theory this can be done either by adjusting the outputs for quality improvements (measured by life years, Quality-Adjusted Life Years (QALYS) or willingness to pay) or by reducing the price deflator applied to the outputs in recognition of the fact that the quality of the service product has improved. The Department's economists identified both forms of adjustment over a decade ago. A third approach is to develop a separate service

---

*The Department was unable to find a way of measuring primary care activity that did not suggest a persistent decline in efficiency. Under the new 2003 GP contract the agreement on a raft of quality indicators should make it much more feasible to adequately measure trends in efficiency in this sector.
† While the efficiency index was showing, or was expected to show, 'acceptable' improvements, there was no interest within the department (or outside) in mounting a major review.
‡ Unit cost data based mainly on health resource groups (HRGs), detailed activity classifications similar to diagnostic resource groups (DRGs).

effectiveness growth measure. This was encouraged by the 2002 Spending Review, which set a target to improve value for money in the NHS by at least 2%, with annual improvements of at least 1% in both cost efficiency and service effectiveness.

Since 2002 (and therefore strictly beyond the period under consideration) the combination of rapid growth in public expenditure and an apparent decline in public sector productivity has spurred major efforts to improve the measurement of productivity across government. In late 2003, the Atkinson Review was established to look at the measurement of productivity in the whole public sector. In its Final Report it recommended that in the health field the measurement of output (and hence productivity) should be extended to include a number of dimensions of quality, with the results weighted together by marginal social valuation.[6] Separately the Department has commissioned a major research project on measuring NHS outputs and productivity from the University of York and the National Institute of Social and Economic Research.[7]

Setting efficiency targets

A brief history

The setting of efficiency targets in the NHS pre-dated the establishment of a system for monitoring aggregate trends in efficiency, even of a crude kind. For the years 1981–82 and 1982–83, health authorities were set specific national efficiency savings targets of £30 million and £35 million, respectively. These sums represented about 0.5% of total revenue allocations.[8] By the second year not only was there a substantial shortfall between reported and target savings, but it was clear that only 50–60% of reported savings resulted from the more efficient use of resources. Recognising the shortcomings of this approach, in 1983 the Department abandoned top-down target setting and instead introduced a 'cost improvement programme (CIP)', under which each district and region was expected to incorporate a plan for cost improvements within its short-term planning programme. The improvements could be either cost releasing or productivity improving. In the first two years of the new programme (1984–85 and 1985–86) the reported savings were equal to 1.1% and 1.4% of total current expenditure on hospital and community health services. The programme continued for another two or three years, but there was growing scepticism about how far the reported savings reflected real efficiency gains rather than service reductions. Without systematic and comprehensive measures of efficiency in hospital and community health services at district level, the Department had to rely on self-reporting and the infrequent investigations of the National Audit Office. Towards the end of the 1980s, attention swung back to 'cash-releasing efficiency savings', in part because they were easier to monitor than efficiency improvements that took the form of providing more healthcare for the same cost.

 With the announcement of the internal market reforms in 1989 there was an increase in the Treasury's expectations about the size of realisable efficiency improvements. The NHS Management Board at first opposed setting regional efficiency targets, on the grounds that they could undermine incentives for rigorous local contracting. However, the Treasury was insistent that a national efficiency target should be applied to hospital and community health service expenditure as a whole, and that the chances of delivery would be increased if efficiency targets were agreed with each of the 14 regions and monitored through an efficiency index that was capable of being applied at sub-national level. In anticipation of these pressures, the Board established a working party led by a senior Departmental economist to make recommendations on how the national HCHS efficiency index could be developed to be capable of application to both purchasers and providers, and at regional, district and unit level. The 1990s saw a number of reviews of the methodologies used for monitoring efficiency at sub-national level and those used to set sub-national targets. However, despite strong choruses of complaint there were no major changes until 1998.

Labour came to power in 1997 committed to ending the use of the HCHS efficiency index. Nevertheless, the new government was still determined to set efficiency targets for the NHS. Although a more sophisticated way of measuring activity was under development using case-mix-adjusted health resource groups (HRGs), the initial coverage was too limited for it to replace the old cost-weighted activity measure. However, to ensure that the pressure for efficiency improvements did not undermine quality and responsiveness, a new approach to the setting of sub-national efficiency targets was agreed in the 2000 Spending Review. The cost of care commissioned from trusts that performed well against indicators of access, quality and responsiveness became the benchmark for the whole NHS. All providers were expected to reach the level of the best over the next five years. At the national level, measurement of trends in efficiency continued to rely on the traditional efficiency indicator. Since 2002 the Department has been developing a new measure of NHS efficiency (or productivity) that covers a much wider range of NHS activity and will take account of quality. When operational it should finally support the old CWAI-based index..

Policy issues

This brief history hides a number of intense and at times protracted policy debates about how efficiency targets should be calculated and set, and about how the adverse effects could be minimised. The most important arguments can be reviewed briefly under five headings:

1 top down or bottom up
2 appropriate jurisdiction
3 ambition
4 allowing for quality
5 distortionary effects.

Top down or bottom up?

Over this whole period Departmental officials showed a fairly consistent preference for allowing regions, districts and providers to set their own efficiency targets. However, the pressure from the Treasury for delivery on increasingly demanding national targets required the Department to ensure that these targets were cascaded down to lower levels. In practice, in the second half of the 1990s evaluations found no relationship between trust published targets and changes in unit costs. The published targets set for individual health authorities and hospitals were rarely the actual targets that were agreed with district or regional management, and the monitoring of performance against targets was at best indirect.[9] Given that the Department's approach to performance management generally tightened as the 1990s progressed, it is unlikely that the cascading of efficiency targets was any more effective in earlier years. However, in view of the uncertain success of the bottom-up approach to efficiency target setting in the 1980s (as reported earlier), the available evidence would not suggest that either approach is invariably superior to the other.

Appropriate jurisdiction

The trend has been to disaggregate national efficiency targets into regional targets, district targets and finally hospital and other provider unit targets. This disaggregation has required the development of increasingly complex methodologies for setting differential targets for lower management units and an increasingly sophisticated monitoring system. In practice, as noted already, the targets set for lower levels on the basis of national methodologies have frequently been replaced by targets that have come out of local planning negotiations. In addition, at the end of the 1990s the Department's monitoring systems proved unable to keep up with the frequent changes in the way in which targets were defined.

Ambition

National efficiency targets have been agreed for every year since the late 1980s, first in the annual public expenditure rounds and latterly in the two-yearly spending reviews. The target began at an annual 1% of hospital and community health service expenditure, but after the internal market reforms it was raised rapidly to 3% in 1995–96. It remained at that level until 2000–01. After two years at 2%, the 2002 Spending Review replaced the efficiency target with a 'value-for-money' target at the same level, but to be made up from annual improvements of 1% in cost-efficiency and 1% in service effectiveness.*

The size of the national efficiency target was initially set largely by looking at the past efficiency record. The introduction of the internal market sparked a period of increasing optimism. For example, it was noted that while efficiency improvements had averaged 1.6% per annum in the 1980s, they had risen to 1.9% in the post-reform years up to 1994–95. In 1994, a detailed Departmental review of the sources of past efficiency improvements and the scope for further improvements concluded with the judgement that 'average efficiency gains of the order of 3% would probably be achievable in the health and community health services over the next few years'. (The Treasury's judgement was that greater gains – 4% a year or more – were achievable.) In 1997–98 a further review of the scope for efficiency improvements was almost equally optimistic. However, in practice 1994–95 proved to be the last year in which recorded efficiency gains approached 3%. In the four years from 1996–97 to 1999–2000 the recorded improvement never reached even 1% per annum, and in three years it was negative.

What went wrong? In the mid-1990s retrospective analysis by the Department's economist showed that almost all of the improvements in efficiency recorded by the HCHS efficiency indicator in the 1980s and early 1990s could be

---

* The 2004 Spending Review agreed a more ambitious target of 2.7% per year for 2005–06 to 2007–08, made up of a mix of cost efficiency and service improvement.

accounted for by the reduction in the average hospital length of stay and the growth in the number of hospital day cases. With hindsight the mistake of the exercises in futurology from 1994 onwards was to underestimate how quickly reductions in average length of stay would slow down, and how rapidly the rise in day-case rates would also decelerate. The speed with which other potential sources of savings could be exploited, such as variations in staff productivity and the cost of supplies, was also probably exaggerated. In retrospect it is hard to resist the conclusion that it was a particular set of technological advances – notably new anaesthetics and minimally invasive surgery – that were responsible for the great bulk of the efficiency gains over the last 20 years. They were aided and abetted (and the 'whole-system' savings were exaggerated) by the introduction of non-NHS sources of funding for long-term care and by policies for moving long-term care patients into the community. Central efficiency initiatives, most notably the internal market, may have speeded up the impact of these technology and policy developments, but there is little clear evidence that they had a substantial long-term additional effect.

Allowing for quality

As noted before, there was early recognition that the HCHS efficiency indicator was at best a partial measure of technical efficiency, because it took no account of the changing quality of delivered services. The attempts to adjust for this have been outlined earlier. They remain far from complete, but the quality indicators that we do now have and the experience of the USA, with much better information, both suggest that the HCHS efficiency indicator has been significantly under-counting the real improvement in efficiency (i.e. after allowing for improvements in the quality of services and their impact on health outcomes). For the future it will be even more important to capture these effects. Much of the investment under the NHS Plan is not aimed at increasing health service activity but at improving the safety and quality of services. Unless and until these quality effects can be picked up, it will be unsurprising if measures of technical efficiency show performance to be deteriorating or at best static.

Distortionary effects

For the first decade of its existence the HCHS efficiency index received little adverse comment either from the NHS or from policy analysts. However, once it was converted from a retrospective analytical exercise into a management tool it attracted a barrage of criticism. Some of the technical criticisms were addressed by a working party in 1991 and a further review in 1993. However, other criticisms continued right through until the CWAI-based index was dropped for target-setting purposes at the end of the 1990s.

The more persistent criticisms included the following.

1 Attaching rewards to counts of particular activities led to reporting drift, reclassification and at worst statistical dishonesty.
2 Ignoring variations in the base level of efficiency between regions, districts and hospitals was unfair and discouraged effort among the efficient.
3 Important areas of efficiency improvement were uncounted or under-counted because they involved a shift of activity from the hospital sector to the primary care sector.

4 Targeting technical efficiency in the hospital sector undermined the aims of allocative efficiency (which were thought to require a shift of services into ambulatory settings) and was inconsistent with the overall strategy of the health service, which was to place greater emphasis on improving the health of the population.
5 There was an incentive to shift costs to budgets outside the HCHS, such as social services.

Many of these criticisms were well made and generated much study within the Department and some remedial action. Although improvements in counting were to be welcomed they, like relabelling and straight fraud, made interpretation of trends very difficult. The Departmental responses of clearer definitions, incentives for statistical quality and increasingly severe sanctions for dishonesty may have controlled the problem, but they did not eliminate it. The second problem, namely the importance of taking into account the efficiency starting points of different regions, districts and provider units, was tackled by developing cross-sectional indices. These permitted the setting of differential targets that took into account the performance of units relative to their peers.

The third issue, namely the leakage of activity into areas that were not adequately counted, such as minor surgery in GP practices, was recognised as early as 1993. However, despite the best efforts of various working groups it remained a major problem. In 2003 it was still being quoted as one reason why both activity and efficiency in the NHS were under-counted. In this and other respects the Department's databases failed to keep up with its rapidly changing policy concerns.

The fourth charge – that of undermining allocative efficiency and the overall strategy of the health service – also proved difficult to remedy. Simulations indicated that the index was not inherently biased against community care. However, as it was believed that allocative efficiency required a shift of activity from hospital to ambulatory settings, it was clearly unsatisfactory to use costs weights which implied that the current balance of activity was optimal. The proposed solution was to develop measures of the quality and effectiveness of care so that allocative efficiency could be assessed alongside technical efficiency. However, as noted earlier, progress proved difficult and slow.

The fifth issue, namely cost shifting to social services budgets, was the subject of internal departmental debate but was never accurately quantified. It is clear that the reductions in the length of hospital stays for long-term care patients in the 1980s and 1990s were facilitated by the growth of social security and social service expenditures on these patient groups. The HCHS efficiency index did therefore significantly exaggerate the system-wide improvements in efficiency over that period. As a corollary, efficiency improvements in the social services were under-counted.

In retrospect it is apparent that, in the words of some early critics, turning the efficiency index into a target was 'like placing a lantern in a jungle on a dark night . . . and . . . resources are attracted to targets like moths to a flame'.[10] The Department struggled to light other lanterns for effectiveness, quality and responsiveness, but they rarely burned as brightly. However, if the index did at times distort behaviour, it also exerted continuous pressure to search for new areas for efficiency savings. Although 'tweaked' from time to time, for 20 years neither internal analysts nor external critics could come up with a better measure. Nor have other countries had more success. In international terms, the CWAI-based efficiency index is unique in its comprehensiveness and longevity.*

The role of analysts

In a vast organisation like the NHS, the level and rate of change in efficiency will depend on the decentralised actions of the million or so people who work in the service as managers, doctors, nurses and other staff. The centre can contribute at the margin by funding skills and training, providing incentives, imposing regulations, establishing governance arrangements, evaluating innovations, helping to develop and disseminate good ideas (and impede bad ones) and developing information systems that will allow performance to be monitored and compared. The focus here is on the role of analysts in relation to the last of these potential functions.

In the early to mid-1980s, Departmental operational researchers played a major role in converting the 1981 Performance Indicator Initiative into a tool that was user-friendly for districts, regions and the centre. They developed the expert systems that allowed the indicators to be linked into a potentially powerful diagnostic tool. In retrospect the tool was ahead of its time. There were too few analysts in the districts who could use it, and the centre's soft approach to performance management gave districts insufficient incentive to strengthen their analytical capacity.

The Department's analysts can take credit (or blame!) for most of the development of the HCHS efficiency index over its long history, and for the technical work necessary to convert it into a target capable of being used at regional, district and provider levels. Economists initiated the work on the original HCHS efficiency index in the early 1980s, and an economist-led working group developed a credible indicator for regional target setting in 1991. Subsequent reviews of the calculation of the efficiency index and targets were sometimes led from the NHS, but always relied on Departmental analysts. Analysts led the work on developing a broader set of indicators of quality and outcomes to put alongside the efficiency index. Departmental economists also broke down the measured efficiency improvements into their component causes.

The first involvement of external analysts in this area came with work commissioned in 1998 to develop a better measure of relative efficiency at trust level. Subsequently external economists, particularly the York Centre for Health Economics, were used extensively to evaluate the robustness of the trust-level indicator and the effect of trust-level targets on performance.

Another area where internal analysts dominated was in international comparisons of efficiency. Although the OECD databases are in the public domain, the Department's responsibility for supplying the UK data meant that internal analysts were generally more aware than their external peers of both its strength and, latterly, its weaknesses.

Internal operational researchers were also involved in convincing the Treasury that the NHS cannot run at 100% capacity because of the need to allow some

---

* For instance, in New Zealand at the time of writing (2004), the most comprehensive indicator of efficiency relates only to inpatient acute hospital activity, and it is monitored intermittently.

'slack' to cope with unpredictable peak loads, and later in convincing Departmental Ministers and senior management that, for similar reasons, rigorously enforced 100% targets were likely to be exorbitantly expensive.

If the Department's analysts can take credit for promoting measures of efficiency and developing operational efficiency targets, they must also take some responsibility for their weaknesses. Analysts can point to a good record in terms of putting forward proposals to deal with the various weaknesses in the indicators and targets. The biggest weakness was the absence of adjustments for changes in effectiveness or quality of care. However, for many years the slow development of outcome measures meant that it was easier to point to the weakness than to remedy it. It also proved difficult to persuade Treasury (and DH Ministers) that claims of uncounted quality improvements were not simply special pleading. Departmental analysts made these claims with increasing force from about 1998 onwards, but it required several years of flat or negative efficiency increases, as traditionally measured, before they were taken seriously.

With hindsight, the biggest error of internal analysts (or more accurately my biggest error) was in being over-optimistic about the scope for further efficiency and productivity improvements, or more precisely about how easily these could be achieved. The Department's economists began arguing strongly for a lower national efficiency improvement target from about 1999. However, analyses showing the dependence of earlier claimed efficiency savings on one-off reductions in hospital length of stay for geriatric and mental illness specialties were throwing up warning signals as early as 1995. Recognition of these signs was effectively buried by a sophisticated analysis of variations in hospital unit costs in 1997, which found larger than expected differences. It was only when the signs of a flattening out in hospital lengths of stay became apparent across all patient groups, and further analysis raised questions about the statistical significance of the hospital cost differences, that a concerted effort was made to convince Ministers of the need for lower efficiency targets.

The big questions

It would be inexcusable to write a chapter on the development of efficiency measures and targets without commenting on the following two policy questions that have been at the heart of the debate over NHS efficiency for most of the last 20 years.

1 How efficient was and is the NHS?
2 Have efficiency targets improved the efficiency of the NHS?

How efficient was and is the NHS?

This question is easy to ask but much more difficult to answer. For most of the last two decades the prevailing assumption among national and international policy analysts has been that the NHS 'was and is a remarkably cost-effective institution'.[11] Arguably, over most of this period the Department had a strong interest in playing up the efficiency of the NHS. In speaking to the public it could be used to explain and justify the UK's low expenditure on healthcare relative to other countries, and in negotiating with the Treasury it could justify arguing that improvements in services must depend heavily on obtaining more resources. After 2000 it became less important to emphasise the NHS's efficiency, because the Government had accepted the need for a major injection of resources. At the same time, the Department was able to convince the Treasury that the scope for further unit costs reductions was less than had been assumed for the previous decade or more.

The public and political debate about the efficiency of the NHS has frequently used two concepts interchangeably, namely the absolute level of efficiency and the rate of change in efficiency. Much of the central effort that has gone into measurement has been concerned with establishing the rate of change. The main exception is benchmarking (national and international), which can be and has been used to compare both levels and rates of change.

What evidence has the Department used to judge the efficiency of the NHS? A prime source of information on absolute levels of performance has been international comparisons. Through the whole period up to the late 1990s it was possible to argue that the UK's almost uniquely low inputs into health services (whether measured in terms of expenditure, skilled personnel or hospital beds) produced health outcomes that were broadly comparable with those of other countries. The explanation appeared to be simple – analyses of OECD data showed that the NHS used resources more intensively than most foreign countries. For example, bed turnover rates were the highest in the OECD and doctor caseloads (measured by admissions and patient consultations) appeared to be at the top of the international distribution. Another commonly quoted illustration of efficiency was the NHS's very high level of use of generic drugs.

International comparisons suggested that not only was the NHS more efficient than other health services, but also its efficiency was improving faster than elsewhere. Some fairly heroic calculations showed that hospital unit costs were falling faster in the UK than in other countries for which the OECD provided (highly aggregate) data. The absence of foreign efficiency measures comparable to the HCHS efficiency indicator made it difficult to challenge the assertion that efficiency in the NHS was improving as fast as or faster than abroad.

Another 'common-sense' reason for believing that the NHS was relatively efficient was its low administrative costs. It was intuitively appealing to claim that countries with multiple payers and greater reliance on user charges must face higher management costs than the NHS. In fact there have been no good studies of comparative administrative costs outside North America.* And there have been even fewer that have looked at the relationship between administrative costs and technical (or allocative) efficiency. This research gap is all the more surprising given the frequency with which both governments and their political opponents put forward administrative reform as a sure-fire way of saving costs, with beneficial or at least neutral effects on overall efficiency.

In addition to foreign comparators, two other broad comparisons have frequently been used to support conclusions about the efficiency of the NHS. In both cases the focus has been on changes over time. The first comparison was with the economic performance of the whole UK economy and of major sectors within it.

---

*There have been no studies at all that have directly compared either central (Ministry) or local management costs in England with the comparable costs in other countries. Proposals by the Department's analysts for such studies were ignored (*see also* the discussion in Chapter 9).

For example, using the cost-weighted activity indicator it was shown that from the mid-1970s up to the late 1990s, HCHS labour productivity matched productivity in the wider economy, averaging around 2% per annum. The second comparison was with trends in the private health sector. Such comparisons are difficult to make because of differences in the coverage of the services provided. However, whenever comparisons were attempted they consistently showed NHS unit costs rising less rapidly than those in the private sector.

One further important source of evidence gave more mixed messages. This was the variation in performance within the NHS. From the earliest development of comparable hospital indicators at the beginning of the 1980s, almost every measure of efficiency at the hospital or district level showed wide variation. This was as true of catering and cleaning unit costs as of day-surgery rates and of nurse-to-bed ratios. Detailed analyses within the Department and by the National Audit Office, and later by the Audit Commission, concluded that many of the differences could not be attributed to circumstances that were beyond local managers' control. Sustained campaigns from the centre succeeded in levelling up performance in some areas (e.g. day-surgery rates and procurement costs), but progress often appeared to be painfully slow. In other areas (e.g. use of operating theatres and bed management) there remain large unexplained variations, even though the overall level of performance has risen.[12] Throughout the entire period active benchmarking remained a minority pursuit among health authorities and hospitals. One reason for this was the lack of case-mix severity adjustments which made (and still makes) much benchmarking ambiguous and potentially misleading. Another reason was the lack of analytical skills in the management cadres of the NHS, a weakness that continues to the present day.

The good record in international and sectoral comparisons could be reconciled with persistent wide variations in performance within the NHS by arguing that there was always scope for any organisation to do better. Implicitly officials also assumed that at the local level efficiency performance in other health systems must be even weaker than in the NHS. The few micro-comparisons available (e.g. operating-theatre use in Sweden and England) tended to support this assumption.

In retrospect, how robust were the arguments for the 'outstanding' efficiency of the NHS? Recent evidence suggests that the picture of efficiency presented to Ministers in the 1980s and much of the 1990s was probably too rosy. There are two main reasons for this, namely gaps in evidence and comparisons that subsequently turned out to be flawed. The gaps related primarily to health outcomes. It was not until the late 1990s that disease-specific data on survival rates and mortality showed that the relatively satisfactory information on aggregate health status hid health outcomes that compared unfavourably with many other countries. Around the same time, better information on patient hospital experiences and on hospital waiting times also suggested that the UK was 'off the pace' compared with many of its foreign peers.*

The second reason for judging that the picture of the efficiency of the NHS was too rosy is that some of the international comparisons used inconsistent data. There are two key examples. First, for many years the England hospital

---

*These outcome weaknesses do not imply that the NHS was technically inefficient. They do suggest that the level of efficiency was not sufficient, as had earlier been assumed, to compensate for the NHS's low level of funding.

admissions data reported to the OECD was in terms of finished consultant episodes (FCEs), while every other country was using direct counts of spells in hospital. Secondly, the reported data on England (and UK) acute hospital admissions commonly added together day-case and overnight admissions, while most other countries were only reporting overnight admissions. Because of these definitional differences, England and the UK appeared to be achieving lower average hospital lengths of stay, higher bed turnover rates and higher hospital admissions than was actually the case.* Correcting for these definitional differences, the NHS performance is still good but it is not as outstanding as it appeared to be at the time. It is also clearer now that some of the apparently good performance (e.g. the exceptionally high bed turnover rates) contributed to other problems (e.g. the difficulty in providing rapid emergency care, and unsatisfactory patient treatment). In short, cost efficiency was bought at some price to the quality of care.

What then is the short answer to the question that introduced this section? Looking back at 20 years of sifting the evidence, my answer would be that the NHS was relatively efficient by international standards, and on available operational measures it remains so. However, it was not and is not (quite) as efficient as the Department, the NHS and most Ministers have chosen to believe. On the other hand, relative to the UK economy as a whole the NHS productivity performance has almost certainly been better than claimed. Here the historical comparisons have understated the NHS's performance by failing to take account of quality improvements, and by tending to compare a measure of labour productivity in the wider economy with a measure closer to total factor productivity in the NHS.

Looking to the future, the more important question is what scope there is to improve the efficiency of the NHS. My judgement is that there remains much scope, but that it will be harder to mine than the past 'big wins' of reduced length of stay and shift to day cases. However, there may still be more gains in these directions. For example, the Kaiser experience[13] suggests that significant further reductions in average hospital lengths of stay should be possible without detrimental effects on health outcomes. However, achieving these benefits will probably require major changes in operational processes, including relative expansions in the roles of both primary and post-acute care. Other potential areas for efficiency improvements include skill mix changes, redesign of hospital and clinical processes, service reconfigurations and greater use of information technology.† However, both past and international experience suggests that levering improvements in these areas will not be easy. And one lesson of the last 20 years is that any new efficiency initiatives should be accompanied by more comprehensive measurement of performance, particularly clinical quality and patient experience, as well as by system-wide (not provider-specific) measurement of changes in costs.

---

*These inconsistencies were not of course deliberate, but reflected unique statistical practices in England, the vagueness of some OECD definitions and the very limited resources that the Department put into quality-assuring the data sent to the OECD.

† As others have noted, medical practice and process design is still dominated by custom and practice, rather than by evidence, and mechanisms for best practice transfer are severely under-developed compared with most other sectors.

Have efficiency targets improved the efficiency of the NHS?

It is not possible to give a confident evidence-based answer to this question. There are several reasons for this. First, as already noted, current measures of efficiency are confined to expenditure on hospital and community health services and do not take account of improvements or deteriorations in quality. Secondly, there are no good measures of the counter-factual (i.e. what efficiency would have been in the absence of targets). Thirdly, the efficiency targets introduced at the beginning of the 1990s were accompanied by a raft of other reforms referred to as the 'internal market'. There are consequently major problems of attribution.

However, although firm answers are ruled out it is possible to speculate. Targets have been set at different levels (national, regional, district and provider) and for aggregate expenditures and for specific activities (notably day surgery). The impacts of these different types of targets can be considered separately.

National aggregate targets have certainly served to focus Departmental policy and analytical thinking on the scale of inefficiency in the NHS and its sources. They have encouraged the Department to identify areas in which new policies or management actions look likely to improve efficiency. One example is procurement, where the Comprehensive Spending Review identified major opportunities for reducing costs. Other Departmental reviews of efficiency led to proposals for better provider efficiency indicators and the (re)launching of benchmarking as a way of encouraging management action at the local level. There are two more recent examples of the benefits of setting targets for efficiency improvements. The first is the encouragement given to the search for new sources of improved efficiency now that reductions in the length of average hospitalisations appear (probably temporarily) to have come to an end. The second example is the general recognition that improvements in quality can be as important a source of efficiency improvements as reductions in unit costs, and therefore a new generation of efficiency measures is urgently needed. These features may seem unremarkable, but they are not commonly found in publicly funded health systems without formal efficiency targets.*

It might have been expected that these benefits would be reinforced by the setting of efficiency targets at lower levels in the NHS. However, at sub-national level considerable management energy has been diverted into arguing about the fairness of particular targets. The frequency with which targets have changed and the failure of higher levels of management to monitor progress or to take action when they are not met has also reduced their impact. At the trust level the best evidence is that, over the six years 1994–95 to 1999–2000, published targets showed no relationship to changes in unit costs and, even more surprisingly, there was no reduction in the variance of unit costs between acute trusts.[9] Moreover, targets were more likely to be met by 'firefighting' actions than by longer-term reforms such as service reconfiguration or re-engineering. From this and other studies there are strong messages about how efficiency targets should be improved if they are to continue to be used at the local level. In particular they should be clearly defined and relatively stable over time, they should be seen as

---

* For example, as of 2004 New Zealand has no centrally led programme to improve health service efficiency. There are no national efficiency targets, although current measures of efficiency have recently been recognised as inadequate.

fair and locally owned, they should be monitored, and they should be backed by adequate incentives.

Perhaps the major advantages of single-aspect efficiency targets, such as procedure-specific day-case rates, are that they are usually clear, stable and easy to monitor. A major disadvantage, of course, is that individually they can only cover a very small part of total health expenditure and may divert management action away from areas that offer larger benefits. However, a decade or more of experience suggests that the advantages of ease of understanding and of monitoring outweigh the disadvantages.* Single-aspect efficiency targets also have one other major advantage – they usually point at where, and indeed by whom, action needs to be taken. It is probable that a persistent focus on day-case rates and the setting of increasingly demanding targets has accelerated the growth of day surgery and contributed to the marked reduction in the variance of day-case rates across acute trusts. For the future there will inevitably be continued performance management interest in developing better summary measures of the comparative efficiency of NHS providers and commissioners. However, it is likely that benchmarking around carefully chosen single-aspect targets will prove more effective in driving performance improvements. Such targets are most likely to be effective if they are backed up by systematic processes for identifying and transferring best practice.

References

1 Griffiths R *et al.* (1983) NHS Management Inquiry. Letter dated 6 October to the Secretary of the State, Norman Fowler.
2 Parliament (1956) *Report of the Committee of Enquiry into the Cost of the National Health Service (Chairman, CW Guillebaud)*. HMSO, London.
3 Rivett G (1998) *From Cradle to Grave: fifty years of the NHS*. The King's Fund, London.
4 Ministry of Health (1968) *Report for the Year 1967*. HMSO, London.
5 Parsonage M, personal communication, July 2003.
6 Office of National Statistics (2005) *Measurement of Government Output and Productivity. Final report*. Office of National Statistics, London.
7 A first report was published in 2004. Dawson D *et al.* (2004) *Developing New Approaches to Measuring NHS Outputs and Productivity*. CHE Technical Paper Series No. 31. Centre for Health Economics, University of York, York. A final report is expected in 2005.
8 Robinson R and Judge K (1987) *Public Expenditure and the NHS: trends and prospects*. The King's Fund Institute, London.
9 Dawson D and Jacobs R (2001) *Hospital Efficiency Targets. Report for the Department of Health*. Centre for Health Economics, University of York, York.
10 Donaldson L, Kirkup W, Craig N and Parkin D (1994) Lanterns in the jungle: is the NHS driven by the wrong kind of efficiency? *Public Health*. **108**: 3–9.
11 Organisation for Economic Co-operation and Development (OECD) (1994) *Economic Surveys: United Kingdom*. OECD, Paris.
12 Audit Commission (2003) *Acute Hospital Portfolio*. Audit Commission, London.
13 Ham C, York N, Sutch S and Shaw R (2003) Hospital bed utilisation in the NHS, Kaiser Permanente and the US Medicare Programme: analysis of routine data. *BMJ*. **327**: 1257–60.

*The advantage of ease of understanding is confirmed by the focus in single-aspect efficiency measures, particularly day-case rates and average length of hospital stay, in reports to the public on hospital efficiency. *See*, for example, Meikle J (2005) Why hospital throughput is a matter of trust. *The Guardian*: Supplement on measuring health. 15 June 2005 p. 6.

Chapter 6

'Doing the right thing': allocative efficiency in the NHS

Introduction

In their desire to meet the needs of the public and the electorate at the lowest tax costs, governments strive both to 'do things right' and to 'do the right things'. The previous chapter considered the first of these objectives, namely technical efficiency. This chapter reviews the contribution of analysis to improving allocative efficiency or 'doing the right things'.*

In any health system, decisions affecting resource allocation are made at many levels and in numerous contexts. A key judgement for analysts wishing to improve resource allocation is where to aim their fire. Should it, for example, be at decision making in the National Health Service or should it be at decision making in the centre, in the Department of Health? Again, should it be focused on undertaking detailed cost-effectiveness studies or should it attempt to change the processes and language of decision making? Other layers of choice concern the level and type of expenditure. Should the focus be on appraising individual capital projects, on new technologies and treatments, on broader healthcare policies and programmes, or on the overall balance between major health and healthcare sectors and programmes? One of the purposes of this chapter is to indicate how the Department's analysts addressed these choices.

The role of analysis and particularly of economics in the allocation of health service resources has grown remarkably over the last 20 years. Part of the reason for this is that the environment has been made more favourable by developments in medicine and healthcare management. There have also been major advances in analytical tools. The chapter therefore begins with a short overview of these contextual developments. It then considers in turn each of the areas where analysis, particularly economic analysis, has come to play a larger role, namely investment appraisal, technology appraisal, policy and programme appraisal, and cross-sector prioritisation. Attention is then given to the role of internal and external analysts in improving allocative efficiency. The chapter ends with short reflections on three questions. First, has allocative efficiency in the healthcare sector been improved (are more of the 'right things' being done)? Secondly, why

---

* Economists commonly define technical efficiency as minimising the cost per unit of output and allocative efficiency as optimising the mix of outputs. In practice the distinction is not always clear-cut. For example, it will be influenced by how outputs are defined. Some may argue that two of the areas of decision making discussed in this chapter, namely investment appraisal and health technology assessment, are mainly concerned with technical efficiency. As they draw on the same broad economic tools as policy and programme appraisal and the comparison of sectors, I have chosen to include them here.

did the systematic use of economic appraisal spread so slowly in the Department of Health? Thirdly, would allocative efficiency have improved more rapidly if the Department's analysts had focused on improving decision making in the NHS, rather than decision making in the Department?

Policy context

At the beginning of the period under consideration the NHS Management Inquiry, led by Sir Roy Griffiths, noted that 'economic evaluation of . . . [particular] practices [is] extremely rare'.[1] Griffiths was referring to the NHS, but he might equally well have been referring to the policies of the Department of Health. Twenty years later, economic evaluation and the language of economics were commonplace both in the Department and in the NHS, although the rhetoric sometimes ran ahead of the reality.

A large number of factors contributed to the revolution in the use of economic analysis in decision making. Some of these, such as the increasing pressures to prioritise in the face of tight resource constraints and the introduction of managerialism, have already been referred to in earlier chapters. Together these developments highlighted the need to look at healthcare outcomes and costs together if resources were to be efficiently deployed. Research studies showing large and apparently inexplicable variations in medical practice and a lack of scientific evidence for a substantial proportion of medical and healthcare practices also helped to make room for economists and operational researchers at the decision-making table. Belief in medical omniscience and clinical autonomy declined both outside the medical profession and within it. One response to growing public doubts about the scientific basis for some medical practices was the movement towards evidence-based medicine. This gave economists both outside the Department and within it the opportunity to argue that healthcare should be not only clinically effective but also cost-effective. Information should be gathered on costs and cost-effectiveness as well as on clinical outcomes and patient experience.

Assessment of the relative cost-effectiveness of different interventions required the development of better measures of outcomes and standardised approaches to the measuring of costs. The last 20 years have seen major progress in both areas. The more difficult problem has been the development of utility, and latterly monetary, measures of health outcomes. These 20 years saw various utility measures, most notably the quality-adjusted life year (QALY), move from the research drawing board to wide use by health economists and broad acceptance by policy advisers and Ministers. The broader economic concepts of cost-effectiveness and opportunity costs also moved from the wings to centre stage in the rhetoric of decision making.

The spread of systematic decision making

A common device used by DH analysts to improve resource allocation in the health sector has been to argue that decision making should be systematic and explicit. Systematic decision making requires clarity about objectives, careful identification of alternatives, assessment of options in terms of full benefits and costs, and awareness of opportunity costs. In retrospect it has taken an enormous amount of energy to spread these simple ideas throughout decision making in the Department and the NHS, and there is still further to go. In the early 1980s, Departmental analysts were vaguely aware of how many resource allocation decisions were made in ad-hoc ways, often with little or no relevant evidence of benefits or costs. No grand strategy was developed for correcting this situation. Instead, the approach adopted was pragmatic, looking for opportunities to show that systematic appraisal methodologies, particularly those that pushed out the boundaries of quantification, could lead to different, better or more defensible solutions.

Unsurprisingly, the spread of economic and analytical methodologies did not follow a straight line. Initial successes in some areas could be followed by years of stagnation or even retreat. The earliest widespread advance was in the appraisal of new capital investments. The second area of broad advance was in health technology assessment. The development of systematic approaches to appraising health policies and programmes followed rather later. Balancing and comparing value for money across sectors and programmes (e.g. primary and secondary care or healthcare and health promotion) has yet to be regularly and properly systematised.

These four major areas of decision making are discussed below in roughly the order in which economic analysis came to play a major role.

Investment appraisal

Large capital-spending decisions were the first area in which the Department was convinced of the need for a systematic assessment of costs and benefits. As advocates of such an approach, the Department's economists were able to call on the authority of the Treasury, which had been recommending investment appraisal in the public sector for many years. A case for investment appraisal in the NHS was first successfully pressed during the 1979 Review of Capital. This led to the writing of the first guidance on what came to be called *option appraisal*. As recounted by Jeremy Hurst, the successful trialling of the guidance on the re-provision of facilities for the epileptic inmates of St Faith's Hospital in Essex led to option appraisal being made mandatory for large construction projects.*

Revised and improved guidance on option appraisal was issued on several subsequent occasions in later years, including 1987, 1994 and 1999. Assessing the option appraisals (later known as business cases) for large NHS and DH capital projects became a routine task for Departmental economists. As the policy context changed, so did the guidance (e.g. to cover the Private Finance Initiative, the separation of purchasing and provision under the internal market and the growing number and scale of IT capital projects). There were also recurrent attempts to spread business case skills in the NHS by the dissemination of best-practice materials and the organising of training workshops. In order to speed up learning, 'post-project evaluations' formally became mandatory on large projects

---

*Hurst, drawing on a personal communication from Martin Buxton, notes that it was because this first investment appraisal came up with a proposal that was both different from the preconceived solution and acceptable to various parties, that sceptical officials were convinced of the value of the methodology. *See* Hurst J (1998) The impact of health economics on health policy in England, and the impact of health policy on health economics 1972–1997. *Health Econ.* 7(**Suppl. 1**): S47–62.

from 1995, although this requirement was honoured more in the breach than in the observance. (Individual hospitals saw little advantage in learning from infrequent decisions, and the Department was unwilling to establish a separate evaluation budget.)

Learning was particularly slow in relation to information technology projects – precisely the area where a series of audit reports pointed to the largest mis-allocation of capital spending. The lesson here was that even the best guidance is of little value if those responsible for applying it doubt its value and see it as primarily a bureaucratic hurdle. It took many years for health IT professionals, including some in very senior positions in the DH, to accept that the benefits of IT proposals were not self-evident and had not only to be properly identified and assessed but also to receive the full support of the clinicians and managers who would be affected by them. Indeed, at the time of writing, new IT systems in the UK and overseas are still being criticised for involving insufficient consultation with users or for failing to take account of how clinicians actually work.[2]

Health technology assessment

In the period under consideration, economic assessments moved from being an occasional source of information on new health technologies to becoming a formal criterion for decisions on what technologies should be publicly funded. Although economic assessments of health technologies in England can be traced back to the 1960s,[3] it was not until the mid-1980s that economists could point to examples of economic analysis informing major national decisions on the rate of dissemination of healthcare technologies. The breakthroughs were in relation to heart transplants in 1985 and breast cancer screening in 1986.[4] These seminal studies were the forerunners of the systematic incorporation of cost-effectiveness and cost-utility analysis into the Department's research on new technologies. A major step forward was the setting up of a Standing Group on Health Technology Assessment in 1993 under the chairmanship of Sir Miles Irving, with several economist members.* At about the same time the DH funded a new NHS Centre for Reviews and Dissemination at the University of York to aid the dissemination of quality-assured studies of the effectiveness and cost-effectiveness of healthcare interventions.

It was also around this time that Departmental economists began working with the Association of the British Pharmaceutical Industry (ABPI) to develop guide-lines for the economic evaluation of pharmaceuticals. The aim was to encourage the industry to give a higher priority to economic considerations and particularly to cost-effectiveness in funding research on new medicines, and to help to improve the quality of such studies. Joint guidance was issued in 1994.[5] The next three years saw work on more rigorous appraisal standards, proposals for a pharmaco-economic research centre to help to build up the capacity and tech-niques of cost-effectiveness studies, and exploration of the case for introducing a cost-effectiveness 'fourth hurdle' to add to the three hurdles of safety, quality and efficacy. The proposals for a pharmaco-economics research centre were not progressed, but the arguments against using cost-effectiveness as one decision

---

* One of the perennial roles of the Department's economists was (and is) to advise on the economist membership of such groups.

criterion in the public funding of new medicines (but not in their licensing) were rapidly overridden when the Labour Government came to power in 1997.

Parallel to the infiltration of cost-effectiveness into the DH's thinking about the funding of pharmaceuticals, Ministers agreed in 1996 to the establishment of a National Screening Committee under the Chief Medical Officer, Sir Kenneth Calman. From the beginning it was accepted that cost-effectiveness should be one of the criteria used to judge what screening campaigns should be endorsed by the Committee.

As part of the 1998 Comprehensive Spending Review (CSR), officials were asked to look at ways of improving efficiency and effectiveness in the NHS. A working group chaired by a senior Departmental economist recommended that new machinery should be developed for ensuring the clinical and cost-effectiveness of both new and existing technologies. It proposed a systematic and national approach to the appraisal and management of technologies built around the following five tasks:

- early identification of new technologies
- timely assessment of clinical and cost-effectiveness
- clear appraisal and communication of the implications for the NHS
- managed implementation in the NHS
- rigorous monitoring of compliance.

In relation to the first two tasks, the recommendations amounted to a pulling together and rationalising of existing activities. The proposals for the third and fourth tasks were much more radical. The group recommended a public commitment that NHS resources would increasingly be restricted to technologies for which there was good evidence of clinical and cost-effectiveness. It proposed that a national body should issue policy guidance on the use of technologies, taking into account both clinical and cost-effectiveness. Although the early focus would inevitably be on costly and contentious new technologies, as resources allowed the scope of the reviews should be expanded to existing technologies. The policy guidance should initially be seen as guidance, not direction, but it could become mandatory if voluntary compliance was not forthcoming. Ministers accepted these recommendations and also the conclusion that monitoring mechanisms should be applied to clinical guidelines and guidance on new technologies from the start.

The ground had been prepared for this major step forward in the role of cost-effectiveness information by the Government's White Paper, *The New NHS: Modern, Dependable*, published in December 1997.[6] The White Paper stated that 'to ensure consistent access to beneficial care right across the NHS, the Government believes stronger arrangements are needed to promote clinical and cost-effectiveness both for drugs and other forms of treatment'. It went on to announce the establishment of a new National Institute for Clinical Excellence (NICE) which, *inter alia*, would produce and disseminate clinical guidelines based on relevant evidence of clinical and cost-effectiveness. In the light of the CSR Report, the government decided to extend the remit of NICE to include assessing and providing guidance on the clinical and cost-effectiveness of both drugs and other technologies.

Departmental economists provided some early support to the establishment of NICE, but their role is now primarily one of warning of any tendency for the analysis to neglect economic principles. For example, on occasion there has been concern that clinical guidelines have failed to apply incremental cost-effectiveness tests or to assess the expenditure impact on the NHS. A second and continuing area of concern has been the cost-per-QALY criterion or 'pass mark' used to judge the cost-effectiveness of technologies. At times this appears to have been too lenient relative to the criteria used to inform other resource allocation decisions in the NHS, raising the possibility that resource allocation may be distorted rather than improved.*

Six years after its establishment, it seems probable that NICE has accelerated the dissemination of many technologies that it has judged to be cost-effective (e.g. taxanes for cancer and nicotine replacement therapy for smoking). However, there has been less compliance with other recommendations (e.g. on new drugs for arthritis and schizophrenia).[7] It has also been less successful in identifying cost-ineffective treatments and in discouraging the use of such treatments. The Government has sensibly introduced a programme of action aimed at improving the implementation of NICE guidance and at giving greater priority to the identification of treatments for disinvestment.[8] Ministers will need to show considerable courage if they are to support NICE in this last task. If it is not supported, NICE could effectively become an instrument for perpetuating poor value for money in healthcare.

As has already been noted, there is also some concern that the criterion being applied to distinguish between cost-effective and cost-ineffective interventions – described as a range rather than an arbitrary threshold[9] – may be too generous given the criteria used to make decisions in other parts of the NHS.[10] This highlights the problems that arise if cost-effectiveness techniques are applied across the healthcare sector with different degrees of rigour or different thresholds. Allocative efficiency may be improved within particular areas, but at the cost of distorting allocations between major policy areas or types of intervention.† The Department needs to do more work on this problem. An even broader issue is whether cost-effective thresholds or ranges should be set to exhaust a given budget, or whether the NHS budget should be set according to how many treatments pass an (optimal) threshold.[11] Historically governments, and particularly the Treasury, have always favoured the first approach. However, the 2002 Wanless Report implicitly adopted the second one.

Policy and programme appraisal

Overseeing investment appraisal and promoting technology assessment have always been a small part of the Department of Health's responsibilities. A far larger share of administrative resources has gone into the development of policies and programmes for particular disease areas, client groups or types of healthcare. Bringing economics and rigorous analysis to bear on these decisions has proved

---

* Economists tend to split between those who believe cost-effectiveness calculations should *make* or determine policy decisions and those who believe they should *inform* such decisions. DH economists generally took the latter view, accepting that there is bound to be a role for social value judgements.
† The issue is not unique to England. For example, it appears to arise in a stronger form in New Zealand, where cost-effectiveness criteria are applied rigorously to drug expenditures but not to other technologies.

much harder. Decision making has gradually become more systematic, analytical and informed by proper costing and awareness of opportunity costs, but progress could be best described as intermittent. Even today coverage is not complete.

In retrospect, Departmental analysts have tried to ensure that new policies and programmes improve resource allocation through four main approaches:

1 encouraging systematic and quantified approaches to the appraisal of new policies and programmes
2 providing information on the cost-effectiveness of policy options
3 advocating that guidance from the centre on clinical effectiveness pays attention to cost-effectiveness and to resource implications
4 ensuring that National Service Frameworks are properly costed and that their recommendations take account of evidence on cost-effectiveness.

It is worth saying a little more about each of these approaches in turn.

Attempts to persuade the Department to adopt a systematic approach to the appraisal of new policy proposals date back at least to 1981. At that time the DHSS agreed to apply a consistent set of objectives and criteria to the appraisal of social security policies. A proposal that health and personal social service policies should similarly be systematically appraised in terms of a set of agreed criteria (including effectiveness, efficiency, cost, manpower and equity) was considered by the Department's Cross-Sector Policy Review Group, but was not endorsed. Apparently it was concluded that policy leads in health, unlike their social security peers, did not need to be guided or constrained by best-practice checklists or guidelines. Judging by the Department's subsequent actions, or lack of them, this belief persisted throughout the 1980s and 1990s and may continue today.

Undiscouraged, the Department's analysts made several further attempts to systematise best practice. In 1992, the Health of the Nation White Paper announced that a policy appraisal guide would be produced to assist other government departments in assessing the health impacts of their policies.[12] Departmental economists hoped that it would be at least as useful for internal policy makers in the DH as for their peers in other departments. The guide, *Policy Appraisal and Health*, was published in 1995.[13] Follow-up monitoring suggested that it was used in only a minority of other departments. In the DH it was seen as something that should be used by others, but not internally (an example of a general law of administration that regulations should be applied to others but not to oneself). This myopia was all the more remarkable given that later in the same year Ministers expressed dissatisfaction with the way in which major issues were being presented to them, particularly those with a significant economic and/or financial dimension. In response, the Department set up a (short-lived) 'Major Business Case Team' to adopt a systematic approach to the appraisal of all policy changes with significant expenditure implications. The team was also requested to prepare and circulate guidance for use by staff generally. The EOR completed a *Guide to the Appraisal Process for Major Business Cases* in 1996, but it was never formally endorsed and used. Senior finance colleagues thought that it either stated the obvious or infringed on their responsibilities.

As the analytical standards of some policy submissions continued to be poor, the EOR made a further attempt to produce useful guidance in 1999 under the slightly amended title *Guide to Making Submissions with Major Resource Implications*. This attracted interest and support from some policy divisions but again it was never formally endorsed. In 2001–02, a major policy division was persuaded to take the lead in codifying experience with policy appraisals, and more particularly with the development of National Service Frameworks, by developing a guide to National Service Framework development. Finally, in 2004, a new unit was set up, the Policy Hub, charged, inter alia, with promoting good policy making. It has issued a Policy Tool Kit and re-issued 'Policy Appraisal and Health'.

A second way in which the Department's economists have tried to bring cost-effectiveness information to bear on policy and programme decisions is by presenting the growing body of cost-effectiveness studies in an easily assimilable form. As early as 1986, proposals were made to develop a register of cost-effectiveness studies to assist the Department's health policy group in identifying treatments or practices which should be expanded, those that should be contracted, and those for which so little was known that they should be priorities for further research. At the time, policy colleagues judged the proposal to be too risky. In 1991 the proposal was revised. It was taken forward slowly using internal EOR resources, and was finally published by the Department in August 1994.[14] Responsibility for quality assuring and updating the register was then handed over to the NHS Centre for Reviews and Dissemination at the University of York. The register is still in existence and is regularly updated. Another example of the way in which cost-effectiveness information was disseminated to inform decision making was the guidance issued to NHS purchasers in 1995 on the effectiveness and cost-effectiveness of interventions to reduce mortality from coronary heart disease (CHD) and stroke.[15] This also provided guidance on 'target effectiveness' (i.e. on the scale of the contribution that various interventions were likely to make to the Health of the Nation target of a 40% reduction in CHD and stroke death rates for the under-65s).

The third approach was to climb on to the wave of interest in evidence-based medicine and to argue that in a resource-constrained healthcare system, improving clinical effectiveness required account to be taken of costs and cost-effectiveness. In 1994, the DH established a multi-professional Clinical Outcomes Group chaired by the Chief Medical Officer (CMO) and the Chief Nursing Officer (CNO) to help the NHS to improve the outcome of clinical care through clinical audit, clinical guidelines and a clinical effectiveness programme. The Group included several Royal College presidents, as well as senior NHS managers, patient representatives and academics. With the support of the CMO and the CNO, the Group had two debates on why work on clinical effectiveness should take account of cost-effectiveness considerations. The Group broadly accepted the arguments put forward by the Department's economists. It subsequently agreed that work on developing clinical guidelines should incorporate cost and cost-effectiveness considerations. The NHS Executive was persuaded to give similar status to cost-effectiveness in its wider plans to improve clinical effectiveness.

However, by the time the Government changed in 1997, there were increasing concerns about whether the Department's strategy for clinical effectiveness had enough teeth. Internal analysts were not alone in asking if it included the information, regulatory mechanisms and incentives necessary to change clinical practice at a politically acceptable speed. The foundations were therefore laid for the new Government to announce that 'stronger arrangements are needed to promote clinical and cost-effectiveness both for drugs and for other forms of treatment'. It went on to announce that 'a new National Institute for Clinical

Excellence (NICE) will be established to give new coherence and prominence to information about clinical and cost-effectiveness.'[16] The first task of NICE would be to produce and disseminate 'clinical guidelines based on relevant evidence of clinical and cost-effectiveness'. Another new institution, the Commission for Health Improvement, was expected to systematically review the guidelines developed by the Institute.

The fourth way in which the Department's economists contributed to improving resource allocation within policies and programmes was by collecting and collating studies of cost-effectiveness relating to particular diseases. The value of a disease-based approach was probably first recognised in work on a Value-for-Money Initiative for the Chief Medical Officer in 1989. This work was subsequently used to help to identify areas for health targets in the health promotion strategy later announced in the Health of the Nation White Paper. It was agreed that all targets should be backed by evidence of cost-effective interventions. As has already been noted, in the case of coronary heart disease and stroke this evidence was subsequently disseminated to NHS purchasers.

The early experience of taking a disease-based approach to collating and comparing evidence on cost-effective interventions proved extraordinarily helpful when in 1997 the new Labour Government announced a programme of evidence-based National Service Frameworks (NSFs) setting out the patterns and levels of service for major care areas and disease groups. The EOR was able to offer to work with clinical advisers on prioritising possible interventions in terms of their cost-effectiveness. With experience, the approach adopted has come to have broad similarities with the Programme Budgeting and Marginal Analysis (PBMA) technique advocated by many health economists for deciding purchasing priorities at local health authority level.[17] Box 6.1 illustrates the approach as it was applied to the coronary heart disease NSF. The approach is information and analysis intensive. For example, providing estimates of the costs and benefits of expanding services requires more detailed information than is often available on what services are currently being provided and to whom. It is also knowledge intensive, as it requires analysts to work very closely with clinicians and to understand the clinical literature almost as well as the economics literature. Only a small number of Departmental analysts have risen to this challenge.

Box 6.1 Economic analysis and the Coronary Heart Disease National Service Framework, March 2000

1 An expert External Reference Group developed a list of recommended interventions for the prevention, diagnosis and treatment of coronary heart disease and the standards to be applied to each intervention.

2 Working with medical colleagues, Departmental economists estimated how current intervention levels compared with the recommended standards.

3 For each intervention, a Departmental economist split the resulting estimates of required additional activity into estimates of staff inputs and facility capacity.

4 By attaching costs to the input requirements, estimates were made of the total cost of each intervention.

5 As the total costs of the initial list of interventions greatly exceeded the initial, current and anticipated budgets, estimates were made of the cost-effectiveness of expanding activity under each intervention. A Departmental economist put these together. Strong support for the attention to costing and cost-effectiveness came from two Departmental doctors, Nick Hicks and Peter Doyle, and from a special adviser.

6 The cost-effectiveness estimates were used to inform judgements about the interventions recommended for inclusion in the NSF, the priority with which those recommendations were to be rolled out, and the scale of resources required to support the NSF over the next 10 years.

7 Because of this work, Departmental economists were later readily able to provide Derek Wanless with estimates of the scale of additional expenditure on coronary heart disease that could be justified on cost-effectiveness grounds.

Despite the challenges, or perhaps because of them, National Service Frameworks look to be the most effective way yet developed of prioritising services at the national level. For the client groups and disease areas that they cover, they require comparisons of the cost-effectiveness of allocating additional resources to prevention, primary care or secondary care. Similarly, they provide a framework for prioritising all forms of intervention, whether in the form of screening, vaccinations, pharmaceuticals, surgery or nursing care. They therefore provide an appropriate context for considering advice issued by the National Institute for Clinical Excellence.

As noted earlier, the Department was strangely resistant to capturing NSF best practice in the form of a template or guidelines. This may explain why the same injunctions about their development had to be repeated from time to time. For example, in the course of the preparation of the mental health NSF in 1999, DH Ministers assured Treasury Ministers that NSFs would include full information on the cost-effectiveness of interventions. Three years later, Derek Wanless thought it necessary to recommend that 'future NSFs should be fully costed to incorporate detailed information about the cost-effectiveness of interventions',[18] a recommendation that was repeated in his 2004 report.[23] Sometimes institutional memories in the public sector can be very short.

Comparing sectors and programmes

There is logic to looking last at the attempts to improve allocative efficiency by rebalancing resources between major sectors, such as primary and secondary care, or between major programmes, such as healthcare and health promotion. Without information about the cost-effectiveness of a representative sample of interventions within individual sectors or programmes, decisions to switch resources between them would be based on faith or feel rather than on evidence. However, there is another reason for leaving these levels of decision to last. Over the 20-year period under consideration they received far less serious study than the lower decision levels discussed earlier.

The Department's potentially most useful tool for raising questions about the allocation of resources between major sectors and client groups was invented, developed and abandoned by the beginning of the 1980s. One of the earliest tasks for the Department's first health economists was the construction in 1971 of a programme budget.[19] Structured around the main 'client groups' served by the health and social services, it showed trends in activity, unit costs and expenditure: 'This allowed for exploration of issues concerning broad allocative efficiency in the NHS.'[19] By the mid-1970s, the programme budget had developed into a forward-planning device and had become a keystone in the new 'planning cycle' for the NHS. It was attributed with enabling 'decisions to be taken to pull back on growth for acute services while transferring funds to primary care, children, the elderly and the handicapped.'[20] However, the NHS planning cycle was scrapped by the incoming Conservative administration in 1979. The programme budget survived only as a retrospective device, supplied annually in the evidence to the Social Services (later the Health) Committee.

Even with the formal ending of the NHS planning cycle, the annual Public Expenditure Survey (PES) discussions could have used the information in the programme budgets to explore issues of allocative efficiency. In the 1980s and 1990s this was rarely done. Fundamental reviews of resource allocation were discouraged by generally tight budgets, strong Ministerial views on priorities and little clear evidence for the relative benefits of marginal increases or reductions in client group or sector resources. However, there were occasional scoping studies of the desirability of shifts in resources between the major expenditure blocks. Two issues that attracted particular attention from time to time were the balance between primary and secondary care and the balance between healthcare services and health promotion.

For most of these 20 years there was an implicit or explicit assumption that it was desirable to shift services out of hospitals and into the community and/or primary care. The 1980s and most of the 1990s saw a rapid run-down in hospital beds of all types, powered by large reductions in the average length of hospital stays. However, as hospital admissions rose rapidly and hospital care became more capital intensive, there was a relatively modest shift in resources out of the hospital sector. In 1993, policy leads responded to the modest changes by asking the Department's analysts to look at whether the balance between service provision in primary and secondary settings was appropriate and cost-effective, and whether there was evidence that resource allocation could be significantly improved by changing the balance. The resulting review concluded that on the basis of the hard evidence alone it was impossible to determine which sector showed the greater inefficiency. However, the authors' judgement was that a further shift of the balance towards primary and community care was likely to improve resource allocation. To supplement existing proposals to strengthen research on the primary/secondary care interface, they recommended that emerging shifts in services should be monitored and evaluated, protocols should be developed on the appropriate location of services, barriers impeding the movement of services to cost-effective locations should be identified, and there should be a single budget covering primary and secondary care services.

Although some of these recommendations were implemented, learning was very slow. In 1999 when the National Beds Inquiry revisited the same broad issue, the research evidence still did not allow it to reach firm conclusions about what balance of hospital and other services would be most effective and cost-effective in improving the welfare of older people.[21] However, a national consultation found almost unanimous support for the development of 'care closer to home', implying a continuing shift of services out of hospital.[22]

Between 1993 and 1999 there were several further partial attempts to look at the scope for reallocating hospital resources. One approach was to identify inappropriate or ineffective hospital treatments and to estimate how much could be saved if interventions were reduced to the 'appropriate' level. However, it proved impossible to persuade clinicians to agree on what was the 'appropriate' level. A more ambitious EOR-led initiative looked at whether treatments that were expanding very rapidly could be justified on cost-effectiveness grounds. Studies of both pharmaceuticals and surgical interventions that met this criterion suggested that most of the increases could be justified on cost-effectiveness grounds, and that there was no obvious strong case for changing the broad balance between surgery and pharmaceuticals. Nevertheless, there were wide variations in the cost-effectiveness ratings for different pharmaceuticals and surgical interventions, raising questions about the balance of expenditure between individual procedures and individual medicines.

The Department has had even greater difficulty in assessing the balance to be struck between expenditure on health promotion and expenditure on healthcare services. In 1984 and again in 1989, Departmental economists were asked to assist in building up evidence on the cost-effectiveness of preventive programmes, including health education and promotion. Proposals were made for the development of a new analytical tool, and a small number of cost-effectiveness assessments were conducted. However, both exercises fizzled out, overtaken by demands for work on higher policy priorities. The same story tended to be repeated in the 1990s. Policy divisions responsible for prevention and health promotion usually either showed fleeting interest in developing evidence of cost-effectiveness, or their requests were trumped by higher-priority demands from other parts of the Department. Further initiatives were also discouraged by the resistance of some public health professionals, both within the Department and outside it, to the application of rigorous cost-effectiveness frameworks to their favoured interventions.

In the 20 years up to 2002 there was no sector-wide systematic attempt within the Department to compare the relative cost-effectiveness at the margin of activities aimed at prevention or promotion with interventions in mainstream healthcare. The 1998 Comprehensive Spending Review might have been used to undertake such an assessment, but the opportunity was missed. A report for the Review noted the limitations in the evidence base on health promotion effectiveness and cost-effectiveness, including: a lack of consensus about the nature of health promotion activity; the length of time between intervention and benefits; a lack of agreement about what evidence to use in order to assess effectiveness; and different views on appropriate methods and tools for reviewing effectiveness. However, on the fringes of the CSR an experienced and knowledgeable Departmental economist did identify a range of preventive interventions that appeared to be cost-effective relative to many healthcare treatments. These included universal flu vaccinations for those aged 65 years or over, statin therapy for middle-aged people with existing CHD or at high risk of CHD, screening for chlamydia infection, nicotine replacement therapy for smokers wishing to stop, and increased expenditure on counselling smokers. All of these particular examples are now being implemented.

The 2000 NHS Plan drew attention to the importance of self-care, which could be seen as either an extension or the natural ally of prevention and health education.* However, although there were significant initiatives (e.g. the Expert Patient), it was not until 2003 that a specific part of the Department was given policy responsibility for self-care. Advocacy of its potential benefits and the identification of policy options have largely been left to operational research staff in the EOR (*see* Chapter 8). Arguably this is an extreme illustration of the rather peripheral status that in practice has generally been accorded to health promotion in the Department.

It required an external study, namely the Wanless Report, to focus policy attention on the potential benefits (including benefits to future healthcare resource costs) of larger investments in public health, health promotion and support to self-care. Much of the evidence that was drawn on when developing the first Wanless Report's 'full public engagement' scenario came from the EOR. The second report by Derek Wanless, *Securing Good Health for the Whole Population*,[23] identified the barriers to achieving that scenario, including the reasons why the Department had made little progress in comparing the cost-effectiveness of preventive and public health interventions with more traditional interventions in healthcare.† The Report's recommendations included better target setting in public health, more research and evaluation on the key determinants of health, and the adoption of a consistent framework to evaluate the cost-effectiveness of interventions across healthcare and public health. Implementing these recommendations should greatly increase the probability that NHS funding will be allocated efficiently between healthcare and public health.

Role of analysis

The central role of Departmental economists in promoting the use of cost-effectiveness and the language of cost-effectiveness in Departmental policy making should already be clear. What deserves a little expansion is the symbiotic relationship between Departmental economists and external health economists. It should also be recorded that the drive to apply economic concepts and techniques to the allocation of health resources received support from powerful allies within the Department.

The work of external academic economists supported the proselytising activities of the Department's economists in two main ways. First, they took the lead in creating the methodologies necessary for assessing the cost-effectiveness and cost-utility of different healthcare interventions. In the 1980s and 1990s, huge strides were made in developing and applying a standardised measure of

---

* In 1996, an EOR study trip to the USA, Canada, Australia and New Zealand had concluded that supporting self-care was one of four major areas where health policy in England was 'off the international pace'. The conclusion was discussed at senior levels in the Department, but follow-up action was limited.

† The reasons included the limited evidence about the cost-effectiveness of public health and preventive policies, which in turn was related to the difficulties of research, restricted research funding and the slow acceptance of economic perspectives within public health.

health needs and health benefits that could combine quantity and quality of life and enable comparisons to be made across a range of patient populations. The quality-adjusted life year (QALY) evolved from being a concept intelligible to and supported by only a small handful of economists, to being part of the day-to-day language of most health managers and policy makers and many clinicians. In the Department, QALYs similarly advanced from being a term that invited scorn or hilarity among policy and medical colleagues to being part of the currency of day-to-day policy making. For Ministers they similarly advanced from being a term whose name should not be spoken to being a term that was expected to be used when justifying a new policy or technology. Although the Department supported research work on QALYs from the 1970s onwards, including support-ing a major survey of the public's valuation of different health states, it was academics who acted as the shock troops in convincing sceptical clinicians and health service managers of the value of QALYs as an aid to decision making.*

The second major contribution of external economists was to apply cost-effectiveness analysis to an ever-expanding range of interventions.†. This not only provided Departmental economists with the evidence that they needed in order to make comparisons between alternative policy options, but also helped to sensitise clinical and policy customers within the Department to the concepts of economics. The EOR's 1994 register of cost-effectiveness studies relied almost entirely on external studies. Similarly, the cost-effectiveness analyses that became a required element of National Service Frameworks also drew overwhelmingly on external studies. It was the growing number of external economic studies of technologies of all kinds, from new pharmaceuticals to screening interventions, that enabled the Department's economists to convince policy colleagues and Ministers that cost-effectiveness should become a criterion in the funding first of national screening campaigns and then of all new technologies.

More recently, in line with the general development of cost–benefit analysis and the search for methods of comparing value for money across sectors as well as within them, the Department's economists have supported research into attach-ing monetary values to health benefits.[24] Methods of deriving monetary values such as willingness to pay are currently as politically suspect as methods of quantifying QALYs were 10 to 20 years ago. But as the competition between health and other public expenditure programmes becomes ever more intense, the pressure for a common monetary currency is likely to prove irresistible.

While external economists made an indispensable contribution to the Department's adoption of the techniques and language of cost-effectiveness, there were also a number of distinguished clinicians who played vital roles. Within the Department two Chief Medical Officers assisted in moving cost-effectiveness considerations from being at the margins of policy discussions to being a core criterion for decisions. Both Sir Donald Achieson and Sir Kenneth Calman recognised the importance of taking account of resource constraints and opportunity costs, and helped to ensure that economists were invited to the policy

---

* Of the many economists and contributors from other disciplines (notably Dr Rachel Rosser) who contributed to the development and dissemination of QALYs, special mention must go to Professor Alan Williams. Not the least of his contributions was to take head on and to rout those critics who claimed that using QALYs for priority setting was unethical.

† Tribute should be paid to the role of the Health Economists' Study Group (HESG) in both raising the quality and assisting the dissemination of these analyses.

table. Sir Kenneth Calman's ready acceptance that new publicly funded screening programmes should pass tests of cost-effectiveness set a precedent that could be used to good effect in arguing for a similar decision criterion in the funding of new technologies, and in the development of National Service Frameworks. Sir Michael Peckham, the charismatic Departmental Director of Research and Development from 1991 to 1995, showed similar farsightedness in supporting health economics research and in using economists to improve the effectiveness of NHS and Departmental research. A number of distinguished clinicians outside the Department also argued for the importance of taking account of opportunity costs when making resource allocation decisions. The role of Sir Leslie Turnberg, then President of the Royal College of Physicians, in convincing colleagues in the Clinical Outcomes Group that work on clinical effectiveness should incorporate resource and cost-effectiveness considerations comes particularly to mind. So, too, does the contribution of the late Dr Anthony Hopkins (Director of the Research Unit, Royal College of Physicians) to the education of doctors in the value of the QALY, and the education of economists in the value of the medical perspective.*

Interesting questions

This last section briefly reflects on three questions that continue to puzzle the author.

1 Has health economics improved the effectiveness of the NHS? Are we doing more of the 'right things' (and fewer of the 'wrong things')?
2 Why did it take so long for cost-effectiveness considerations to be incorporated into Departmental decision making?
3 Would there have been faster progress towards cost-effective care if the economists employed by the Department had focused on improving decision making in the NHS, rather than decision making in Department?

Has health economics improved the effectiveness of the NHS?

To an economist, an 'effective' healthcare system is one that provides the largest social benefits for any given level of social costs. Put more prosaically, it is one that serves the community as well as it could by delivering the maximum health and healthcare benefits for a given level of public and private costs. Can health economics claim to have moved the NHS towards this goal? I think that the short answer is 'yes', but it is difficult to judge how far down this road the health service has moved and how much further it still has to go.

Health economists can reasonably claim to have improved the effectiveness of the NHS in three ways:

1 by increasing information on what interventions represent good value for money (i.e. are cost-effective)
2 by promoting incentives to do the 'right things' (i.e those that are cost-effective)

---

* An example of this work is Hopkins A (ed.) (1992) *Measures of the Quality of Life and the Uses to Which Such Measures May be Put*. Royal College of Physicians, London

3 by changing the behaviours of policy makers and clinicians so that cost effective interventions are substituted for ineffective interventions.

The evidence for the first of these benefits is the most impressive. There has been a huge mushrooming of information on the effectiveness of healthcare interventions, procedures and policies of all kinds, and on their cost-effectiveness. Economists have not, of course, been alone in pressing for better measures of the outputs and outcomes of healthcare, but they have taken a leading role. The development of generic measures of health outcomes, notably the QALY, has been left largely to economists. In the Department it was economists who were asked to chair the first working groups that were developing indicators of the general effectiveness of the NHS and of the effectiveness of primary care. Within the Department the careful costing of care interventions and more particularly their cost-effectiveness has been left almost entirely to economists and operational researchers. Compared with 20 years ago, we now know vastly more about what types of interventions and treatments are effective and cost-effective and what types are ineffective and poor value for money.

Economists can also rightly claim to have taken the lead in proposing ways of strengthening incentives for decision makers to incorporate cost-effectiveness considerations in their decisions. Such incentives can be strengthened in several ways (e.g. by direct regulation, by removing barriers that discourage consideration of cost-effective alternatives, and by financial incentives). Economists have been particularly successful in pushing for regulations on cost-effectiveness. For many years before NICE was set up, academic economists had been arguing that all new publicly funded technologies should be not only demonstrably safe and efficacious but also cost-effective.[25] Within the Department it was economists who led the working group that recommended the extension of NICE's remit to include providing guidance on all technologies (both new and existing). The same working group also recommended that NICE's advice on both guidelines and technologies should be monitored to see whether behaviour was being affected. External and internal economists have also been strong supporters of the ending of segmented budgets (e.g. between hospitals and primary care) and in general of the development of budget holding by both hospital clinicians and GPs (the latter first through fundholding and then through primary care trusts).

However, improving information and strengthening incentive does not necessarily change behaviour. Evidence of cost-effectiveness has certainly affected Departmental policies – for example, by influencing the form of some screening campaigns (e.g. breast cancer), by accelerating the adoption of some interventions (e.g. statins) and by discouraging the adoption of others (e.g. primary angioplasty for heart attack). The impact of cost-effectiveness evidence on the behaviour of clinicians is less clear. Clinicians have rapidly adopted some interventions that have been promoted by NICE or the Department as cost-effective, recent examples being flu vaccinations and taxanes. As has already been noted, there is less evidence that information alone or even information plus strong guidance has a rapid impact on reducing the use of interventions that have been judged to be cost-ineffective. However, it is relatively early days – NICE is still developing its implementation strategy, and a full evaluation is still some way in the future.

As major new technologies are automatically assessed for their cost-effectiveness, the proportion of total healthcare activity that does represent 'doing the right thing' should steadily increase. However, decisions about technologies are only one of the ways in which allocative efficiency can be improved in the NHS. There are also major choices about the ways in which services are organised and delivered. Economists have so far been far less effective in improving these decisions. As noted earlier, for example, the evidence for the relative cost-effectiveness of delivering many services through hospitals or through primary and community health services 'closer to home' is still weak. In some cases the decision may turn on the weight and value attached to patient preferences.[26]

Why did it take so long for cost-effective considerations to be incorporated into Departmental decision making?

In most though not all of its decision making, the Department now attempts to assess costs and cost-effectiveness with some degree of rigour. This is a huge change from the situation 20 or even 10 years ago. The battle has to be continually re-fought, but today it would be a brave or foolhardy policy lead who put forward a major policy proposal without any reference to cost-effectiveness.

Given that public sector resources have always been constrained and that all governments have an interest in improving value for money, why has it taken so long for cost-effectiveness to become part of the Department's day-to-day language of decision making? There is no shortage of possible explanations, including the following:

1   reluctance (by policy officials, politicians and clinicians) to accept the need for prioritisation, or the value of explicit approaches to priority setting
2   the absence of evidence on cost-effectiveness and the newness of the concept
3   the small number of economists and other analysts in the Department and/or their limited influencing skills
4   the dominant role of doctors as the Department's key professional advisers, and the problem that many of them had in reconciling the professional imperative to do their best by the individual patient with the objective of maximising health for the population as a whole
5   the low level of analytical skills among many Departmental administrators, and their reluctance to admit another group of professionals to a policy-making table already crowded with doctors, nurses and, more recently, NHS managers
6   lately, the very rapid turnover of senior and junior policy division staff combined with the failure of Departmental training to keep up with the increasingly sophisticated nature of decision making, and a perplexing resistance to codifying best decision-making practice
7   the reluctance of Ministers (with one or two notable exceptions) to get ahead of public and more particularly medical opinion about the role of costs and cost-effectiveness in health service decision making.

All of these factors doubtless played a role. The first was perhaps the most pervasive, but the influence of doctors and the lack of information on the cost-effectiveness of alternative options were probably also major initial impediments. In the 1980s, many Departmental doctors were reluctant to engage with the choices required by resource constraints and the implications of such constraints for clinical freedom. However, their gradual acceptance that prioritising interventions in terms of maximising value for money could accelerate improvements in health and healthcare was enormously important in opening doors for the EOR. The leadership role of two Chief Medical Officers has already been referred to above. The leadership extended not only to the Department's doctors but also through mechanisms such as the Clinical Outcomes Group and the National Screening Committee to their peers in the country at large.

In the last six or seven years the major constraint on the fuller and more rigorous adoption of cost-effectiveness techniques has been rapid policy staff turnover combined with a failure to codify best decision-making practice. The major downsizing of the Department in the mid-1990s meant that the new Labour Government inherited an organisation that was not adequately staffed or skilled to carry through an agenda of radical and continuous reform.* The problem was made worse by frequent internal reorganisations and the importing of large numbers of senior staff from the NHS.† NHS managers have many qualities, but a strong grounding in analytical skills or in their management is rarely one of them. These problems could and should have been tackled through major expansions in departmental training programmes and the development and regular updating of guidelines or templates on best-practice approaches to policy appraisal and prioritisation. There was formal and very senior recognition of these problems on several occasions, but up until my retirement in 2002 there had been no effective action.

Although Ministers generally played a fairly neutral role in relation to the dissemination of cost-effectiveness techniques across the Department, this position changed radically under the post-1997 Labour Government. It was Ministers – particularly Alan Milburn – who led the drive that converted cost-effectiveness from an information tool to a decision tool across fields as diverse as the funding of new technologies and the construction of National Service Frameworks.

Would there have been faster progress towards cost-effective care if the analysts employed by the Department had focused on improving decision making in the NHS, rather than decision making in the Department of Health?

Once there were significant numbers of operational researchers and economists working in the Department, a recurrent issue was the balance to be struck between support to the Department and 'seeding' or 'outreach' activities in the NHS. The Department's economists and, more particularly, operational researchers have always spent a certain amount of time working directly with NHS managers and analysts, commonly on investment appraisals or the development of decision tools. In 1984 and on a number of subsequent occasions, consideration was given to whether much greater support should be given to the NHS either through reprioritisation or through additional funding for an outreach analytical service. These reviews did lead to a number of initiatives aimed at building closer links between analysts in the Department and those in the NHS, but in their

---

* Commentators in the future may reach a similar conclusion about the more arbitrary reduction in Departmental staff announced in 2003.
† These practices have continued until the time of writing (2004).

formal forms the links generally proved short-lived. The Department's analysts continued to focus on Departmental decisions.

In retrospect, was this right? In practice it was probably the only feasible course. I and my senior colleagues were unable to convince the Department's senior management to fund an outreach arm even on a seed-corn basis. Should we have argued harder? Many of the problems about the use of analysts in the NHS that were identified in the 1984 review remained true in 2003. For example, analysts were dispersed in small isolated groups, reporting at a low level within health authorities or hospitals, without support from senior managers, often tackling similar problems in different parts of the country without mechanisms for collaboration, and with no good career structure. At the same time the more analytically minded senior NHS managers reported a lack of analytical support on many of the big issues that were facing them.

These weaknesses could probably have been addressed more rapidly and effectively with a beneficial impact on value for money and hence healthcare if additional resources had been found either for an analytical extension service, somewhat equivalent to the Modernisation Agency, or for offering the NHS the equivalent of a Government Economic Service or a Government Operational Research Service. In the absence of a will to find the resources for either development,* hindsight suggests that the focus of the Department's analysts on improving central decision making was probably allocatively efficient. One argument for this is that in a health system that became increasingly centralised, focusing on influencing central decision making must almost certainly have had a greater impact than attempting to directly influence the myriad local decision units. Another argument is that it led to three major indirect benefits to analytical work in the NHS. First, the Department was persuaded to fund large expansions in postgraduate training programmes for health economists and health operational researchers. Secondly, the Department was persuaded to adopt decision tools that have had an enormous impact on the NHS's demand for analysis, such as option appraisal for capital projects and, more recently a cost-effectiveness criterion for the funding of new technologies. Thirdly, internal analysts have helped to convince the Department to expand its funding of economic and analytical research. This has contributed both to the growth of health economics in universities and to the availability of relevant analytical evidence for NHS decision makers.†

In these various indirect ways it is probable that the Department's 30–50 economists and operational researchers made a much larger contribution to improving analysis in the NHS than would have been possible if most or all of

---

* The failure to plan the development of analytical skills in the NHS was arguably part of a wider failure in planning human resource development. For example, up to 2002 there was no attempt to relate the size of the intake of NHS management trainees to any rigorous analysis of the demand for management skills in the NHS.

† A further argument in support of the focus on central decision making is the evidence from a number of countries in addition to the UK that economic evaluation has been more useful in decision making at the central level than at the local level. The conditions that foster the use of economic evaluation (clear decision-making process, clear policy-making objectives, reasonable timelines and resources, and appropriate incentives) are more often found at the centre than locally. *See* Drummond M (2004) Economic evaluation in health care. Is it really useful or are we just kidding ourselves? *Aust Econ Rev.* 37: 3–11.

them had been working directly in the NHS or as part of some kind of NHS extension service.

Nevertheless, the quality and quantity of analysis in the NHS remain poor. There has been rapid growth in the number of health economists working in universities, but many continue to find it difficult to influence NHS decision making at the local level. There remain major challenges to increase the analytical awareness and economic literacy of NHS managers, and to develop career structures or pathways for the still small numbers of analysts who are scattered across primary care trusts and hospitals and invariably work in small and isolated groups. However, it may prove more efficient to recognise that decision makers at the local level will rarely be able to use economic evaluation, but will respond to targets or guidance prepared by a higher decision-making tier.[27]

References

1 Griffiths R *et al.* (1983) NHS Management Inquiry. Letter dated 6 October to the Secretary of State, Norman Fowler.
2 *See*, for example, Koppel R *et al.* (2005) The role of computerized physician order entry systems in facilitating medication error. *JAMA.* **293**: 1197–203.
3 *See*, for example, Pole GD (1969) Economic aspects of screenings for disease. In: TN McKeown (ed.) *Screening in Medical Care*. Cambridge University Press, Cambridge and Nuffield Provincial Hospitals Trust, London.
4 *See* Buxton MB (1985) *Measurement of the Costs and Benefits of Heart Transplant Programmes at Harefield and Papworth Hospitals*. HMSO, London and DHSS (1986) *Breast Cancer Screening (Forrest Report)*. HMSO, London.
5 Department of Health and Association of the British Pharmaceutical Industry (ABPI) (1994) *Guidelines for the Economic Evaluation of Pharmaceuticals*. Department of Health and ABPI, London.
6 Department of Health (1997) *The New NHS: Modern, Dependable*. The Stationery Office, London.
7 *Measuring the Impact of NICE Guidelines in Selected Disease Areas*; www.nice.org.uk/page.aspx?o=200009
8 Department of Health (2004) *Implementation of NICE Guidance*. Department of Health, London.
9 Rawlins M and Culyer A (2004) National Institute for Clinical Excellence and its value judgements. *BMJ.* **329**: 224–7.
10 Maynard A, Bloor K and Freemantle N (2004) Challenges for the National Institute for Clinical Excellence. *BMJ.* **329**: 327–9.
11 Towse A *et al.* (eds) (2002) *Cost-effectiveness Thresholds. Economic and ethical issues*. Office of Health Economics, London.
12 Department of Health (1992) *The Health of the Nation*. HMSO, London.
13 Department of Health (1995) *Policy Appraisal and Health*. Department of Health, London.
14 Department of Health (1994) *A Register of Cost-Effectiveness Studies*. Economics and Operational Research Division, London.
15 NHS Executive (1995) *Assessing Options in the CHD and Stroke Key Area: Health of the Nation*. NHS Executive, London.
16 Department of Health (1997) *The New NHS: modern, dependable*. The Stationery Office, London.
17 Segal L and Chen Y (2000) *Priority Setting Models for Health. The role for priority setting and a critique of alternative models. A summary*. Health Economics Unit, Monash University, Melbourne, Victoria.

18 Wanless D (2002)*Securing our Future Health: taking a long term view*. Final report, HM Treasury, London.

19 Hurst J (1998) The impact of health economics on health policy in England and the impact of health policy on health economics, 1972–1997. *Health Econ.* **7(Suppl 1)**: S47–62.

20 Timmins N (1995) *The Five Giants: a biography of the welfare state*. Harper Collins, London.

21 Department of Health (2000) *Shaping the Future NHS. Long-term Planning for Hospitals and Related Services. Consultation document on findings of the National Beds Inquiry and supporting analysis*. Department of Health, London.

22 Department of Health (2000) *The NHS Plan: a plan for investment, a plan for reform*. Department of Health, London.

23 Wanless D (2004) *Securing Good Health for the Whole Population. Final report*. The Stationery Office, London.

24 For example, *see* Department of Health (1999) *National Air Quality Strategy. Report on economic appraisal of the health benefits*. Deptartment of Health, London.

25 *See*, for example, Drummond MF (1992) Cost-effectiveness guidelines for reimbursement of pharmaceuticals: is economic evaluation ready for its enhanced status? Guest editorial. *Health Econ.* **1**: 85–92.

26 A good example is the recent evaluation of outpatient teleconsultations. *See* Jacklin P *et al.* (2003) Virtual outreach: economic evaluation of joint teleconsultations for patients referred by their general practitioner for a specialist opinion. *BMJ.* **327**: 84.

27 Weatherly H *et al.* (2002) Using evidence in the development of local health policies: some evidence from the United Kingdom. *Int J Technol Assess Health Care.* **18**: 771–81.

Chapter 7

Measuring and managing performance

Introduction

Between 1975 and 1981 the Permanent Secretary of the Department of Health and Social Security was Sir Patrick Nairne. Reflecting on his experiences shortly after his retirement, Sir Patrick wrote: 'The DHSS can, and does, set national objectives . . . but it cannot readily clarify and assess what has been achieved in terms of better care for patients or more effective services at the local level.'[1] He went on to explain that this was because 'in health and welfare the criteria of performance . . . are particularly hard to define, and measures of success or failure are difficult to formulate'. Twenty-years on, the Department and Ministers not only believe that they can assess what is being achieved in terms of better patient care and more effective services, but they also believe that such assessments can be used to reward or sanction organisations and, increasingly, individuals within the NHS. Both sets of beliefs are reflected in actions. This chapter reviews the contribution of analysis to bringing about this transformation in perceptions and behaviours.

The last 20 years have been marked by an almost continuous expansion in the number and range of performance measures and in the roles given to such measures. However, performance measures have been only one of the tools used to monitor and increasingly to drive improved performance. Alongside the growth of performance measures there has been an almost equally rapid increase in the number of instruments or tools used by the Department to promote performance. There has also been a major strengthening in the rewards and sanctions attached to such drivers.

This chapter begins with a summary of the changing policy context for these parallel developments. A brief history of the development of performance measures and performance management since the early 1980s is followed by a discussion of a number of the key themes that have emerged over this period. The next section identifies the contribution of analysts to these developments. The chapter ends with reflections on four questions. First, what has been learned about performance measurement? Secondly, why was the Department so slow to develop a rounded set of performance measures? Thirdly, what has been learned about the relative effectiveness of the different tools of performance management? Fourthly, has the performance of the NHS been improved by the active performance strategies of recent years?

Policy context

Performance management in the NHS has recently been defined as a 'set of managerial instruments designed to secure optimal performance of the healthcare system over time, in line with policy objectives.'[2] The explicit and active management of NHS performance by the centre is a development of the last 20 years. This development has been prompted both by wider approaches to the management of the public sector and by developments specific to health services. A critical Whitehall-wide development was the adoption of the new managerial approach known as the *new public management* (*NPM*). The Department of Health was one of the pioneers in adopting key features of NPM, such as performance measurement, encouraging the adoption of private-sector management styles, the development of relationships based on contract rather than hierarchy, and the setting up of an implementation agency. Within the Department the period of managerialism was largely inaugurated by the Griffiths Report.[3]

The Griffiths Report followed the 1982 restructuring of the NHS, which essentially replaced a three-tier system of local management (regions, areas, and districts) with two tiers (regions and districts). Both the restructuring and the management review put much emphasis on decentralisation and the devolution of responsibilities. The quid pro quo of greater devolution was the need to strengthen systems of accountability and related performance measures. In 1982 it was announced that Ministers would lead annual departmental reviews of regional long-term plans, objectives and effectiveness.[4] Every successive reorganisation of the NHS and purported decentralisation provided another opportunity for a review, and usually a strengthening of accountability arrangements.

In addition to managerialism and devolution, a third and even stronger influence on the development of performance management was the continuing imbalance between policy priorities and resources. All governments over the last 20 years have seen the promotion of greater efficiency and value for money as a way of reconciling rising public expectations with control of public expenditure. The search for levers to improve performance received an added boost under the Blair Government when aspirational policies were increasingly quantified in terms of targets and standards, making it much easier to judge whether the government was succeeding or failing.

In the second decade of the period under consideration, the task of managing NHS performance was complicated by recognition that equity, technical efficiency and cost control were not the only (or even the most important) aspects of health system performance. Increased acknowledgement of both the importance and the measurability of aspects of the effectiveness of care, including quality, clinical outcomes and patient experiences, added to the pressures for new performance measures and new managerial instruments.

Another contextual feature worth mentioning was the frequent reorganisation of the NHS and, to a lesser extent, of the Department itself. Over much of this period the organisational units whose performance was being extensively measured and managed were changing their shape, size or responsibilities as fast as or faster than information systems could be developed or adjusted. However well intentioned they might have been, the frequent changes in organisational units and in their senior management made it very difficult to hold anyone to account, particularly in fields where there were lags in the production of performance indicators or service improvements inevitably took time. In these circumstances, effective performance management was often as elusive as a will-o'-the-wisp. At times effectiveness was further reduced by continual changes in the performance management regime itself.

The shifts in organisation and in management tools often reflected broader changes in the approaches to managing the NHS. The period saw major switches in the philosophy of control between hierarchy (or 'bossiness'), markets (or 'choice') and professional self-regulation (or 'groupism').[5] There were also related shifts in emphasis and belief between centralisation and decentralisation of management. On a different axis there was a growth in the value and influence accorded to consumers, compared with providers (and, more tentatively, purchasers). Although these changes were accompanied by changes in the role given to different performance instruments or levers, there was an uninterrupted increase in the interest in improving performance measures and measurement. Improved information on the costs and outcomes of healthcare has been seen as a complement to all forms of control, whether by regulation or market, centrally led or decentralised, or by consumers, providers or purchasers. The drive for better performance information came from both the demand for greater accountability, which affected all public services, and from recognition of the fact that healthcare is peculiarly affected by asymmetries of knowledge, not only between the public and providers but also – such is the rate of medical advance – between individual health service professionals.

In passing, it is worth noting the contrast between the management of macroeconomic policy, where the focus is nowadays almost entirely on creating stability, and the management of the NHS and the public sector in general, where the order of the day has been almost constant change and upheaval.* The difference is indicative of continuing uncertainty about what performance regime is most appropriate both for the NHS and for the public sector.

A short history

In terms of the development of performance measures and performance management, it is convenient to identify three periods:

1 the early 1980s to 1991
2 1991 to 1997
3 post 1997.

Early 1980s to 1991

To monitor NHS performance in this period, the Department relied on the data generated by the 1981 Performance Indicators Initiative and on those emerging from the subsequent Korner review. The main purpose of these indicators was to facilitate internal control by local managers. Accordingly, they were drawn from routine administrative data sets and focused almost entirely on activities and costs. For reasons alluded to in the above quotation from Sir Patrick Nairne, there were very few measures of outcomes and effectiveness. A review of performance measures in the Department in 1987 found that their development was impeded both by lack of information and by the lack of clear programme objectives. 'Unless and until service objectives can be specified, there are obvious limits on how far the performance of the Hospital and Community Health Services can be

---

*I am grateful to Mike Parsonage for making this point.

meaningfully assessed.'[6] In relation to primary care there were also 'doubts as to whether it was either proper or feasible for the Department to apply performance measures to independent contractors'. The review recommended that the Department should consider developing a strategy for expanding the coverage of performance measures and for integrating such measures into normal management procedures. It was six years before these recommendations began to be followed up.

Despite the dearth of data on outputs and outcomes, there was an annual accountability review process from 1982 onwards. The Department or latterly the NHS Management Executive annually reviewed the plans and performance of the 14 regions. Each in turn was expected to review the performance of its districts. Although in theory a command and control system, it has more accurately been described as management by exhortation. Despite conscious efforts to move away from detailed controls of inputs and to place more emphasis on performance, data deficiencies and a lack of clarity on policy objectives made it hard for senior Departmental managers or their analytical support team to reach firm judgements. (For example, when it was discovered that there was a fivefold variation across Districts in terms of cataract operation rates, no one could decide whether this was an acceptable or unacceptable variation.) With Regional Chief Executives reporting to a Regional chairman and not to a Departmental manager, the absence of a clear and effective chain of management command also constrained the actions that the Department could take to improve performance. The focus of many of the reviews on regional ten-year plans that were out of date almost as soon as they were written, because of resource constraints, also undermined the effectiveness of the management process.

Primary care performance monitoring and management were even less effective. Information was collected and compared on aspects of the administrative performance of Family Practitioner Committees, but up until the 1987 Primary Care Review it was not regarded as either proper or feasible for the Department to apply performance measures to the activities of independent GP and dental contractors. Instead of the hierarchical structure that in theory applied to hospital and community health services, there was a broadly competitive approach to performance, with independent primary care contractors influenced by the structure of fees and allowances in central contracts and by patient choice. While the Primary Care Review commissioned work on the development of service-wide measures of performance it was prophetically noted at the time that 'quantifying objectives for the Family Practitioner Services is likely to prove a lengthy process'.[6] It was eight years before a set of indicators was identified, and 16 years before a set was operationalised.

1991 to 1997

The introduction of the internal market acted as a huge spur to the development both of performance indicators and of new approaches to driving up performance. To ensure that the efficiency benefits of the new competition were captured and locked in, the Treasury successfully pressed for the conversion of the existing aggregate efficiency indicator into a target. As the target was ratcheted up to more and more demanding levels, there was increasing concern that the quality of care might be at risk. Responding to these concerns, in 1993 the NHS Management

Executive set up a group 'to consider what measures of quality, effectiveness and health outcomes and patient satisfaction can be used as systematic measures of NHS performance for the national accountability process'.[7] The group was specifically asked to identify a small number of indicators ('around six') that could inform future performance contracts with regional health authorities. In two reports in 1993 the group identified a set of summary indicators that could be used to monitor progress under the Executive's then key strategies, namely public health, community care, effective purchasing, the Patient's Charter, clinical quality, strengthening the scientific base, and giving choice and influence to health service users. In subsequent years further working groups identified additional potential indicators, most importantly in relation to primary care.[8] Progress in introducing these new indicators was slow and was not helped by the abolition of regional health authorities and the need to extend the centre's information base and performance management to the 100 or so new district health authorities. In early 1997, work began on developing an assessment framework to pull together the proliferating indicator sets.

Although on the NHS front-line the focus of performance monitoring continued to be on efficiency, there was some progress in publishing indicators of performance in other fields. Most importantly, the 'Patient's Charter' announced in 1991 included the first set of performance indicators specifically aimed at informing the public about the performance of their local health service. In addition to waiting times, they also included data relating to vaccination and immunisation rates and cervical cytology screening.

While the development of new performance indicators proceeded at a stately pace, there was more rapid progress in developing new instruments for promoting performance. For the hospital and community health services, markets and competition had been introduced as mechanisms to drive up performance by providers. However, for fear of the political and human costs of 'de-stabilisation' (i.e. service closure), and in recognition of the Government's continuing ownership responsibilities, detailed management controls were relaxed only slowly. The first (and only) regulatory framework for the new internal market was not issued until the end of 1994.[9]

There was no equivalent competition between health authority purchasers, although the development of GP fundholders did create a stimulus for all purchasers to improve their performance. The main focus of the centre's attempts to influence NHS performance switched to the management of health authorities in their purchasing role. Reflecting this new emphasis there was a raft of reviews of different aspects of purchasing, including the nature of contracting, involvement of the public and approaches to prioritisation.

The first attempt to take a holistic view of the centre's instruments and levers for improving NHS performance and to label this a 'performance framework' was in 1995. It is indicative of the way in which interest in performance was broadening that a year earlier a similar review had been labelled an 'efficiency review'. The new performance framework identified three sets of instruments or structures for improving performance, namely levers (which included planning and priorities guidance, the accountability framework and the regulatory framework), incentives (which included the internal market, consumer pressures and professional ethos), and knowledge and skills (which included information, research and development and workforce skills, and was seen as working through mechanisms such as benchmarking). A review of these various drivers of performance raised a range of questions about how they might be strengthened or developed, but there were no clear recommendations on the way forward. The review also found it impossible to quantify the respective contributions of the various levers or their role relative to broader developments such as medical advance and the change to general management initiated by the 1983 Griffiths Report.

Post 1997

When the Labour Government came to power in 1997 with a manifesto commitment to change the focus of performance management away from activity and efficiency and towards quality of outcome, it found that much of the conceptual and analytical work required for such a shift had already been undertaken. Borrowing from the thinking behind the 'balanced scorecard' approach to measuring private sector performance,[10] and from the attempts of US employers to systematically compare the performance of American health plans (the Health Plan Employer Data and Information Set – HEDIS), Departmental analysts and clinicians had already actively explored various approaches to identifying the key domains for performance management and measurement in a health service focused on quality. The objective was to channel indicators, monitoring and management towards those aspects of performance that most resonated with the users and funders of the NHS. In the summer of 1997, Ministers agreed that the new Performance Assessment Framework (PAF) should cover six areas, namely health improvement, fair access, effective delivery of appropriate healthcare, efficiency, patient/carer experience, and health outcomes of NHS care.

The subsequent history of performance indicators has been described elsewhere.[11] Suffice it to say that much energy was put into selecting and consulting on a raft of indicators to populate the new performance domains. In many cases existing, albeit imperfect data sets could be used, at least as interim measures. However, in some areas, notably patient experience, new surveys had to be rapidly mounted. Indicators that had been selected as suitable for raising questions had to be reviewed again for their suitability as measures for rating performance. While lip-service continued to be paid to the Performance Assessment Framework and its growing number of indicators as a balanced overview of health service performance, policy attention quickly shifted to the smaller number of indicators used to assess the performance of NHS hospitals (and later primary care trusts) under the star-rating system introduced from 2002. Most if not all of the indicators also had to be prepared for public reporting.

Having abolished competition as an incentive mechanism, the new Government rapidly recognised that the new performance measurement system which it was developing needed to be complemented by a wider range of management tools if performance was to improve as quickly and radically as it required. Early initiatives can be categorised under three headings:

1 mechanisms for defining standards and targets so that 'stretch' was introduced into the system and poor performance was clearly identified (National Service Frameworks and the work of the National Institute for Clinical Excellence were the prime initiatives in this area)

2   incentives to change behaviour to overcome natural conservatism (four key initiatives to strengthen incentives were the performance rating of hospital trusts and primary care trusts, the offer of operational freedoms or earned autonomy to high-performing organisations, the NHS performance fund to encourage innovation at the local level, and the negotiation of new contracts for hospital doctors and general practitioners that linked pay more closely to performance (including, for GPs, quality of care)

3   support to behavioural change to help those who might want to change but did not know how to do so (the major changes here were the establishment of the Commission for Health Improvement – which later evolved into the Healthcare Commission – and the development of the Modernisation Agency).

These initiatives nested within, and were supported by, the Government's new public-sector-wide framework for performance management, namely the Public Service Agreements (PSAs) first introduced in 1998. For the Department of Health as for other departments these set out key aims and objectives, the budget for the next three years, performance targets for the delivery of services, and a statement of how productivity would be improved. As the PSAs became more sharply focused, they took on the role of the earlier and largely ineffective Priorities and Planning Frameworks as the top level or tier of the Department's performance management system.

More recently there has been an attempt to reintroduce many of the incentives of a market. Patient choice of providers has been greatly extended, the private sector has been invited to help to expand supply capacity, and public hospitals are moving to payment by results through the introduction of a case-mix-based payment system.[12] At the same time, a new framework of standards is being introduced to complement a reduced number of national targets as the main driver for continuous improvement in quality.[13]

Overviewing developments up to the end of 2003, Simon Stevens, then Health Policy Adviser to the Prime Minister, identified no fewer than 12 management instruments in use to improve healthcare delivery in the face of tight supply constraints.[14] The 12 instruments or strategies were grouped under three headings as follows.

1   *Support for providers.* This had led to strategies for growing capacity by expanding the number of health professionals, for modernising infrastructure (particularly information systems) and for supported learning and improvement.

2   *Hierarchical challenge.* This had given rise to centrally mandated changes, including the setting of national standards and targets, inspection and regulation, published performance information, and 'earned autonomy' and direct intervention in the management of poorly performing organisations.

3   *Localist challenge.* The main strategies under this heading included active healthcare purchasing through primary care commissioning, more patient choice of providers, aligned and sharpened provider incentives, new entrants and a mixed economy on the supply side, and local democratic accountability.

Underlying themes

Standing back from the detailed and often ephemeral changes in the evolution of performance measurement and management for the NHS, it is possible to identify a number of pervasive themes. Those identified below are particularly relevant to discussion of the role of Departmental analysts. They are grouped under two headings:

1   performance monitoring
2   performance management.

Performance monitoring

Future historians are likely to recognise at least four main trends in the development of NHS performance measures over the last two decades of the twentieth century:

1   the broadening of the domains of performance subject to measurement
2   a move from 'indicators' to raise questions to 'measures' backed by rewards and sanctions
3   disaggregation of the units being monitored and a switch of interest from purchasers to providers
4   the hiving off of monitoring to an independent agency.

These trends will each be discussed in turn.

Broadening the performance domains and developing performance frameworks

It is commonly asserted that 'what gets measured, gets managed' and 'it is impossible to make improvement without measurement'. The broadening of the aspects of NHS performance that attracted measurement after 1990 is a guide to the broadening of the interests of both politicians and Departmental managers. Although work on developing measures of health outcomes and the clinical aspects of the quality of care began in the early 1990s, it is indicative that there was no serious attempt to monitor patient experiences (outside waiting times) until after 1997, or about 20 years after patients had supposedly been put at the centre of healthcare.[15] Pressure for broadening performance measurement to include indicators of effectiveness and outcomes came from successive Chief Medical Officers, who were concerned that the internal market would lead to cost minimisation and keen to promote evidence-based care, and from Chief Executives of the NHS who were responding to complaints from the field that the focus on efficiency was undermining other policies. The main pressure to expand performance measures to include patient experience came from Ministers.

Once there was political and senior management interest in monitoring NHS performance across a range of aspects, the challenge was to identify ways of presenting a relatively large number of indicators in an understandable way. As already noted, the framework chosen, which became known as the Performance Assessment Framework (PAF), drew heavily on pioneering work in other countries, particularly the frameworks being developed in the USA and to a lesser extent in Australia. An important initial choice was whether the main performance domains should be built around the key policy strategies of the time or whether they should reflect the more generic and long-lasting areas of concern of the principal NHS stakeholders, particularly patients. The latter course was taken when the new framework was announced in 1997.[16] However, it was recognised early on that Ministers might find it difficult to live with a framework that was not focused on their current strategic priorities:

> *An issue requiring further thought is how the PAF can strike a balance between providing a broad overview of the general performance of local health systems/organisations and an assessment of their progress in relation to current strategic priorities. Striking this balance will not be easy, but the long-term success of the Framework may depend on its ability to perform both functions.*[17]

Since 2002, the balanced scorecard approach of the PAF appears to have been largely lost to sight behind a star-rating system with a focus on progress against current strategic priorities. As priorities change one can expect a return to a broader overview of the performance of the health system to complement the monitoring of current priorities.[18] Indeed, at the time of writing, the latest Departmental planning guidance proposes a new framework of seven 'domains' to structure both standards and the whole performance agenda.*

From performance indicators to performance measures

Although the term 'performance measures' was used to cover the development of new indicator sets throughout the 1990s and beyond, in practice the nature of what was being talked about changed dramatically. Before 1997 all of the indicator sets that were proposed (for effectiveness and quality, equity and patients' experience) were seen as 'indicators' to be used only for raising questions, not as 'measures', that were capable of supporting judgements about performance.† This initial caution reflected doubts both about the technical quality of the data and about the interpretations that could be given to it. Many of the members of the initial working parties, particularly clinicians, were only willing to participate if these limitations were acknowledged. The cautions were rapidly forgotten or overruled once the decision was made to compare NHS trusts and latterly primary care trusts using rating systems. Many of the performance indicators that had been developed over some years for raising questions (to be 'can openers') were found to be unsuitable for apportioning rewards and penalties. Ideally much more time should have been given to developing new indicators that could carry the weight required for informing judgements and for allocating rewards and penalties.‡ However, Ministers chose

---

*Department of Health (2004) *National Standards, Local Actions: health and social care standards and planning framework 2005/6–2007/8*. Department of Health, London. The domains proposed (safety, clinical and cost-effectiveness, governance, patient focus, accessible and responsive care, care environment and amenities, and public health) look a hotch-potch and may require further thought.
† This was also true of the performance indicators developed in the 1980s. They were seen as a tool for learning, not for reaching judgements. *See* Gibbs R (2002) Performance indicators: for judging or learning? *Br J Healthcare Comput Info Manag.* 19: 21–2.
‡ I am grateful to Maria Goddard for pointing out that the indicators in the Scottish performance framework have remained as indicators and are not associated with formal sanctions and rewards. The same is broadly true of New Zealand. It would be useful to compare the effectiveness of this approach with that adopted in England.

to believe, probably correctly, that whether treated as indicators or measures, the incentives to develop better information would be stronger and progress would be more rapid if a start was made with the imperfect data to hand. It was also implicitly accepted – without any formal testing – that using indicators for delivering judgements would be as effective as or more effective in promoting learning and a development agenda than using them only to raise questions.

Measurement unit: from purchaser to provider

In the 1980s and the first half of the 1990s the Department's performance management focused on regions. With the abolition of regional health authorities, attention switched to districts. Before district health authorities were abolished, attention began to switch to providers, initially acute and community trusts and then primary care trusts. These changes in focus partly reflected changes in governance arrangements within the NHS, but more importantly they recognised that the concerns of patients and the public were not with the performance of large funding agencies but with the performance of local health service providers.

The change in the units subject to measurement was another major strain on the Department's resources for developing indicators, and raised increasingly difficult questions about the degree to which statistically robust comparisons of organisations could be made. The growing political interest in the performance of individual clinicians or clinical teams has raised these problems in an even more acute form. The public needs to be educated about the limitations of indicators that are based on very small numbers, but the genie cannot and should not be put back in the bottle. It is interesting to note that in the rush to develop indicators of individual provider performance, arguments about official or business confidentiality were almost completely forgotten. Up until 1997 these arguments ensured that little information on the performance of regions and districts was placed in the public domain in an easily accessible form. Since around 2000 the position has been transformed, and there has been relatively little information on the performance of NHS trusts and primary care trusts available to the Department that has not also been placed in the public domain.

Towards an independent agency

The decision to move performance monitoring and performance rating first to the Commission for Health Improvement (CHI) and then to the Healthcare Commission has been presented primarily as being motivated by a wish to demonstrate the independence of the performance-monitoring function and to re-establish trust in indicators of NHS improvement. However, with hindsight an equally important reason for moving in this direction was the evidence that this was the only way of ensuring that the performance-monitoring function was properly staffed and resourced. A later section of this chapter comments on the slow development of new types of performance measures, and argues that one reason for this was the under-resourcing of data collection and analytical capacity in the Department. This problem was apparent in the mid-1990s and became critical once the Labour Government put performance monitoring and performance targets at the centre of its strategy to drive up performance. The downward pressure on Departmental staff numbers and an unwillingness or inability to radically reprioritise the deployment of staff meant that a performance-monitoring function of the range and quality required by Ministers could only be provided by contracting out the function. It is a peculiarity of governments of all complexions that they are quite happy to double or treble the budgets and staff directed to a particular function once it is split off to a new agency. This is exactly what happened when the performance monitoring of NHS trusts moved to the CHI.

Performance management

A number of threads or themes also run through the development of performance management in the NHS over the last 20 years. Some of the most interesting ones can be discussed under five headings.

1 What were seen to be the causes of poor performance?
2 What were the objectives of performance management?
3 What was perceived to be the Department's relationship with the NHS?
4 What strategies were adopted?
5 What was the role for market forces?

These will each be discussed in turn.

The performance problem

The last 20 years have seen numerous initiatives aimed at improving the performance of the NHS. The performance weaknesses of the NHS have been frequently rehearsed,[16,19] and a great deal of effort has gone into developing tools, levers or drivers to improve performance. However, looking back there has been surprisingly little attention given to identifying and understanding the underlying causes of the disappointing performance. To many outside and inside the NHS the answer has been obvious – under-investment. However, no government has seen that as more than part of the problem. In retrospect it is surprising how little attention successive governments gave to setting out what they saw to be the causes of the chronic shortfalls in performance.

In 1989, the Conservative White Paper *Working for Patients* included no explicit discussion of the causes of the poor performance of the NHS, although it implied that the monolithic organisation of the NHS was ineffective and that management was too centralised. Reading between the lines, it can also be inferred that incentives were thought to be too weak and information systems deficient. However, the suggestion by some officials that there should be an introductory chapter setting out why incentives needed to be improved was rejected. In various academic forums Departmental and external analysts subsequently attempted to clarify what were regarded as the underlying causes of the performance weaknesses of the NHS. However, within the Department it would be fair to say that there was a tendency to reach for new management levers without fully exploring why performance was poor. The 'unacceptable' variation in performance up and down the country was seen in 1989 and again in 1997 (in *The New NHS: Modern, Dependable*) as justifying major policy changes, but on both occasions there was no detailed analysis of the reasons for the variation.

The NHS Plan in 2000 was the first major reform document to attempt a systematic explanation of the causes of the poor performance of the NHS. It argued that in addition to under-investment, the causes included a lack of national standards, an absence of clear incentives, a lack of support and intervention procedures (including reliable information), demarcations between staff, barriers between services, over-centralisation, and disempowered patients. More recently the NHS Confederation suggested that the list of problems could be considerably extended, and should include lack of management of clinical areas, failure to successfully engage professionals, inadequate leadership and management, and over-enthusiasm for structural change.[20] There will be differences in view about the relative importance of these various causes, but in retrospect it is clear that the NHS Confederation was right to conclude that there has been much more concentration on defining the treatment than on clarifying the diagnosis. This is still true today. It was even more true in the 1990s.

Objectives of performance management

Over the last two decades of the twentieth century there was a major shift in the Department's objectives in reviewing NHS performance. The initial concern with accountability to the centre was supplemented and partly replaced by a focus on improving performance and delivery. The accountability reviews held with regions from the early 1980s were, as their name implies, primarily directed at establishing what services were being produced, how regional plans were progressing and exploring any problems. As the Department built up its capacity to analyse the performance indicator packages available after 1983, the Management Board was briefed to raise more penetrating questions about regional and district variations. However, the narrow range of performance indicators, doubts about their quality and the absence of national standards or targets all limited the extent to which the centre could probe. The lack of a clear and effective chain of management command from districts, through regions to the Chief Executive and to the Secretary of State also restricted the ability of the centre to require improvements in performance, even when the centre knew what it wanted to achieve.

After 1989, the Department gradually moved beyond accountability reviews to active performance management. Within the department the Regional Liaison Division gave way to the Performance Management Division, and there was increasing talk first of the Department's 'levers' and then of the 'drivers' of improved performance. The number of national targets began to increase and in some cases, notably in the Health of the Nation, went beyond activity and efficiency to include health outcomes. However, well into the 1990s there remained a reluctance to use performance indicators to measure and compare the performance of local management, rather than to raise questions. In 1993, for example, a report on progress in developing indicators of effectiveness and quality noted that they were 'intended to serve as high-level pointers of progress in meeting national objectives and not measures of the achievement of local management'.

In 1995, an attempt to codify a 'new performance framework' can be seen as a further step beyond accountability reviews and towards more active management of the NHS.* The 'new framework' emphasised that, in addition to using the

---

* Although it was called 'new,' this performance framework was almost certainly the first to be formally codified.

incentives of the internal market, the Management Executive was developing and applying a raft of other 'drivers' to improve NHS performance.

The switch in the centre's role in relation to the NHS, from requiring a loose accountability to explicitly driving performance improvement and behavioural change through every conceivable instrument, was taken much further after 1997. Service delivery became the focus of attention not only in the NHS but also across the public sector. In quick progression indicators became first 'measures' and then 'targets' or 'standards'. To further motivate changes in behaviour the targets and standards were backed by an ever-increasing range of incentives, both financial and non-financial. In case the desired behaviour change was impeded by a lack of time or mechanisms to learn from others, there was also a range of initiatives aimed at providing the necessary space and technical support.

At the end of the period under consideration there was a re-emphasis on the importance of accountability, but now it was accountability to local people, through star ratings and other mechanisms of disclosing information on local providers, rather than to the centre.

The Department's relationship with the NHS

Troughout these years there has been a perennial debate as to whether, for performance improvement purposes, the Department should regard the NHS as akin to an industry or a firm. Up until 1989, the NHS was basically treated like a loosely (some would say feebly) managed large firm or nationalised industry, with the Department acting as head office and supported by vertical line management relationships and administrative controls running from the top downwards. The introduction of the internal market sparked a lively Whitehall debate over whether this was still the appropriate model. From 1991 to 1997 it was accepted that this analogy was still broadly valid as far as the demand or purchasing side of the NHS market was concerned. The centre would continue to specify key national policy objectives, and these objectives would be transmitted to the service via the management line running from regions to districts (and later to GP fundholders).

However, under the internal market it was realised that on the supply side the appropriate analogy was no longer the firm but a competitive industry (i.e. a collection of separate units linked to purchasers via contractual rather than management relationships, and often in competition with each other). The main driver of performance was expected to be competition, not management directives from the Department. The implication was that the Department's role in relation to healthcare providers, notably hospitals, should be closer to that of a market regulator than to a 'head office'. The analogy could not be pushed too far, as hospitals remained under public ownership and the Department had a continuing responsibility to ensure that public assets were used efficiently.

These analogies did not prevent hospitals from continuing to be tightly managed by the centre and health authorities, but they did fend off Treasury proposals for even more central management. They also helped to create the space necessary for developing the regulatory framework that was announced in 1994.

In 1997, the new Labour Government initially swung firmly back to treating the NHS like a huge firm, with the Department as head office. Unacceptable variations in service were to be replaced by national standards, and competition between providers was ended. Although health authorities and primary care groups/trusts would continue to have contractual relationships with hospitals, there would also be stronger performance management from the centre. The strong emphasis on centralisation was rationalised (almost certainly correctly) on the grounds that it was the only way in which the Government could drive through change quickly.

Since 2001 the tide has turned again, and the Department has to begun treat the NHS more like a mixed-economy industry. Private providers are being encouraged and so is patient choice and, implicitly, provider competition. The activities of foundation trusts and the private sector are to be governed by an independent regulator. It remains to be seen how wide the remit of the regulator will be (e.g. whether in time it will be extended to primary care) and whether there will be a real reduction in direct management from the centre.

The current political and academic rhetoric is strongly in favour of decentralisation. It is accompanied by welcome recognition that devolved decision making will only work if it is underpinned by stronger capacity in performance management by front-line organisations. However, recent history and the experience of other parts of the world, such as New Zealand and Scandinavia, suggest that for reasons of equity and Ministerial impatience we can expect governments (and the Department) to continue to oscillate between treating the NHS like a firm and treating it as an industry.[21] The oscillation in rhetoric may of course be larger than the oscillation in practice. At the time of writing, many NHS staff remain sceptical about the degree of local freedom that will actually be delivered.

Performance management strategies

Throughout the last 20 years the Department has used a range of instruments to attempt to improve NHS performance. Evidence of effectiveness has generally played little part in the selection of the instruments, and their presentation as coherent strategies has invariably followed rather than preceded their individual development. In the 1980s the instruments included new policies, tight budget constraints, targets, earmarked funds, accountability reviews, executive letters and performance indicators. There were debates about the effectiveness of different instruments, but there were no formal evaluations to compare their relative effectiveness and no attempts to bring them together into a performance strategy or framework.

The internal market brought in a new range of market mechanisms and heated academic and political debates about their effectiveness. In 1991, Departmental analysts suggested a categorisation of the levers then available to the centre under the headings 'incentives', 'information' and 'organisational changes'. They also suggested developing a set of criteria for aiding selection between the management and market instruments. However, as already noted, it was not until 1995 that the Department put forward an explicit 'new' performance framework with the available instruments grouped into three categories, namely 'strategies and levers', 'incentives', and 'knowledge and skills'. Questions were raised about whether each of the instruments within these categories should be pushed harder or more softly, but there was no attempt to assess their relative effectiveness. By neither funding nor encouraging formal evaluation of the internal market reforms, Ministers and senior officials ensured that there was insufficient evidence to make judgements about effectiveness.

Since 1997 there has been a huge increase in both the number of instruments applied to managing NHS performance and the vigour with which they have been pursued. Formal evaluations have at last grown apace, and there have also been determined attempts to learn from the experiences of other countries. There has been some important learning and sometimes relearning. For example, the need to keep the number of key NHS objectives small was learned in the period up to 1997, and when objectives were turned into hard targets it was relearned again after 2001. However, in recent years new management instruments have been introduced faster than it has been possible to learn from older ones. Impatience for quick improvements has overtaken strategic thinking about how performance improvements can be maximised, while at the same time minimising both administrative costs and distortions to other policies.

Various attempts have been made to provide a rationale for the plethora of new management instruments. One has grouped them in terms of mechanisms for defining standards and targets, incentives to change behaviour, and support to behavioural change.[22] Another has classified them in terms of 'guidance, monitoring and response'.[23] In 2004, as noted earlier, Simon Stevens identified 12 tools and classified them under three headings, namely 'support for providers', 'hierarchical challenge" and 'localist challenge'. Although intuitively appealing arguments can be made for each and every one of the instruments, the rate of change points to a government learning on the hoof rather than carefully implementing a considered strategy. Learning on the hoof – sometimes known as 'failing forward' – can be an effective change strategy provided that there is sufficient learning and not too much 'hoof'. Between 1997 and 2002, internal analysts were unable to ensure that this balance was properly struck.

What role for market forces?

In the late 1980s, the Thatcher Government concluded that the best way to improve the efficiency of the NHS and to make it more responsive to consumers was through the injection of market forces. Thus the internal market was born. In 1997 the Labour Government came to power committed to ending the internal market system, which was seen as defined by unfairness and bureaucracy. Five years later the same government was re-injecting market forces into the NHS as a way of expanding consumer choice and increasing supply capacity. However, this was not to be an 'internal' market confined to public suppliers – the entry of private suppliers was actively encouraged. What brought about this apparent policy reversal?

The first point to note is that the Labour Government never opposed provider competition in principle. On the precept of 'what matters is what works', it argued that some key elements of the internal market should be discarded (because they encouraged bureaucracy, service fragmentation and unfairness) but others, notably the separation between the planning and provision of services and the central role in commissioning of primary care, should be retained. In the White Paper *The New NHS* the door was even left open for contestability in hospital services.*

---

* 'Primary Care Groups will be able to make choices about cost-effective patterns of service [and] will be able to signal a change to their local service agreements, where NHS Trusts are failing to deliver.' Department of Health (1997) *The New NHS: modern, dependable.* Department of Health, London.

The second point is that the new Government's early reforms addressed some of its major complaints about the internal market. Both bureaucracy and unfairness were reduced by replacing several thousand volunteer GP fundholders with a universal system of a few hundred primary care trusts. Subsequently, other policy developments advertently or inadvertently tackled some of the specific factors that had limited the positive impact of competition.[24] For example, comparative information on costs and quality was gradually improved, and the announcement of a national price schedule for hospital services meant that purchasers could more easily focus on comparing quality. Steps to reduce hospital utilisation rates and to import capacity from overseas private suppliers meant that there was greater capacity to expand into new markets. And the establishment of autonomous foundation trusts and an independent regulator covering the private sector as well as the new trusts meant that Ministers could, at least in theory, more plausibly distance themselves from the special pleading of providers in difficulty.

The third point is that the government became convinced of the value of choice and competition for its reform agenda. Increased choice and the personalisation of services became a central feature of the general reform of public services. And no one has yet invented a mechanism for giving consumers choice that does not imply some element of competition between providers. However, there were also particular reasons for opening key healthcare sectors to competition. First, in order to meet waiting-times targets, elective and diagnostic capacity had to be expanded at a rate that was only possible by inviting in private suppliers, both domestic and foreign. Secondly, entitling patients to go elsewhere if waiting times were too long was seen as an important way of challenging the restrictive practices of a minority of clinicians in specialties with particularly long waiting times.

At the time of writing it is too early to judge whether this second attempt to inject competition into the NHS will be more successful than the first one. However, there are encouraging signs. Significant numbers of patients are obtaining their operations earlier by opting to go to alternative providers, and private-sector prices are reportedly falling, making the private sector a more competitive alternative to public hospitals. The government is also trying to directly address a major constraint on the adoption of competitive behaviours under the internal market, namely the belief among NHS workers and the public that they are not consistent with traditional NHS concepts of social justice and fairness. It is now argued that a right to choose among hospital providers will give the less well off the same privileges that have long been enjoyed by the rich and those with sharp elbows. Support services are promised to make these choices real.

Overall the prognosis for choice and competition being able to improve healthcare outcomes, at least in certain sectors, is much better than it was in the 1990s. However, there remain formidable imbalances in information in favour of providers, and it is unclear how widely primary care trusts (or patients directly) will exercise the skills and knowledge required to be smart purchasers or choosers. There are also unanswered questions about the long-term costs and equity implications of offering wide-scale choice.

Role of analysis

The Department's economists and operational researchers can reasonably claim to have made a major contribution to the development of performance monitoring and performance management over these two decades. In relation to performance indicators, they worked very closely both with the Department's statisticians and with administrative colleagues responsible for finance and regional liaison/performance management. Operational researchers took the lead in converting the NHS Performance Indicators initiated in 1981 into interactive packages that district health authorities could use for benchmarking. In 1984, the heads of the Statistical, Economics and Operational Research Services jointly proposed the establishment of a small analytical team to support the policy division charged with monitoring and liaising with regions. This team, known as CARP (Central Analysis of Regional Plans), survived in various forms for about 15 years.

It was noted earlier (*see* Chapter 5) that economists led the initial work on the development of an efficiency indicator. An economist was also asked to chair the 1993 working group that attempted to broaden monitoring by identifying high-level indicators of quality and effectiveness. The same economist later led the first groups that were charged with identifying how the performance of primary care and community care services could be assessed. A number of the indicators identified by these initial exercises were still in use in 2004 as part of the star-rating systems run by the Healthcare Commission.[25] Working with public health clinicians, Departmental economists initiated work on developing the framework that became known as the Performance Assessment Framework (PAF).

There were two issues on which Departmental economists persistently acted as advocates within the Department, namely patient experience surveys and public disclosure of comparative performance. The story on both is told in Chapter 8.

Turning to performance management, the Department's economists and operational researchers played important roles as both catalysts and innovators. They developed the industry/firm distinction that helped to clarify the Department's role in relation to the NHS under the internal market. A university economist attached to the Department (Dr Carol Propper) developed the internal-market regulatory framework that was published in 1994. After 1997, Departmental economists had some success in arguing for a strengthening of financial incentives at both organisational and individual levels. The NHS Performance Fund was developed by a group led by a senior Departmental economist, and economists contributed substantially to the strengthening and redirection of performance incentives in the new contract for hospital doctors. The Department's economists were also the leading advocates for the new system of hospital payments – 'Payment by Results' – that was introduced in 2003. Unsurprisingly, they were persistent supporters (when the political climate allowed) of the virtues of choice and contestability as mechanisms for improving efficiency and responsiveness.

The advice offered by Departmental economists did not always go with the flow of Ministerial opinion. For example, recommendations for a loosening of financial constraints on NHS trusts in 1996 were not accepted at the time. In other cases advice was slow to be implemented because of resource constraints or loss of institutional memory. Two examples were the 1998 recommendations that data on the productivity of consultants should be made available to hospital Chief Executives, and that the Department's data systems should be explored to see whether they could provide early warning of adverse outcomes similar to those at Bristol.* Both recommendations were accepted by Ministers at the time, but Departmental resource constraints and staff changes resulted in there being little or no progress for about four years.

From 1989 onwards, internal analysts persistently pushed for evaluation of the various mechanisms of the internal market (as is discussed in Chapter 10). However, external evaluation of performance-monitoring and management tools was not adequately funded until the second half of the 1990s. From then on internal analysts were greatly assisted by external researchers. Particularly notable contributions to the Department's thinking about performance management came from a long series of studies from the Centre for Health Economics at York.† These provided the hardest information available on the effects, including the distortions, of various performance tools. They helped to inject more rigour into the Department's thinking. There were also significant contributions from the Commonwealth Fund of New York and the Nuffield Trust in facilitating access to the latest thinking on and experience with performance monitoring and management in the USA. These foundations were particularly effective conduits for research findings on measuring clinical quality and patient experience.

Some lessons?

What are some of the more important lessons that have been learned about the development of performance measures in a centralised health care system? Why did it take so long for the Department to move from measures of efficiency to a rounded set of performance measures? What has been learned about the relative effectiveness of the different tools of performance improvement? Overall, has the performance of the NHS been improved by the active performance strategies adopted in recent years? Reflections on these questions may be a useful way of ending this chapter.

What has been learned about the development of effective performance measures?

Some of the more important lessons are summarised in Box 7.1. They are spelt out in the Appendix at the end of this chapter.[26]

---

* At Bristol Royal Infirmary cardiac surgeons negligently operated beyond their competence and children died as a result. *See* Kennedy I (2001) *Learning from Bristol: the Report of the Public Inquiry into Children's Heart Surgery at the Bristol Royal Infirmary 1984–1995*. The Stationery Office, London.
† These studies covered many of the tools deployed by the Department, including performance measurement, efficiency targets, devolved budgets, earned autonomy and choice. *See* www.york. ac.uk/inst/che/policy.htm

---

Box 7.1 Developing effective performance measures

1 Developing good performance indicators is a complex and resource-intensive task.
2 Start using the data to hand – do not wait for the ideal indicators to be developed.
3 Different stakeholders require different data sets.
4 For high- level indicators and targets, parsimony is preferable to comprehensiveness.
5 Think 'outcomes' but use 'output' and 'process' indicators as stepping stones or proxies.
6 Governments initially focus on measuring the performance of big planning or funding units, but the public, patients, users and clinicians are more interested in the performance of 'small' providers and in care for particular conditions.
7 The effectiveness of performance measures depends critically on presentation.
8 The effectiveness of performance measures also depends critically on stakeholder ownership.

Why did it take so long to move from measures of efficiency to measures of effectiveness and quality?

As noted earlier, it was in January 1993 that the NHS Chief Executive commissioned a working group to identify systematic measures of NHS performance in terms of quality, effectiveness and health outcomes and patient satisfaction. Reflecting the urgency attached to rebalancing performance monitoring, the group was asked to report back by the end of May on an initial set of indicators that could be used to inform regional performance contracts for 1994–95. The group met its remit through two reports that were delivered in mid-1993. However, indicators of quality and effectiveness were not used to systematically monitor and compare the performance of units in the NHS until 1999–2000. Why did it take so long for the Department to signal that it was as concerned about improving health status, raising the quality of clinical care and improving patient satisfaction as it was with improving efficiency?

In retrospect, the reasons are fairly clear. They can be grouped under two headings as follows.

Cultural and environmental factors

- *Cultural resistance.* As in other countries, there was trust in the medical profession and reluctance to embark on a course that might appear to call that trust into question. In addition, the public's affection for the NHS encouraged complacency over the quality of NHS care. It took time for Departmental officials to wake up to the need for modernisation and reform.
- *Scepticism and sometimes opposition to developing measures of clinical quality among a significant number of the medical profession.* Some consultations with professional groups that had been expected to take months in fact dragged on for years.

- *The technical difficulty of measuring quality and patient experience.* Developing good indicators is a lengthy and time-consuming process. As the 1990s progressed the Department could learn from burgeoning research and experience in the USA.
- *Reorganisation of the NHS.* By 1994, regional health authorities had been abolished and the task was to identify performance indicators that could be applied to 100 district health authorities rather than to 14 regions. Later, further organisational changes switched the interest to NHS trusts and primary care trusts.

Organisational response

- There was limited statistical and analytical capacity in the Department and in the NHS. Initial indicators relied on existing databases. However, as the data had generally been little used, certainly for accountability purposes, much checking was required. Many of the indicators also called for aggregation or manipulation of databases. At a time when the Department was under severe pressure to reduce staff numbers, rapid progress would only have been possible if the work had been given the highest priority.
- Instead there was under-resourcing. Although the 1993 working group was well staffed and resourced, no provision was made for the further costs of implementing its findings.
- There was no provision for monitoring implementation of the 1993 recommendations, and initially no one was tasked with leading the implementation. These shortcomings were later tackled by establishing a standing group on performance measures.

It required the election of a new government with a manifesto commitment to shift the focus of performance management towards effectiveness and quality of outcome to give the work the priority that ensured it was adequately resourced. The new commitment also gave the supporters of reform within the Department the power to place a time limit on professional scepticism, and in the case of measures of patient experience, to override former managerial doubts.

Looking back, this experience illustrates two features of the Department in the first half of the 1990s. First, the ability to produce innovative ideas ran ahead of the capacity to implement them. Secondly, project management skills were in very short supply.

What has been learned about the relative effectiveness of different management tools in improving performance?

The current government has introduced a plethora of management instruments with the aim of improving the performance of the NHS. Nearly all of the instruments can be seen as attempts to tackle the principal-agent problem – that is, the problem of how to align the behaviours of health service managers, clinicians and other workers with the wishes of the public (as interpreted by the government of the day) when the public and health service workers have different objectives, face different incentives and have access to different information. As all instruments that aim to tackle the agency problem have transaction and administrative costs, and most can generate perverse incentives, there is great interest in identifying which instruments are likely to be most effective in improving performance. So far economists and other analysts have been able to give only limited guidance on this critical issue.

At the time of writing (2004), a personal list of policy conclusions would be as follows.

1 Relying on the professional ethics and intrinsic motivation of NHS workers is not enough. Nearly all people want to do a 'good job', but to understand what is a 'good' level of performance they need to be helped to know what others can achieve. To overcome system inertia they need a source of 'constructive discomfort'.[27] And to buy in to the government of the day's direction of travel they need to clearly understand what it is and to be motivated to follow it. So long as it is not overly heavy-handed there is little evidence that the introduction of extrinsic motivation will significantly weaken intrinsic motivation.

2 Given the large number of separate units within the healthcare system and the degree of compartmentalised working, both organisationally and professionally, relevant and reliable comparative information is critical. At the national level good information is vital for judging levels of efficiency and effectiveness. At the unit and the individual clinician level, good information has a critical role in setting standards and providing an incentive for performance improvement. This requirement for better performance measures is independent of whether the political preference is for a health system driven by markets or by regulation, by central action or by decentralisation.

3 The maintenance of tight budgets has been one of the major successes of the NHS. These have produced substantial cost savings compared with the controls in many other countries. However, on their own they supply incentives to minimise expenditure and to satisfice. The experience of the NHS before 1989 suggests that they do not provide strong incentives to continually search for ways of improving efficiency and, in particular, effectiveness.

4 Targets can focus efforts and motivate improvements in performance, but only if they are few, focused on what matters, well crafted (i.e. SMART),* locally owned and supported by incentives. The Labour Government learned these lessons, although it took some time. Econometric evidence from data obtained more than a decade ago supports the conclusion that targets associated with waiting times can have a substantial impact on behaviour in the desired direction.[28] The huge improvement in inpatient and outpatient waiting times between 2001 and 2005 appears to reinforce this conclusion, although it is difficult to disentangle the effects of targets from the large increase in resources, an attribution problem that is common to most of the areas in which targets have been set recently.

5 Public disclosure of performance information can also prompt improvements in performance (primarily by providers), but again the information needs to be accurate, relevant, timely and well presented. Provider organisations and the public need to be assisted in making good use of it.[29,30]

6 Benchmarking can also stimulate significant improvements, but the data have

---

* Specific, Measurable, Achievable, Relevant and Timed.

to be seen to be relevant and important and broken down to a level that can be influenced by individual clinicians or managers. Benchmarking that is poorly resourced or poorly designed is a waste of time.[31]

7 Specifically designed non-financial incentives such as 'earned autonomy' are seen as attractive by NHS managers, but so far there is little hard evidence as to whether they can produce sustained and beneficial changes in behaviour.[32]

8 Well-designed financial incentives, whether for individuals, teams or institutions, are likely to be as effective in the NHS as they have been shown to be in other health care systems – despite years of internal opposition on the grounds that they run counter to professional ethics and the culture of the NHS. The new contracts for consultants and GPs and the new system of financial flows (payments by results) should put this expectation to the test.

9 Support or technical assistance systems such as the Modernisation Agency can facilitate clinical and management networks, and peer review and quality collaboratives. Early studies suggest that they offer considerable potential in terms of improving access and quality of outcomes. However, they are not a panacea, and to retain credibility they must be subject to the same rigorous evaluation that is (or should be) applied to other instruments to improve performance.[33]

10 In health as in other service industries, customer choice and its natural corollaries, contestability and competition, can provide the strongest incentives to providers to improve performance. After 15 years of experimentation, both main political parties appear to accept this conclusion. However, there are probably limits to the health fields to which they can be applied. For example, what is appropriate to elective surgery may not be suitable for emergency care or some types of chronic care. Moreover, if choice and competition are to work in the NHS, there must be adequate safeguards of access and quality, and regulations to address the problems revealed by the internal market and recognised as common causes of failure in the health sector market.*

11 Performance will improve most rapidly if markets and a range of management instruments are used in 'judicious' combination. For example, performance monitoring alone is not enough. It should be based on good information, related to clear standards or targets and backed by appropriate incentives. However, in general there is still little understanding of what are judicious or appropriate combinations – in short, what optimal policy mix or mixes will produce 'constructive discomfort' in the different fields of healthcare.[27] This is an important research frontier.

12 Another priority is the development of performance mechanisms that can work effectively on a system basis, promoting the integrated delivery of healthcare and desirable shifts in the location of care. This points to incentives that straddle institutional boundaries.[34]

13 In any major organisation or industry there are limits to the range of activities in which improvement can be achieved at any one time, and to the speed with which major changes can be successfully implemented. At present we have a

---

* For example, there may be need for an independent regulator to ensure that there is a legally binding lock on provider independence and no scope for hospitals to pass on income losses or cost inflation to their local primary care trusts.[14]

very poor understanding of what these limits are. Governments need to stand ready to ruthlessly reprioritise if they have set their own aspirations too high.

These judgements are necessarily subjective, but I believe they are supported by the current evidence, both in the UK and in other countries. They are also broadly consistent with the conclusions reached from the Government's recent review of its approach to overall performance management across the public sector.[35] It is a tribute to the current Government's enthusiasm for driving up performance that there are now so many different management instruments in place. It is indicative of how recent and frequent the changes have been that there is so little knowledge of their relative effectiveness and efficiency. Experimentation with such a range of instruments should provide a great opportunity for learning. Many of the initiatives are already being evaluated, and it is encouraging that the NHS Service Delivery and Organisation Programme and the Department's own research programme are reportedly developing a coordinated approach to assessing the overall impact and coherence of the different instruments for performance management.

If learning about these performance instruments is to be maximised, it will be important to guard against three main threats.

1   That number of initiatives and the speed with which they are introduced overloads the management and analytical capabilities of the NHS. Perhaps the clearest lesson from the existing evaluation literature is that all of the instruments currently being trialled can have a positive impact if well designed, but their effectiveness is very sensitive to how they are applied (see, for example, the literature on public disclosure, benchmarking and performance targets). There is a real risk that the sheer number of these new instruments will prevent their careful design and proper implementation.
2   That the personal commitment of Ministers (including, in some cases, the Prime Minister) to many of the new instruments or approaches leads to pressure (from officials as well as from politicians) to soften findings that could be interpreted as criticisms of the basic ideas. Similar pressures are found under all governments. Compared with its predecessors, the Labour Government has been particularly courageous in promoting evaluation. It needs to be equally courageous in disclosing and learning from the results.
3   That the changes in the parameters of some of the instruments is so rapid that it may be difficult for evaluation studies to keep up. If the changes reflect accumulating knowledge, there is no problem. However, if they reflect Ministerial impatience based on unrealistic expectations, some costly initiatives may contribute little or nothing to our understanding of how to improve health service performance. They could prove as large a waste of public money as new technologies that add nothing to patient care.

Has the performance of the NHS been improved by the active performance strategies of recent years?

The proliferation of performance instruments is a symptom of a wider change in the government's role in relation to the performance of the NHS. Twenty years ago the Department and the Regional Offices essentially saw themselves as administering the health service. New policies might be announced and new national objectives set but, notwithstanding the Rayner Report and the new public management, there was no sense at the centre that it could or should be actively driving performance. To the extent that it was thought about at all, performance improvement was seen as the responsibility of the medical and nursing professions, aided by local managers. This has now all changed – terms such as 'levering' and 'driving' performance became commonplace in the Department in the 1990s, as did talk of performance strategies, targets and incentives. There have been ongoing debates about whether performance is best improved by market forces or regulation, or through central direction or decentralisation, but there has been no going back on the belief that the Department must take lead responsibility for actively improving NHS performance.

Compared with the relatively passive administration of the 1980s, today's active performance improvement strategies are marked by five new ingredients:

1 clearly defined targets and standards
2 publicly disclosed information on costs, outcomes and patient experience by individual provider (as well as in aggregate)
3 the design of explicit incentives (financial and non-financial) for purchasers, providers and individual clinicians
4 strong support services or technical assistance to expedite the dissemination of best practice
5 independent monitoring and inspection.

Has the adoption of this proactive approach to performance improved NHS outcomes and the health and healthcare of the population?

Like most fundamental questions, this one is extraordinarily difficult to answer. At the time of writing (2005), the services provided by the NHS are improving rapidly on many dimensions, from access to clinical outcomes. There has been a parallel improvement in provider star ratings. For example, the number of acute trusts with 3-star ratings has almost doubled in four years However, these improvements could simply reflect the enormous injection of additional resources. The issue is what has been added by an active performance management strategy. (One thing that clearly has been added is greater awareness of where performance is improving and where it is not. Another is considerable information and transaction costs.) The obvious potential controls are past history and other countries. Of these, the more promising control is international comparisons. England is probably an outlier in the extent to which an active performance management strategy has been adopted at the national level. Most countries rely more on clinician leadership or local management discretion. Some countries appear to be deliberately eschewing active performance management at the national or Ministry level (a current example is New Zealand). In view of the scale of the resources, both national and local, going into performance management, a cross-country comparison that aimed to assess the benefits and costs of active performance management relative to the alternatives would look to be a high priority for further research. One possible way into this might be to compare and contrast recent policies and performance in England, Scotland, Wales and Northern Ireland.*

* It is interesting that, after initial resistance, the Welsh government appears to be following the English example. *See* Welsh Assembly Government (2005) Designed for Life – creating world class health and social care for Wales in the 21st century. Welsh Assembly, Cardiff.

Appendix

1 Developing good performance indicators is a complex and resource intensive task

Those in the Department who began the search for high-level indicators in the early 1990s had no idea how long and complicated the process would prove to be. And the end of the process is still not in sight! Identifying what is important to different stakeholders, selecting measures, identifying and evaluating data sources, launching new surveys and consulting on all stages of the process invariably takes far more time and resources than expected. The rapid growth in research evidence on the design and use of performance measures suggests that the process will not become simpler in the future. The complexities, delays and resource implications need to be properly planned for.

2 Start using the data to hand – do not wait for the ideal indicators to be developed

Whether the purpose is accountability or improved performance, progress will be more rapid if a start is made with the imperfect data to hand. Provided that the direction of travel is clear, using deficient data will stimulate the demand for better indicators, as other countries have found.[36] Waiting for perfect indicators will aid the procrastinators who are sceptical about or frightened by measurement and comparison. However, adapting the indicators to hand should not become an excuse for postponing the search for ideal measures.

3 Different stakeholders require different data sets

Pulling information measures together into a single framework such as the Performance Assessment Framework has major benefits in terms of understanding, consistency and simplicity. However, it should not be allowed to become a straitjacket. Different stakeholders in different parts of the health system will have different interests and different objectives. It is unrealistic to expect to identify sets of indicators that will be equally effective at informing the public, incentivising health service managers and attracting the ownership of clinicians. Attempts to do this, encouraged by resource constraints, may simply generate lack of recognition and ownership by all of the key stakeholders.

4 For high-level indicators and targarts, parsimony is preferable to comprehensiveness

For high-level performance monitoring and for accountability to the public, it is better to strive for a small but balanced number of composite or sentinel indicators than to attempt to cover all aspects of performance. So long as the high-level indicators are well balanced, covering quality and efficiency, the distortions risked by averaging or incomplete coverage are likely to be small in cost relative to the paralysis and incomprehension produced by large sets of measures. Unfortunately, there are usually far more pressures to expand sets of performance indicators than to weed out and prioritise them. The conflicting pressures for more indicators from those who want to make detailed comparisons, and for fewer indicators from those who want simple, clear, overall pictures can be reconciled by developing different sets of indicators for different purposes, perhaps in hierarchical form. In the NHS, one distinction was between 'headline' and 'benchmarking' indicators. Other organisations distinguish between indicators for 'strategy', 'management' and 'peer comparison' purposes. Software tools can help in drilling down from summary measures to detailed components.

5 Think 'outcomes' but use 'output' and 'process' indicators as stepping stones or proxies

When designing performance measures the focus should always be on desired outcomes. The extent to which it will be feasible to use outcome measures will depend on the purpose (e.g. it will be much easier for planning than for accountability purposes), on the organisational unit (e.g. it will be easier for large units than for small ones) and on the available data. Even when the purpose is accountability and the unit is small, outcome measures should be used if possible, notably for assessing patient/carer experiences. In other areas, such as clinical outcomes, it may be necessary to identify output or process indicators that are proxies or predictors of outcomes. For example, for heart attacks re-perfusion rates may be a better guide to performance than mortality. Here there should if possible be good evidence of the link between the proxy measures and the desired outcomes. In the UK, the National Service Frameworks for particular disease areas attempt to provide this linkage and rationale.

6 Governments initially focus on measuring the performance of big planning or funding units, but the public, patients, users and clinicians are more interested in the performance of 'small' providers and in care for particular conditions

Reflecting concerns about national accountability, performance measurement in England initially focused on regional and district health authorities. However, the public and patients are interested in the performance of individual providers, such as hospitals and primary care practices, and in the care that they will receive for particular conditions, such as cancer and diabetes. There is also evidence from the USA and the UK that it is providers and clinicians, not planners and purchasers, whose behaviours is most likely to be influenced by the publication of perform- ance indicators.[37] The message is clear. If performance indicators are to be published either to promote local accountability or to change behaviours, they need to relate to individual providers and/or specific conditions. Indicators that relate to specific conditions are most likely to attract clinician interest and ownership. They may also focus attention on care pathways rather than on particular organisational forms.

7 The effectiveness of performance measures depends critically on presentation

Poorly presented performance indicators can and will be ignored, whether their purpose is accountability or improving performance. The investment and skills required to present performance indicators in ways that are comprehensible to their audiences and that stimulate changes in behaviour are invariably under- estimated. These presentational investments may need to be complemented by programmes aimed at educating the public and providers in interpreting the new performance indicators. In the NHS, for example, software programs have been developed to help hospitals to understand their comparative clinical performance and to trace the causes. Where the objective is to inform the public, recent developments in the UK suggest that media-based private organisations (e.g. Dr Foster*) may have a comparative advantage over public bureaucracies in stimulating interest in performance measures. Imaginative approaches are also required to summarise performance measures – 'spider diagrams' have been found to be particularly helpful.

8 The effectiveness of performance measures also depends critically on stakeholder ownership

Patients, clinicians and managers must believe that performance indicators are relevant and of high quality if their interest is to be gained and maintained. In 2001, the Department announced a process for developing improved indicators on a systematic basis, including annual public consultation on what performance information should be collected and published. The Commission for Health Improvement and the Healthcare Commission have continued this practice.

A few professional groups (e.g. Royal Colleges) have long worked on their own clinical benchmarking systems, but it has taken highly publicised examples of clinician failure (e.g. Bristol[38]) to persuade the organisers to make the activities mandatory and public. Clinical databases developed from audit projects now hold out the prospect of a major step forward in the monitoring and comparison of clinical quality across hospitals and clinical teams. For example, the Myocardial Infarction National Audit Project (MINAP), developed by the Royal College of Physicians and the British Cardiac Society to support implementation of the cardiac NSF, is expected to deliver a range of sophisticated and detailed clinical indicators for heart attacks.[39] Clinicians are likely to regard such indicators as more relevant and useful than the administrative data collected by the Department. This should encourage local ownership and local action.

References

1 Nairne P (1983) Managing the DHSS elephant: reflections on a giant department. *Polit Q.* **62**: 243–56.
2 Smith PC (2002) Performance management in British health care: will it deliver? *Health Affairs.* **21**: 103–15.
3 Griffiths R (1983) *NHS Management Inquiry Report.* Department of Health and Social Security, London.
4 Rivett G (1998) *From Cradle to Grave: fifty years of the NHS.* The King's Fund, London.
5 For this typology, *see* Hood C. (1998) *The Art of the State.* Oxford University Press, Oxford.
6 Economic Adviser's Office/Operational Research Service, DHSS (1987). *Performance measurement in DHSS HQ – A Progress Report.* Unpublished internal report.
7 NHS Management Executive (1993) *Indicators of Effectiveness and Quality That Could Inform the Consideration of NHS Performance in 1994/5 and 1995/6.* Two unpublished reports from the Working Group on Quality and Effectiveness Measures, London.
8 NHS Management Executive (1995) *Report of the sub-group of primary care effectiveness and efficiency.* Unpublished paper, London.

---

*Dr Foster has produced a number of reports comparing the performance of hospitals and clinicians, which have been widely distributed in national newspapers.

9 NHS Executive (1994) *The Operation of the Internal Market: Local Freedoms, National Responsibilities*. NHS Executive, Leeds.

10 Kaplan R and Norton D (1992) The balanced scorecard – used to drive performance. *Harvard Business Rev*. **January–February**: 71–9.

11 For the history up to the end of 2001, *see* Smee CH (2002) Improving value for money in the United Kingdom. National Health Service: performance measurement and improvement in a centralised system. In: *Measuring Up: improving health system performance in OECD countries*. OECD, Paris.

12 Department of Health (2004) *The NHS Improvement Plan. Putting people at the heart of the public service*. The Stationery Office, London.

13 Department of Health (2004) *National Standards, Local Action: health and social care standards and planning framework 2005/06–2007/08*. Department of Health, London.

14 Stevens S (2004) Reform strategies for the English National Health Service. *Health Affairs*. **23**: 37–44.

15 Department of Health and Social Security (DHSS) (1979) *Patients First*. DHSS, London.

16 Department of Health (1997) *New NHS: modern, dependable*. The Stationery Office, London.

17 Smee C (2000) '*The Performance Assessment Framework: where did it come from and where is it going*. Health Care UK, The King's Fund, London.

18 Such an approach is endorsed in Leatherman S and Sutherland K (2003) *The Quest for Quality in the NHS*. The Nuffield Trust, London.

19 Department of Health (1989) *Working for Patients*. HMSO, London.

20 NHS Confederation (2001) *Why Won't the NHS Perform Better?* Paper by NHS Confederation, London.

21 *See*, for example, Pederson K (2002) *Reforming Decentralized Integrated Health Care Systems: theory and the case of the Norwegian reforms*. University of Oslo, Oslo.

22 Smee C (2002) Improving value for money in the UK National Health Service: performance measurement and improvement in a centralised system. In: *Measuring Up: improving health system performance in OECD countries*. OECD, Paris.

23 Smith PC (2002) Performance management in British health care: will it deliver? *Health Affairs*. **21**: 103–15.

24 For a list of such factors, *see* Smee C (2000) Reconsidering the role of competition in health care markets: United Kingdom. *J Health Politics, Policy Law*. **25**: 945–51.

25 Healthcare Commission (2004) *Performance Ratings for the Star Ratings 2003/04*. Healthcare Commission, London.

26 The lessons draw heavily on Smee C (2002) Improving value for money in the UK NHS: performance measurement and improvement in a centralised system. In: *Measuring Up: improving health system performance in OECD Countries*. OECD, Paris.

27 Stevens S (2004) Reform Strategies for the English NHS. *Health Affairs*. **23**: 37–44.

28 Gravelle H *et al*. (2003) Performance signals in the public health sector: the case of health care. *Oxford Econ Papers*. **55**: 81–103.

29 Marshall M (2003) Public reporting of information on health care performance in the UK. In: S Leatherman and K Sutherland (eds) *The Quest for Quality in the NHS*. The Nuffield Trust. London

30 Cutler D *et al*. (2004) *The Role of Information in Medical Markets. An analysis of publicly reported outcomes in cardiac surgery*. National Bureau of Economic Research, Cambridge, MA/Working Paper 10489.

31 Audit Commission (2000) *Getting Better All the Time. Making benchmarking work*. Audit Commission, London.

32 www.york.ac.uk/inst/che/policy.htm

33 Ham C *et al*. (2003) Redesigning work processes in health care: lessons from the National Health Service. *Millbank Q*. **81**: 415–39.

34 For worries about current incentives, *see* Dixon J (2004) Payment by results – new financial flows in the NHS. *BMJ.* **328**: 969–70.

35 HM Treasury and the Cabinet Office (2004) *Devolving Decision Making: 1. Delivering better public services: refining targets and performance management.* The Stationery Office, London.

36 For example, for the Australian experience, *see* Corden S and Luxmore J (2000) Managing performance for better results. In: A Bloom (ed.) *Health Reform in Australia and New Zealand.* Oxford University Press, Oxford.

37 Marshall M, Shekell EP, Leatherman S and Brook R (2000) What do we expect to gain from the public release of performance data? Review of the evidence. *JAMA.* **283**: 1866–87.

38 Kennedy L (2001) *Learning from Bristol: the Report of the Public Inquiry into Children's Heart Surgery at the Bristol Royal Infirmary, 1984–1995.* The Stationery Office, London.

39 Keogh B and Kinsman R (2002) *National Adult Cardiac Surgical Database Report 2000–2001.* The Society of Cardiothoracic Surgeons of Great Britain and Northern Ireland, London.

Chapter 8

Discovering the patient

Introduction

The creation of the NHS was based on the presumption that the producers of health services, rather than the consumers, knew what services should be provided.[1] The rise of consumerism posed a growing challenge to the paternalism and provider-centredness of the service. Improving responsiveness to patients or consumers was the mantra of politicians and policy makers throughout the 20 years covered in this book. This chapter is about the role of Departmental analysts in encouraging and facilitating this shift in influence, a shift that still has a long way to go.

There is now wide acceptance that greater responsiveness to patients is essential if the NHS is to survive. There is also increasing acceptance that the greater involvement or engagement of patients is essential if the quality of healthcare is to improve.* However, in many respects over most of the period covered in this book the patient and the public were ignored or managed, rather than being involved.† This chapter focuses on three aspects of the relationship between healthcare professionals/providers and patients where there has been some progress, albeit slow. These are listening to the views of patients (and carers) and enlisting their feedback, providing information to patients and the public to help them to be informed consumers and active citizens, and involving them in the delivery of healthcare, particularly by promoting self-care.

The chapter begins with a summary of the underlying influences that prompted the 'discovery' or recognition of the role that the patient should be playing in these three areas. There is then a short history of the Department's attempts to listen to patients, provide them with information and engage them in their own care. The next section discusses the role of Departmental economists and operational researchers in developing the Department's thinking and policies in these three areas. The final section addresses the question of why it took so long for the Department of Health and the NHS to set up systematic processes for listening to the views of patients and the public, to begin to inform them about the quality of different healthcare providers, and to facilitate and encourage self-care.

---

*Although the relationship between involvement and quality is neither straightforward nor, currently, does it have a good evidence base.

†In important respects GPs can rightly claim to be an honourable exception. GPs have always had to be careful listeners to patients if they were to avoid losing some of their practice. From the outset the Royal College of General Practitioners had patient involvement and patient liaison committees. I am grateful to Dr Geoffrey Rivett for pointing this out.

Underlying influences

The rise in consumerism has posed major problems for all public services. The growing value attached by the public to choice, convenience and speed of service, ease of access and personal tailoring has challenged all monolithic providers. The challenge for the NHS has been particularly acute, as it was developed as a monopoly and enshrined long-term beliefs in medical paternalism and huge asymmetries in information. By ruling out price rationing, the NHS had to rely on non-price rationing to keep services in line with resources. The obvious criteria for non-price rationing were (and are) clinical need and ability to benefit, and on both of these criteria clinicians were (and are) generally seen as the best informed and most trusted decision makers. The NHS cannot therefore escape from a certain element of producer dominance.

The dilemma for the Conservative Governments of the 1980s and 1990s was how to respond to the consumerist pressures and reduce the extent of paternalism while holding down public expenditure and maintaining equity and efficiency. In healthcare as in many other public services, the Thatcher/Major Governments' response was to try to promote choice, to introduce elements of competition (the internal market), to clarify standards of care (the Citizens' Charters) and to give the public and consumers more information. In one form or another, these policies were largely continued by the Labour Government. Progress was further and faster largely part because of a decision to relax cost-containment through a major injection of additional resources. There was therefore less need for rationing and more scope for both meeting consumer service expectations and delivering improved clinical effectiveness.

Related to the rise in consumerism has been the rise in the quality movement. In all services it has come to be recognised that it is the customer, not the provider, who ultimately defines quality. Recognition of this simple reality came later to healthcare than to most other services. The last 20 years have seen a continuing struggle to ensure that the perspective of the patient on quality is given equal weight to that of the professional and the manager. In some parts of the NHS this struggle has still not been won. In healthcare as in other fields, the increasing weight attached to the patient or customer perspective on quality partly reflects a general reduction of trust in professionals. There is also some, albeit still limited, evidence that patient involvement in care decisions can improve outcomes.

Another factor contributing to the 'discovery' of the patient has been the persistent tendency for demands on health services to run ahead of public resources. Governments have come to see engaging and informing patients not only as a means of improving health but also as a way of controlling demand on publicly funded health services. The belief is that better-informed patients will engage in preventive action, will take on greater responsibility for their own personal treatment and care, and will make more appropriate use of public services.

A further important development has been the growth in new technologies, particularly the Internet, giving patients and the public unparalleled access to medical information and knowledge. Medical professionals can no longer pre-scribe treatments without risk of patient challenge. They can also no longer assume that patients will take the quality of their care for granted. Computer power and new information systems are increasingly allowing patients to compare the performance of hospitals, specialties and individual clinicians.

A final factor is the line taken by government in response to changing public expectations. Public expectations are not immutable – they can be built up or dampened down by government actions and statements. From 2000 the Labour Government was much more proactive than any of its predecessors in building up expectations of a timely, convenient and personalised NHS.* It may have believed that it had no alternative if the NHS was to survive. Interestingly, governments in some other countries with publicly funded health systems have appeared to deliberately hold down expectations.† By choosing to talk up expectations, the Labour Government has certainly accelerated efforts to put the patient at the centre of healthcare. However, the policy may have political costs. The real benefits of service improvements can be cancelled out – in economists' utility terms and in the minds of the electorate – if expectations rise at the same or a faster rate.

A short history

This chapter describes how governments and the Department gradually came to recognise that people who use the NHS should have a say in it. Writing in 1988, Sir Patrick Nairne, a former Permanent Secretary at the Department, noted that the NHS was a most important public service, but that no public service thought less about the public. He argued that the NHS should treat people as responsible individuals and take them into its confidence.[2] Before and more particularly after 1988, attempts to involve patients and the public in the NHS took many forms. Here I use the model of involvement adopted by the Commission for Health Improvement, and I distinguish between three different degrees of involvement, namely information, feedback (or listening), and influence.[3] These forms of involvement can take place at either the individual level or the collective level. The history of each dimension will be discussed briefly in turn.

Feedback or listening to patients

'Voice' and 'exit' are the two ways in which consumers can influence a service. At the start of the period under consideration, opportunities for exit within the NHS were limited to (bureaucratically constrained) freedom to change GPs. There were theoretical opportunities to move outside the NHS to the private health service, but in the absence of public subsidies this was a very costly option for

---

* On this the government appears to have led rather than followed public opinion. The available survey evidence suggests that in 2001 people in the UK rated their healthcare system as more responsive (for both inpatient and outpatient care) than did the populations of the majority of a sample of 16 developed countries. Responsiveness was judged on seven domains, namely autonomy, choice, communications, confidentiality, dignity, prompt attention and support/basic amenities. *See* Valentine NB *et al.* (2003) Patient experiences with health services: population surveys from 16 OECD countries. In: C Murray and D Evans (eds) *Health System Performance Assessment. Debates, methods and empiricism.* World Health Organization, Geneva.

† New Zealand is one such example. Under both major parties the population has been convinced that demand for elective care will inevitably exceed affordable supply, and that it is therefore acceptable to wait at home under the care of a GP until a hospital specialist is able to see them in 6 months or less.

most people. Without effective exit options the role of voice was therefore critical if the consumer was to carry any weight in the NHS. The simplest way in which patients can make their voice heard with regard to what is right or wrong with services, and how they can be made more responsive, is by being asked. There are several ways of doing this, but perhaps the most straightforward is through a sample survey. This approach was specifically commended by the Griffiths Report on the NHS Management Inquiry in 1983. However, it was 15 years before the recommendation was followed up on a systematic and national basis.

In the 1980s there were small-scale local surveys of patient views. The Community Health Councils also did their best to make the voice of the consumer and the community heard. However, at the centre the only consistent and comparable information on patient views came from the annual British Social Attitude Survey run by the consultancy Social and Community Planning and Research (SCPR). Departmental funding ensured that this included a number of questions on health. Over the years these could be used to generate a time series of public and patient satisfaction with the NHS. The survey's results related to England as a whole, focused on broad levels of satisfaction with services rather than detailed experiences, and were usually largely ignored by Department officials, apart from a small number of research and analytical staff.

Although the Conservative Government's review of the NHS in 1988 was partly motivated by a belief that the NHS must be more responsive to consumerist pressures, the Department did not take the opportunity to commission market research. However, the review was able to take account of a major survey of consumer opinion of the NHS conducted by SCPR and Royal Institution for Public Administration (RIPA).[4] Despite its title, the outcome of the review, *Working for Patients*, contained no specific recommendations about strengthening feedback from patients. However, follow-up work aimed at improving the quality of hospital services included recommendations that the quality of services should be monitored, in part through consumer satisfaction surveys. Nothing concrete came out of this recommendation, nor out of similar recommendations for more systematic patient feedback that were made in 1993 as part of the Secretary of State's 'Initiative on Quality'.

At this time an internal paper noted that:

> *Traditionally, the NHS's priorities and the way in which the service has been delivered have been determined by managers and professionals, rather than being influenced by the public. This is perhaps not surprising given the nature of the service being provided. To date we have not given sufficient attention to what patients and their families want from the service.*[5]

The same paper raised the question 'What do patients want?', and went on to note that although some of the answers were known in general terms, much more work was required. The importance and potential value of obtaining systematic feedback from patients and the public were considered and vigorously debated by officials on several other occasions between 1993 and 1996. However, for reasons that will be discussed later, no effective action was taken.

The introduction of systematic patient surveys aimed at providing regular and comparable information on patient experiences at health authority and national level was finally announced by the new Labour Government in November 1997. In the words of the White Paper, *The New NHS: modern, dependable*:

For the first time in the history of the NHS there will be systematic evidence to enable the health service to measure itself against the aspirations and experiences of its users, to compare performance across the country and to look at trends over time.[6]

Subsequent policy statements reinforced the role of patient feedback by linking it to the new performance assessment framework and to the incentive systems being applied to both NHS trusts and primary care trusts. In 2000, the NHS Plan announced that all local NHS organisations would be required to publish the ratings they had received from annual surveys of patients and carers, and that they would be rewarded in line with the results of the Annual National Patients Survey. More recently, responsibility for conducting these surveys has been passed to first the Commission for Health Improvement and then the Healthcare Commission.* The form of the surveys will doubtless continue to evolve, but there now appears to be general agreement that regular and robust measurement of patient views must be an integral part of any strategy to monitor and improve the quality of patient care. Indeed 'improving patient experience' as measured by national surveys has been a Public Service Agreement (PSA) target for the Department since 2004.

Information for patients and the public

At the beginning of the 1980s there was little easily accessible information on what services local GPs and hospitals provided, and generally nothing in the public domain about aspects of service quality, whether measured in terms of structure, process or outcome. Regional information services were expected to provide information about the availability of local services, but public knowledge of this service was often limited. In the few areas where patients could exercise choice, most notably choice of GP, it was generally informed by personal experience or the recommendations of friends.

When *Working for Patients* introduced an internal market to the NHS, the government recognised that greater choice, either by patients or by health authorities or GP fundholders acting as agents for the patient, required the provision of more information about alternative suppliers. The Patient's Charter, which was introduced in 1992 as part of the Citizens Charter initiative, codified a set of patients' rights, including the right to information about conditions and treatments. The Charter also included commitments on maximum waiting times. These were revised from time to time and extended to cover cancellation of operations and arrangements for hospital discharge. Performance against the new commitments was monitored by health authority (and in some cases by hospital), and the results were published in national league tables that were introduced in 1994. Initial plans to extend the league tables into non-acute areas and to include measures of patient satisfaction and even measures of clinical outcomes were not progressed. The reforms of the early 1990s also included linking the 14 regional information services into a national health information service.

---

* At the time of writing the five most recent surveys (on adult inpatients, young patients, primary care trusts, ambulances and mental health services) were published in August 2004. *See* www.healthcarecommission.org.uk

The original league tables had a short life and attracted surprisingly little attention, perhaps because they were under-funded and under-marketed. Evaluations of the performance of the internal market concluded that although patient choice did not increase, there was a limited improvement in the amount of information given to patients. Evaluations of the Patient's Charter concluded that it had been successful in raising awareness among NHS staff of patients' needs, issues and rights. On the other hand, the information provided under the Charter only partially matched patients' concerns.

In 1997, the new Labour Government radically expanded the range of information available to patients by announcing the launch of NHS Direct, a 24-hour telephone advice line staffed by nurses and aiming to provide information about health and illness as well as about medical services. The new service expanded from three demonstration projects in 1998 to cover the whole of the country by the end of 2000. By 2004 it was handling over half a million telephone calls a month. The expansion in communication channels and in the scope of the services offered was equally remarkable. The initial telephone line was complemented first by an Internet service, NHS Direct Online, and then by digital television, the NHS Direct Digital TV Information Service. In addition to providing high-quality health information and advice, the service is now being integrated with GP out-of-hours services and is expected to play an increasing role in supporting emergency services and electronic booking and choice.

One direction in which NHS Direct has not expanded is in the provision of information on the comparative quality of different service providers.* When the new Labour Government came to power in 1997, it did not initially build on the league tables of information for patients that were developed in the mid-1990s. Instead the focus was on indicators and information systems to inform the management of health authorities and trusts, notably through the development of the Performance Assessment Framework. However, around 2000 the Government's interest in developing better information on the health services widened to include making that information available to patients and the public in user-friendly ways. Responding to examples in Scandinavian countries, waiting-times data were made available on the Internet in user-friendly form. Other information on the quality, effectiveness and responsiveness of services in individual hospitals was brought together and publicly disclosed as part of a new approach to assessing and motivating improved provider performance. However, it was Dr Foster, a private media-based organisation, that took the lead in collating and presenting information in a really user-friendly form, initially at the hospital level and then at the specialty and consultant levels. The Government quickly recognised Dr Foster's superior media and presentational skills, and sanctioned active cooperation with it by Departmental officials and the NHS.

Giving patients influence and choice

The last 20 years have shown that it is much easier to obtain feedback from patients on what matters to them than it is to allow patients to have real influence by doing something about the information that they provide.[7] The early 1990s

---

* A move in this direction would have overloaded an already stretched organisation.

saw some attempts to complement the work of the Community Health Councils and to expand the influence of the public and patients on NHS decision making. Apart from the Patient's Charter, perhaps the most noticeable initiative was 'Local Voices', a bid to assist purchasers in the new internal market to reflect the views of their local populations. By 1996, one of the six medium-term priorities for the NHS was defined as to 'give greater voice and influence to users of NHS services and their carers . . .'. In line with this objective, the Patients Partnership Strategy published in 1996 suggested that health authorities and providers should make greater use of consumer views to establish what services users wanted and to inform choices about their treatments. These initiatives undoubtedly led to innovative and imaginative attempts to engage some patients and members of the public in health service decision making. However, the great majority of patients and the public almost certainly remained unaffected and unaware of them.

After the change of government in 1997, reforms to improve the influence of patients took three separate but related forms. First, there was recognition of the value of self-care and the building of NHS support for it.* NHS Direct became a powerful mechanism for giving patients more information about looking after themselves and their families at home, as well as a mechanism for improving access to publicly funded care. Alongside use of the telephone and the Internet, the NHS has now moved into digital television as an additional channel for encouraging and supporting self-care and the more appropriate use of the NHS. For patients with chronic diseases, the Expert Patients initiative is being used to encourage patient organisations to develop patient-led self-management courses.† The scope for developing other forms of cost-effective self-care is also being explored. The jury may still be out on the argument of the Wanless Report, *Securing Our Future Health: Taking a Long-Term View*, that a strategy for self-care offers the potential to significantly lower the long-term trajectory of health service expenditure, but at least the issue is beginning to be explored.

The second way in which the Government has expanded the influence of patients is by offering them greater choice. It was at the very end of the period under consideration (through 2002) that empowering patients and users with effective rights of 'exit' (while remaining within the NHS) emerged as a new government priority. Before the 2001 Manifesto commitment that 'we will give patients more choice' a number of important steps had already been taken. NHS Direct, Walk-in Centres and booked hospital admissions were all moves towards greater choice, although they were not initially developed with this objective in mind. The decision to go much further partly reflected a government-wide view that in order to be attractive public services must offer the attributes associated with successful private services, including choice and personalisation of care. It also reflected a view that monopolistic behaviour by some hospital clinicians, particularly with regard to elective waiting times, could only be effectively challenged if patients were enabled to walk away.

In 2003, the Labour Government announced the beginning of a journey towards an NHS 'where participants can choose how, when and where they

* The NHS Plan recognised NHS support to 'self-care' as one of the key elements of its vision. *See* Department of Health (2000) *The NHS Plan*. The Stationery Office, London.
† This initiative builds on a long history of voluntary led user involvement in some chronic disease areas, such as mental health and physical disability.

get treated, on the basis of good information and a partnership of respect between them and their clinician.'[8] This will be a long and costly journey,* but offering patients the rights of exit – that is, the ability to walk away from poor providers – will also greatly strengthen the influence that they can exert through voice. It will also lock in and require further improvements in the information on the performance of individual healthcare providers that is available to the public.

The third element is the establishment of a range of new organisational structures to facilitate patient and public involvement in healthcare. These include the establishment of a Patient Advice and Liaison Service and a Patients' Forum in every trust, a new national Commission for Patient and Public Involvement in Health,† and the granting of powers to local authorities to review the planning, provision and operation of health services.

Role of departmental analysts

In retrospect, the 'discovery' of the patient was an area in which the Department's analysts (both operational researchers and economists) made one of their largest contributions to both the speed of policy development and, in some respects, the directions that it took. This may not seem a natural area for analysts to carve out an important role. Their contribution undoubtedly partly reflected the personal interests of a few influential individuals. However, disciplinary training probably also played a part. For economists brought up on the dangers of monopoly and the virtues of providing customers with either exit or voice, the Department's (and the NHS's) neglect of the 'customer' was surprising and at times shocking. Similarly, operational researchers trained in systems analysis, scenario planning and horizon scanning were well placed to think about the rapidly developing role of the consumer as a key player in (and indeed as a key resource for) the whole healthcare system, about alternative channels to access it, and about the potential uses of new information and communication technologies. The external links of both groups also enabled them to pick up new ideas faster than the rest of the Department. For most of this period the absence in the Department of an effective forward-thinking or strategy group left a lacuna into which the analysts were happy to move.

What were the particular contributions of the Department's analysts? Again each of the three forms of patient involvement will be considered in turn.

Listening to patients and obtaining feedback

From the mid-1980s onwards the Department's economists were the most persistent advocates of the value of patient surveys as a guide to the performance of the NHS and as a source of ammunition for the annual public expenditure round. Economists were regularly in the lead in drawing the attention of senior

---

* So far as I am aware, no estimates of its long-term cost have appeared in the public domain. Choice was not explicitly incorporated into the costings for the 2002 Wanless report.
† The commitment to this element of the strategy has proved somewhat mercurial. Eighteen months after establishing the Commission, the government announced that it was to be abolished. *See* Department of Health (2004) *Reconfiguring the Department of Health's Arm's-Length Bodies*. Department of Health, London.

colleagues and Ministers to the health results from the SCPR Social Attitudes Survey. From the late 1980s onwards they acted as a persistent lobby for the introduction of a systematic national survey of patient experiences. Recommendations to this effect were made to the NHS Board in 1993, 1995 and 1996. It was argued that national surveys of patient experience disaggregated by regional or district health authority had an important role to play in improving both accountability and health service performance. As the 1990s wore on, it was contended that better feedback would support the priority given to improving responsiveness. It was also noted that in this area the NHS was 'off the pace' compared with Australia, New Zealand, the USA and Canada. None of these arguments succeeded in overcoming the scepticism of senior colleagues. The go-ahead had to await the arrival of Alan Milburn, who picked up the idea with alacrity and made a new national survey of patient experience one of the key themes of the White Paper, *The New NHS: Modern, dependable.*

Departmental analysts also helped to lock patient surveys into the Department's mainstream performance-monitoring and quality-improvement activities. Economists and operational researchers played a leading role in the initial design of the Performance Assessment Framework, and were strong advocates of making 'patient/carer experience' one of the six domains of performance. They were the first to propose using national patient surveys to monitor progress with National Service Frameworks. Departmental economists were also strong champions of including the patient's perspective in the successive initiatives on quality improvement throughout the 1990s. A good understanding of the US quality literature strengthened both their views and their influence.

In addition to drawing on the burgeoning US literature, as the 1990s wore on Departmental analysts were able to 'pray in aid' the work of an increasing number of UK experts. In early 1995, a survey of hospital patients by Brian Jarman and colleagues was quoted internally as 'an example of the market getting on with it while the centre lagged behind'. Later, the work of Angela Coulter was frequently quoted. The organisation that she came to lead, the Picker Institute, played a key role in the eventual development of national surveys of patient experience.

Informing patients

In this area Departmental analysts made significant contributions on two fronts – first, in advocating and developing projects for the exploitation of new channels of patient communication, and secondly, in supporting the public disclosure of information on the quality of care.

Towards the end of the period under consideration, the Department's operational researchers carved out a unique niche as proponents of new channels of both communication and service access for patients and the public. In 1996 the Department had been alerted to the potential benefits of telephone advice lines staffed by nurses. A senior analyst's study tour of North America had drawn attention to their increasing use in the USA, and independently a working party on emergency care outside hospital led by the Chief Medical Officer proposed the trialling of a nurse helpline. However, it was the Department's operational researchers who worked up the idea of a nationally accessible 24-hour telephone advice line and who invented its title, NHS Direct.* As a reward for these endeavours, one of the operational research branches was given responsibility for arranging the piloting of the scheme and its initial roll-out. The operational research branch remained responsible for NHS Direct until it was able to establish more conventional management arrangements late in 1998. By 2000, NHS Direct had developed from a small pilot programme to national coverage in line with the schedule and budget planned three years previously.[9]

The rapid expansion and success of NHS Direct can be partly attributed to its promotion as both a response to patient demands for improved access to primary care and a mechanism for promoting self-care and reducing the inappropriate use of publicly funded primary and secondary care. Training in whole-systems thinking enabled operational researchers to be the first to make these linkages. Operational researchers were also the first Departmental staff to identify and assess the options for using digital television as a further communication channel, leading to the announcement of plans for a £5 million digital TV pilot programme in May 2000. Once again operational researchers were given the task of managing the piloting of their idea. The pilots proved sufficiently successful in disseminating targeted health information, particularly to populations not reached via the telephone ot the Internet, for Ministers to commit to a full national NHS Direct digital TV service to commence broadcasting in 2004.

Analysts also played a role, albeit a smaller one, in adding to the momentum for the public disclosure of information on the quality and performance of healthcare providers. Perhaps because of their belief in the virtues of transparency and incentives, Departmental economists had long been advocates of putting more information on the performance of the health system into the public domain. As new information became available for central management and performance accountability purposes, Departmental analysts consistently supported its publication in user-friendly formats. When it became clear that the Department was unwilling or unable to invest the resources and skills necessary to develop patient- and media-friendly presentations of the new indicators of quality, such as peri-operative mortality rates, cooperation with a private company, Dr Foster, was championed as providing an alternative mechanism for disclosing NHS data. A senior member of the EOR acted as the Department's observer on the advisory ethics committee set up by Dr Foster.

Involving/engaging patients in healthcare decisions

The contribution of Departmental analysts in this area relates mainly to the idea of 'self-care'. A study tour in 1996 drew attention to the interest being shown by US-managed care organisations in promoting self-care. Behind this lay recognition that, in terms of events, 90% of healthcare involved self-care by individuals, families and friends and only 10% involved the provision of care by healthcare

---

* The first use of the term 'NHS Direct' was by the Head of Operational Research, Geoff Royston, in a minute dated 30 September 1997. In it he advocated addressing the question 'What would an NHS look like that was radically reconfigured so that demand was handled wherever possible by . . . direct means such as the use of the telephone, television and the Internet?' Less than three months later, in December 1997, NHS Direct was announced in the White Paper *The New NHS* as one of three developments symbolising the new government's approach to modernising the NHS.

professionals. Small changes in this balance might have major impacts on public healthcare costs. These ideas influenced the development of NHS Direct, but it was not until the publication of the NHS Plan in 2000 that self-care was formally acknowledged as a major part of the government's vision for a health service designed around the patient. It was the Department's operational researchers who marshalled and pressed the arguments for self-care – and in particular for NHS support for it – most strongly and ensured that those arguments were reflected in the NHS Plan.

From around 1999 the Department's analysts reviewed studies of the cost-effectiveness of interventions aimed at promoting and supporting self-care. These reviews appeared sufficiently encouraging to be quoted in Derek Wanless's Report in 2002 as indicating that 'for every £100 spent on encouraging self-care, around £150-worth of benefits can be delivered in return'.[10] Increased self-care was seen as one element of the 'fully engaged' scenario put forward in the Report as holding out the promise of a lower long-term profile for healthcare expenditure. Although there were other developments with regard to self-care (e.g. the 'Expert Patient' initiative launched by the Chief Medical Officer in 2001*), still no part of the Department had formal policy responsibility for this area. It was not until 2003 that a series of presentations to senior officials and contributions to Ministerial speeches finally led to self-care being given a formal policy home.

Why did it take the Department so long to 'discover' the roles of the patient and the public?

From at least the late 1970s, government policy statements emphasised the need to improve the responsiveness of the NHS to patients and the public and to involve them in healthcare decisions at a range of levels. More than 25 years later, after three years of inspections and research, the Commission for Health Improvement noted that 'the NHS is, on the whole, improving in some aspects of patient and public involvement, such as providing information for patients and undertaking qualitative and quantitative exercises in getting feedback from patients'.[11] However, it also concluded that patient and public involvement 'is not part of everyday practice' and it saw 'few successful examples of where patient and public involvement had entered the corporate bloodstream' of the NHS. Why has progress been so slow?

The reasons obviously vary across the many different forms of activity covered by the term 'patient and public involvement'. Changing the culture of the NHS is a far larger task than changing the thinking of the Department of Health. Here we can only throw light on the factors that hindered progress in the Department on the initiatives with which internal analysts were particularly involved. The focus is primarily on the slowness in seeking systematic feedback from patients. It is difficult to see how a service can begin to move away from paternalism and producer dominance if the views of its customers are not actively sought.

In the 1980s, many civil servants saw market research as out of character for a public service. For the NHS it was also thought to be unnecessary, given the

---

* Departmental OR analysts were also heavily involved in the piloting and evaluation of this initiative.

generally high level of patient satisfaction reported by, for example, the 1979 Royal Commission and the SCPR Social Attitude Surveys. There was acknowledgement of patient complaints about waiting times, but in the constrained public expenditure conditions of the time these could be dismissed as the cosmetic demands of the middle classes that must take second place to meeting the medically assessed needs of the whole population, particularly the inarticulate and underprivileged.

In the early 1990s the arguments against giving patients 'voice' through systematic feedback began to change. It was recognised that patient satisfaction levels were falling, and the government was now committed to using a range of policies, including market forces, to respond to consumerist pressures across the public services. However, although there was greater acceptance of the importance of finding out what patients and the public wanted, the emphasis on devolution of management responsibility led policy colleagues to argue that the solution lay in local patient surveys. If these were run by health authorities or the new NHS trusts, they were more likely to generate ownership and remedial action. The evidence from, for example, the Audit Commission that local efforts at feedback were undermined by poor coverage, poor research methods and standards, irrelevant questions and lack of direction and coordination was either unacknowledged or ignored.[12] The arguments, strong in theory but weak in practice, for leaving market research and patient feedback to local providers continued to be raised for the rest of the decade both by officials and on occasion by Ministers. They continue to be raised today. They have been and are based on an over-optimistic view of the survey and analytical skills of many providers. If local surveys are used as the only approach, there will be no development of comparisons either across time or between providers.

In early 1993, the NHS Management Executive accepted that there should be some systematic monitoring of progress with the quantifiable aspects of the Patient's Charter as well as, in principle, some wider measures of patient experience/satisfaction. These measures were needed at regional or district health authority level for performance management purposes. However, when later in the year specific proposals were put to the Board, it resisted the idea of moving towards a national patient survey somewhat similar to one that had been already trialled in Scotland. The minutes of the meeting recorded only that alternative approaches should be explored. However, in the discussion there was a strong consensus against moving towards a national survey, on the grounds that 'we might not like what we found'. There were fears that a survey endorsed by the Executive could raise expectations in ways that could not be met, and could therefore embarrass both Ministers and NHS managers.

After this decision, the next two or three years saw effectively no work on identifying what issues were important to patients. The next formal presentation to the NHS Executive on the arguments for systematic patient feedback was in 1996, in the context of a broader discussion of where the NHS appeared 'off the pace' in comparison with health policies in other major English-speaking countries. Proposals for a more standardised approach to assessing patient experiences were presented as supportive of Ministerial and NHS policies to both improve quality of care and give greater voice and influence to users of the NHS. This time there was a more sympathetic reaction from the Board, but follow-up action was overtaken by the 1997 General Election.

One other factor contributing to the slow acceptance of arguments for systematic patient feedback was probably the relatively low profile and priority given to policy work on patient involvement in the years prior to 1997. The Departmental unit with policy responsibility in this area was generally lightly staffed, staff turnover was quite rapid, and recognition and support from senior management were limited. As a consequence, analysts who were pushing for a more proactive line received little support from the policy colleagues who should have been their natural allies.

Several of the factors discussed above also played a part in the slowness in informing patients about the relative characteristics and quality of different providers. Perhaps the most prevalent of these was a fear of raising expectations to unsustainable levels and of highlighting problems that might embarrass NHS managers and/or Ministers. In trying to avoid embarrassing Ministers, officials were sometimes 'more royalist than the King' – a common occurrence in the public services. For example, in 2001 officials initially advised against the dissemination of the individual hospital results from the national patient survey on coronary heart disease, on the grounds that this might embarrass some hospitals and/or Ministers. The judgement was quickly overruled when the Secretary of State's Private Office was finally consulted.

However, there were additional factors underlying the slow progress. Initially there was an absence of information of a type and level of disaggregation that was interesting or useful to patients. Early work on performance indicators was aimed at health authority managers, and it took time to recognise that patients, the public and the media were more interested in indicators on individual providers, specialties and even clinicians. Another constraint was a failure to recognise how much investment was needed to make performance indicators helpful or even interesting to patients, the public and the media. When this became clearer, it was gradually realised that the Department lacked the skills and was unwilling to commit the resources necessary to make the performance information readily comprehensible to 'the man on the street'. Effectively this function has now been handed over to private agencies, most notably Dr Foster. Unsurprisingly, the early activities of Dr Foster met with some resistance both from officials in the Department and from some NHS managers. The former disliked a private body manipulating 'their' statistics, and the latter objected, legitimately, to being surprised by unfavourable media comparisons and, less legitimately, to having a spotlight put on their weaknesses. Without strong Ministerial support for public disclosure it is most unlikely that a cooperative relationship between the Department and Dr Foster would have developed, let alone survived.

Self-care has come into prominence much more recently, and has been subject to rather different barriers. At first it was seen in some quarters as undermining or diminishing the role of the Department and the NHS. To the extent that self-care can substitute for publicly funded services, it may be seen as weakening arguments for additional resources for the NHS. Spending departments do not normally choose to highlight policies that could reduce their need for larger budgets! Secondly, with no formal policy lead in the Department and no large group of professionals with a vested interest in self-care, there have been no internal or external pressure groups pushing for new programmes in this area. The limited exceptions are chronic care patient groups and far-sighted clinicians who recognise that the quality of chronic care can be improved with active patient participation. Thirdly, there have been concerns about the political 'sale-ability' of self-care. Presented badly it can appear to be a policy either for blaming the patient or for excusing cutbacks in the funding of health services. A final barrier has been the quality of supporting evidence, particularly on the cost-effectiveness of interventions to promote self-care. Although evaluations have been undertaken, they have not been as numerous or as well funded and well publicised as studies of formal health service treatments.

The Department's barriers to discovering and engaging the patient have grad-ually been overcome. There remains the much more formidable task of tackling the barriers to change within the NHS. A subgroup of the NHS Modernisation Board recently reviewed progress with patient engagement and identified no fewer than nine barriers to change.* Tackling these would look to represent a full agenda for the next 20 years.

Critical to the rate of progress will be the attitudes of clinicians. Patient empowerment can be very threatening to those brought up in a tradition of clinical freedom, patient deferment and huge information advantages. Antipathy and indeed outright hostility on the part of some clinicians have delayed progress in all of the aspects of patient and public involvement discussed above. At the same time, other clinicians have been among the strongest advocates of patient empowerment. A major responsibility of the clinical professions in the years ahead should be to resolve these tensions. This will involve addressing difficult questions such as identifying the matters on which patients can make their own decisions, identifying which should be discussed with a professional, and ascertaining how the patient can distinguish between the two.

References

1 Klein R (1983) *The Politics of the National Health Service*. Longman, London.
2 Nairne P (1988) The NHS: reflections on a changing service. *BMJ*. 296: 1518–20.
3 Commission for Health Improvement (2004) *Sharing the Learning on Patient and Public Involvement From CHI's Work*. Commission for Health Improvement, London.
4 Lipsey DL *et al.* (1988) *Focus on Health Care: surveying the public in four districts*. Social and Community Planning and Research, London and Royal Institute for Public Adminis-tration, London.
5 Department of Health (1993) *Outline of Policy Document for Secretary of State's Initiative on Quality*. Department of Health, London.
6 Department of Health (1997) *The New NHS: modern, dependable*. Department of Health, London.
7 Commission for Health Improvement (2004) *Sharing the Learning on Patient and Public Involvement From CHI's Work*. Commission for Health Improvement, London.
8 Department of Health (2003) *Building on the Best. Choice, responsiveness and equity in the NHS*. Department of Health, London.
9 A fuller discussion of the contribution of operational research to the establishment of NHS Direct can be found in Royston G, Halsall J, Halsall D and Braithwaite C (2003)

---

*Cayton H (2003) *Patient engagement and patient decision-making in England*. Paper prepared for the Commonwealth Fund/Nuffield Trust Conference, 'Improving Quality of Health Care in the United States and the United Kingdom: Strategies for Change and Action', Pennyhill Park, July 2003. The barriers included contradictory messages, disempowered front-line staff, professional demarcations, poor use of patient feedback, and confusion about roles of new organisations aimed at promoting patient engagement.

Operational research for informed innovation: NHS Direct as a case study in the design, implementation and evaluation of a new public service. *J Operat Res Soc.* **54**: 1022–8.

10 Wanless D (2002) *Securing Our Future Health: taking a long-term view.* HM Treasury, London.

11 Commission for Health Improvement (2004) *Sharing the Learning on Patient and Public Involvement From CHI's Work.* Commission for Health Improvement, London.

12 Audit Commission (1993) *What Seems to be the Matter: communication between hospitals and patients.* NHS Report No. 12. Audit Commission, London.

Chapter 9

Organisational change

Introduction

In the two decades up to 2002 the biggest source of work-related stress for staff throughout the Department of Health was the uncertainty caused by ever more frequent organisational change. Organisational change was not, of course, an invention of the 1980s. Commenting on his experiences in the 1970s, Sir Patrick Nairne noted that 'there are no clear criteria by which to judge what a Department should be investing in staff administration', but nevertheless 'the over-simple yardstick of cuts in staff numbers is likely to remain the principal virility test for establishment officers – and the most politically cogent way of demonstrating to Treasury Ministers and Parliament that Departmental management is effective'.[1] Both of these judgements remain true today. Commenting on the penchant for structural reorganisation in the Civil Service in the 1970s, Sir Patrick also noted a popular Whitehall saying: 'It is a mistake to take out a man's appendix when he is moving a grand piano'. Whatever the truth behind this saying, it continued to be disregarded in the 1980s and 1990s. Major policy changes were normally accompanied by radical changes in the organisation of both the Department and the NHS.

Reorganisation of the Department (and, although this is not covered here, the NHS) has been a perennial theme over the last 20 years. That Sir Patrick's observations continue to resonate is an indication of how little has been learned about organisational change and efficient organisational structures. In part this may reflect the inherent difficulties of these issues – organisational design is a very inexact science – but in the Department's case it also reflects the weight that decision makers attached to personal experience and personal judgment and the lack of importance attached to evidence, analysis and evaluation. Overall, reorganisation and restructuring are probably the areas in which the Department's analysts have been least successful in improving decision making and increasing learning.

This chapter focuses on the organisational changes that have been introduced within the Department. The even more numerous reorganisations that have affected the NHS are only referred to if they impacted on the Department itself. The next section discusses the policy context for the frequent attempts to reorganise the Department. This is followed by a brief history of the reorganisations since around 1990, and a commentary on some of the underlying themes of those changes. Next there is a short discussion of three analytical issues raised by the history of reorganisation. First, has the Department (or the NHS) had an excessive level of management or management costs? Secondly, have organisational changes improved the efficiency of the Department or the effectiveness of the NHS? Thirdly, what have been the main lessons learned about how organisational change should be introduced? The final section discusses the limited role of analysts in the various Departmental reorganisations.

Wider policy context

The American public management authority, Allen Schick, has noted that politicians can draw from 'a body of developing and accepted ideas concerning the organisation and operation of the public sector'.[2] These include the notions that performance improves when managers are told what is expected of them and results are measured against these expectations, when managers are given flexibility in using resources to carry out assigned responsibilities, when operational authority is devolved from central agencies and departmental headquarters to operating levels and units, when government decisions and controls focus on outputs and outcomes rather than on inputs and procedures, and when managers are held accountable for their use of resources and the results that they produce. Arguably lip-service was paid to all of these ideas in the Department of Health by the late 1980s or early 1990s. They were all seen as part of the new 'managerialism' that was sweeping Whitehall and that had been given an early start in the Department of Health by the Griffiths Report.[3]

Lip-service is not of course the same as effective action. The 'Working for Patients' reforms announced in 1989 could be seen at the time as the latest in a number of attempts to devolve operational authority from the Department to operating levels and units, and to give local managers greater flexibility in the use of resources. After 1990 the Department's expectations of local managers were raised, and accountability was strengthened, as has already been discussed in Chapter 7.

The biggest challenge to the Department's formal organisation and ways of working came not from these 'accepted' ideas but from others, including those that in Schick's view are still 'contested or untested'. Foremost among them in terms of its impact on the Department has been the idea that service delivery should be separated from policy making. In proposing the establishment of an NHS Management Board to take over 'all existing NHS management responsibilities' in the Department, the 1983 Griffiths Report anticipated the Next Steps initiative[4] and laid the foundations for the establishment of a separate internal agency within the Department, namely the NHS Executive. The government of the day accepted the argument that a separate management agency would promote managerial dynamism and through greater efficiency enable public spending to be contained while still meeting the public's rising expectations of the NHS.

Another strand of broader government thinking that impacted on the Department was the belief that Civil Service costs could be significantly trimmed by dispersing staff from London to parts of the country with lower rental and wage costs. Like several of the other beliefs affecting organisational reforms, interest in this issue has gone in cycles. In 2004 the Lyons Review[5] returned to the issue of the savings that could be generated by relocating civil servants outside London.

Under the Blair Government other public-sector-wide initiatives have influenced the organisation of the Department. There has been a return to the concerns that underlay the Next Steps initiative, with a renewed emphasis on policy implementation and service delivery. As in several overseas countries, around 2000 the government's focus shifted from 'strengthening policy making to upgrading line operations, the delivery of services, the productivity of the public service and the responsiveness of government to the interests of citizens/ customers'.[2] Improving delivery is part of a new style of 'active government'. The aims laid out in the White Paper *Modernising Government* published in March 1999[6] are to ensure that policy making is more joined up, strategic and evidence based, to make the users of public services the focus, and to deliver high-quality and efficient services. These aims are thought to require significantly different behaviours from civil servants, including a culture of continuous improvement, innovation, responsiveness and collaboration.

Brief history

In the years since the Department of Health was separated out from the Department of Health and Social Security in 1989 there has been an almost continuous series of reviews of its functions, organisation and ways of working. A selective listing of the reviews is given in Box 9.1. It is selective because it is based on my memories and those of my colleagues in 2001. As many of the reviews produced no permanent changes, it is almost certain that a few have been forgotten!

Box 9.1 Department of Health: major reviews of functions, organisation and ways of working during the period 1990–2001

- *Functions and Structure of the Department of Health (Gwynn Report)*, 1990
- *Review of the Functions and Organisation of the Management Executive (Malone-Lee)*, 1991
- *Internal Services Review (Market Testing)*, 1991–92
- *Managing in the New Management Executive (MINME)*, 1991
- *Job-specific Selection*, 1991
- *Managing the New NHS (Kate Jenkins)*, 1993
- *Managing the New NHS: Functions and Responsibilities in the New NHS (Alan Langlands)*, 1994
- *Review of the Wider Department of Health (Banks Report)*, 1994
- *Public Health in England: Roles and Responsibilities of the Department of Health and the NHS*, 1994
- *Upward/360-Degree Reporting*, 1993–2000
- *Better Ways of Working*, 1995
- *Review of Appraisal/Reporting System and Performance-related Pay*, 1996
- *Shaping the Future*, 1995–97
- *Review of Analytical Services*, 1997
- *Investors in People*, 1996 onwards
- *Delivering Ministers' Objectives*, 1998
- *New Ways of Working*, 1998–99
- *Developing the Department's Capacity/Getting the Right Skills/Skills Audit*, 1998–2000 onwards
- *Open Government*, 1998

- *Valuing Diversity*, 1998
- *Peer Review of Business Activities*, 1998
- *Modernising Governments*, 1999
- *The New Understanding*, 1999
- *Modernisation Action Teams/Task Forces*, 1999–2000
- *Ministerial Review*, 2000
- *Review of Analysis and Modelling (RAMG)*, 2000
- *Departmental Review*, 2001.

Most of these reviews were about changing ways of working. A minority were about making major structural changes to the organisation of the Department. The most important of the latter are listed below.

1   *The Gwynn Report of 1990 and the related Malone–Lee Report of 1991*. These reviews took stock of the collective impact of the split of the former Department of Health and Social Security, the creation of the NHS Management Executive within the Department, and the decision that the Management Executive should relocate to Leeds in 1992. The Gwynn Report proposed a tripartite or trefoil organisation for the Department with three main components, namely a health and social service 'policy group', an NHS Management Executive Group responsible for NHS management and operational matters, and a central resource group responsible for 'common services'.[7]

2   *The Jenkins, Langlands and Banks reviews of 1993 and 1994*. The background for these reviews was the evolution of the NHS internal market, the wish of ministers to tighten monitoring of the NHS while reducing the size of regional bureaucracies, and recognition that the attempt to separate the responsibilities for policy and implementation in the NHS had failed. The reports proposed, among other things, reducing the number of regional offices from 14 to 8 and bringing them within the NHS Executive, and reorganising the Department around three business areas, each combining responsibility for policy and implementation. Policy on health services was transferred to the NHS Executive, while the remainder of the Department was restructured into a social care group, a public health group and a support services group.[8] There was also to be a 20% cut in the number of staff at the centre, although the impact on headline staff numbers was largely offset by bringing regional offices within the Department.

3   *The Departmental Review of 2001 and the follow-up Change Programme of 2003–04*. The background to these changes was the ministerial decision announced in the 2000 NHS Plan to devolve responsibility to the NHS 'front-line,' and a strong belief among Ministers that the Department was over-staffed and not well focused on delivering its policy agenda. Regional offices were abolished and 100 district health authorities were replaced with 30 strategic health authorities. In addition, the Department was reorganised in terms of three groups that were responsible for 'standard of quality' (or policy), 'health and social care delivery' and 'strategy and development' (or common services), respectively. At the same time it was announced that staff numbers would be

cut by close to 40%, with half the reduction being accounted for by transfers to arm's-length agencies. Interestingly, with one or two significant exceptions the 2003–04 changes left the Department with a high-level organisational structure which was very similar to the trefoil proposed by the Gwynn Report in 1990.*

Looking across these major organisational reviews and a host of more narrowly focused reform exercises, it is possible to identify three or four main themes. These are centralisation versus decentralisation, integrating or separating policy and implementation, integrating or devolving centrally provided services, and changing behaviours or ways of working. Each will be discussed briefly in turn.

Centralisation versus decentralisation

The central thrust of the Griffiths Report in 1983 and of 'Working for Patients' in 1989 was that more responsibilities and freedoms should be decentralised to hospitals, districts and primary care groups. One consequence should have been a decimation of staff at the centre. In practice, arguments about the need for capacity to actively manage the NHS and to implement the major changes involved in the NHS internal market enabled the Department to avoid large staff cuts until the Banks Report was published in 1994. Shortly after those cuts took full effect, the new Labour Government introduced a new set of reforms that amounted to the most ambitious attempt to centralise management in the history of the NHS. It is not altogether surprising that a staff complement designed for a decentralised healthcare system failed to meet ministers' new expectations. The switch back to decentralisation and 'localism' after 2001 completed another circuit of what Rudolph Klein has called the 'revolving door of NHS policy making'.[9] As Klein has also noted, it remains to be seen whether the new localism is compatible with old-style central funding and the huge weight attached to equity, access and common standards across the NHS. Although its many advocates are convinced that decentralisation is the way of the future, it is worth remembering that neither NHS history nor the experience of health systems in other countries suggests that it is necessarily associated with higher performance.†

Policy and implementation

Here there is another revolving door. In the 1980s a view that management and policy implementation had been neglected in the NHS led to the establishment of a separate management agency within the Department. In 1994, health policy and management were reunited in one group. In 2003, they were separated again into two major organisational groups within the Department. The new separation presumably reflects concerns similar to those in the 1980s, namely that in integrated arrangements the attractions of policy making could lead to neglect

---

*The major difference is that in the 1990 proposals the 'Policy Group' also had responsibility for management and executive action with regard to social care and public health.
† The World Bank has a useful review of experience with health-sector decentralisation in developed and developing countries; *see*: http://web.world bank.org/WBSITE/EXTERNAL/TOPICS/EXTHEALTH NUTRITION Apart from equity issues, problems can be caused by information asymmetries and local management capabilities.

of delivery, and moreover the two functions require different types of skills. The key problem of separation – that policy making may lose touch with the NHS's capacity to deliver – was to be tackled in 2004 by a similar mechanism to that proposed in 1990. In 2004 it was called a 'policy hub'. In the Gwynn Report it was called a 'policy-coordinating team'.

Multi-purpose department or devolved agencies?

The Department has always been supported by a number of bodies at arm's-length. Since 1997 there has been major growth in both their number and their total complement. By 2004 there were 40 such bodies with a total staff of 24 000.[10] Ten years earlier the Banks Report identified only 14 'agencies and other [bodies]' with a total staff of 1630. These figures may not be exactly comparable, but there is no doubt that the growth has been very substantial. The major justifications for this growth have been to signal new policy initiatives and to improve NHS efficiency and effectiveness. Unfortunately, with the urgent need to get the new agencies up and running, cost control frequently went out of the window.

Another revolving door seems to be in motion with the recent decision to significantly reduce both the number and size of the arm's-length agencies. In establishing such agencies the principle of 'getting it right first time' has been honoured more in the breach than in the observance.

Changing ways of working

The need to change the Department's ways of working has been a persistent cry over the last 15 years. Memory suggests that the 'new ways of working' required at the time of writing (2004) are very similar to those identified at the beginning of the 1990s. They include operating through teams and task forces, corporate and integrated working, more strategic thinking, and trusting and empowering. However, there are two new emphases – on the end users' or patients' perspective, and on consultation with delivery partners. There has also been continuity in several of the proposals for improved organisational procedures and areas of focus. A need for a greater focus on scanning and strategy was raised by the 1994 Banks Report and has been a recurrent theme ever since. Banks also identified radical scope for improving the processes for dealing with correspondence and parliamentary questions, another area of perennial scrutiny. The repetitious nature of many of these reviews raises questions about why they appear to have been so ineffective. In the absence of evaluations, the questions remain unanswered.

Analytical issues

Many of the organisational reviews and reforms for the last 20 years have been based on one or both of the following assumptions – first, that management costs in the Department (or the NHS) are excessive, and secondly, that changes in organisational structure or behaviour will improve the efficiency of the Department or the effectiveness of the NHS. It is therefore worth asking what evidence there is to support either of these assumptions. In view of the scale and frequency of organisational reform in the Department, it is also worth asking what has been learned about the process of managing organisational change. These three issues will each be discussed in turn.

Has the Department (or the NHS) suffered from excessive management costs?

When in opposition, politicians of all parties assume that public-sector management/administrative costs must be too high. There are good theoretical arguments for assuming that in the absence of competition bureaucracies will inflate their costs. To combat these behaviours all governments use a range of mechanisms to put downward pressure on administrative costs, including setting separate budgets, establishing efficiency targets, monitoring trends over time and using audit mechanisms to compare and benchmark costs. Despite this panoply of tools, Oppositions (and sometimes Ministers) regularly assume that there must be fat that can be cut from administration, both in departments like the Department of Health and in the NHS. These beliefs are so strong or so politically expedient that politicians do not usually seek evidence to support them. Throughout the period under consideration there has in fact been very little hard evidence on which to make judgements. Ideally, to gauge where costs are excessive requires a knowledge both of the costs and of the marginal benefits or added value to healthcare (or to Ministers) produced by those costs. For the NHS (but not for the Department) it has been difficult to identify what are current management or administrative costs, although somewhat arbitrary definitions are now used for monitoring purposes. However, for both the Department and the NHS it has so far proved impossible to quantify the benefits (or benefits foregone) associated with marginal additions or reductions in administrative costs.

In the absence of the kind of cost-effectiveness evidence on administrative interventions that is now commonly expected of medical interventions, attention has focused on cost alone. One approach is to look at trends over time. Because of definitional and functional changes it is not easy to put together time series of Departmental administrative costs or staff numbers. Table 9.1 attempts to compare Departmental staff numbers using the three definitions most commonly quoted in the Departmental annual reports. The major impression is of the stability of staff numbers over the 15 years since the Department was split from the Department of Health and Social Security in 1988–89. For example, the 'gross control area' total was 4143 in 1989–90 and 4123 in 2002–03. However, the apparent stability masks many changes in central responsibilities and shifts in function between the centre and arm's-length or regional bodies. For example, on the one hand the former regional functions have been brought within the Department, but on the other there has been a major expansion of special arm's-length bodies. The crude time trends do not allow any judgements to be made about whether the Department has become more or less efficient, particularly when it is remembered that the expenditure for which it is responsible has more than doubled in real terms over this period. However, given this relatively stable history, the continued high rate of growth of expenditure on the NHS and the rapid evolution of health and healthcare policy, the cuts of 38% in 'core DH' staff proposed for 2004–05 were ambitious in the extreme. If they prove to be too ambitious, the consequences could be poorly designed policies in areas such as practice budgets, payment by results and choice. Weaknesses in these areas could impede service development for years to come.

Table 9.1 Staff numbers in the Department of Health, 1989–90 to 2004–05

Year	Total DH	Gross control area	Core DH
1989–90	4399	4143	—
1991–92	4992	4587	—
1993–94	5093	4638	—
1995–96	4543	4083	—
1997–98	4804	4247	—
1999–2000	5101	4341	3753
2001–02	5723	4715	3809
2002–03	5032	4123	3390
2003–04	(5036)	(4123)	(3355)
2004–05	(3698)	(3005)	(2272)

Total DH = core DH + NHS Pensions Agency + Medical Devices Agency (MDA) + Medical Control Agency (MCA) + Medicine and Healthcare Products Regulatory Agency (MHRA) + National Health Service Purchasing and Supply Agency (NHSPSA) + NHS Estates.
Gross control area = total DH – (NHS Estates + MCA).
( ) = planned.
Source: Annual DH Departmental Reports.

Another possible approach is to look at whether management costs are out of line with those of other countries. Unfortunately, the OECD database has been seriously deficient with regard to this aspect of health service performance, reflecting the very different ways in which member countries define and measure management/administrative costs. With the adoption of comparisons based on the System of Health Accounts (SHA) the position should now radically improve, at least for overhead health administration expenditure.* There have also been few research studies on this issue that have included the UK. A McKinsey study in 1996 concluded that total health system administrative costs were much lower in the UK than in the USA but might be slightly higher than in Germany.[11] However, it is probable that the UK and German estimates used different definitions. A more detailed but partial internal Departmental study in 1997, using US definitions of administrative costs, found that in NHS hospitals expenditure on administration was around 16% of total expenditure, compared with 26% in hospitals in the USA.

International comparisons of central departmental costs are even rarer. The 1990 Gwynn Report commissioned a short study of the functions and organisation of central health departments in Finland, France, Germany and Sweden. This study was mostly qualitative, but it collected some information on the relative sizes of the health departments in these countries. Since then there

* An initial comparison of 13 countries is given in Orosz E and Morgan D (2004) *SHA-Based National Health Accounts in Thirteen OECD Countries: a comparative analysis*. OECD Health Working Papers. OECD, Paris. The UK should be added to the comparisons in 2006.

has been no further serious attempt to compare departmental costs. Personal observation and experience of working in or with the central health departments of the USA, Canada, New Zealand and Australia would suggest that the Department of Health has generally been parsimoniously staffed compared with its peers.

For the NHS, an alternative to international comparisons is to look at variations in administrative costs by health authority, hospital or primary care trust. In the early to mid-1990s there were certainly large variations in administrative costs as a share of total expenditure for both hospitals and district health authorities. Attempts (of varying degrees of sophistication) to find a relationship between these costs and measures of health service outputs or outcomes met with no success.[12] The most straightforward implication of these findings is that some providers or purchasers did have excessive administrative costs. A more charitable interpretation would be that it was not possible to adequately allow for differences in the value or range of outputs.

For Departmental costs, another approach has been to look at how the size of the Department (in terms of head count) compares with that of head offices in other organisations. However, differences in the nature of the businesses and in the functions of head office have prevented the drawing of any useful conclusions. It might be more rewarding to compare the size of Whitehall departments. The recent Gershon Review of efficiency across the public sector can be seen as a first step in this direction.[13]

In the absence of firm evidence that expenditure on management/administration was high relative to some comparator, efficiency exercises have sometimes focused on identifying particular functions that appear to add no value or might be re-engineered to significantly reduce costs. This was the approach of the 1994 Banks 'Review of the Wider Department of Health'. More recently it was also the approach adopted by the Gershon Review. In between these two studies, conclusions about the scope for administrative savings both in the NHS and in the Department appear to have relied on political or management judgement. Given the potential costs to patients if staff reductions undermine the effectiveness or quality of health service policies, to say nothing of the pain inflicted on the affected staff, it is to be hoped that the future will see a more rigorous approach to assessing the efficiency of marginal (or major) changes in administrative costs both in the Department and in the NHS.[14] There are unexplored opportunities for both national and international benchmarking.

Have reforms to the organisation of the Department improved its efficiency or the effectiveness of the NHS?

The direct answer to this question is that we do not know. Very few of the reviews set out in Box 9.1 earlier in this chapter have been formally evaluated. Only two studies come to mind. The first was a study of the costs and benefits of moving the NHS Management Executive to Leeds. Unlike most of the other reforms, this was first subject to an ex-ante option appraisal which indicated that it could reduce the Department's running-cost budget. Four or five years later an ex-post evaluation was carried out, which confirmed that there had been savings, although they were less than anticipated, with break-even taking longer than originally planned.* The other change to be followed up was 'Investors in People'. In some parts of the Department its introduction appeared to be associated with an improvement in training and human resource development policies. The original accreditation in 1999 was renewed in 2002.

It is unsurprising that there were no evaluations of the numerous attempts to change the ways in which staff worked. The objectives of these programmes were often somewhat vague, and after enthusiastic launches they almost invariably lost active senior management support and were left to fizzle out. The most extreme example was the Skills Audit at the end of the 1990s, which was so poorly designed and received so little cooperation from staff that the survey was effectively never completed. The extent to which some of the reviews and reforms replicated each other also suggests that little was changed. The obvious examples are *Managing in the New Management Executive* (1991), *Better Ways of Working* (1995) and *New Ways of Working* (1998–99), all of which were about developing roughly the same kinds of skills.

Formal evaluation of the impact of some of these reforms would have been difficult. For example, there are real methodological problems concerning how to quantify (let alone value) the more intangible effects of management reform, such as changes in the quality of policy advice. However, that was not the main reason why formal evaluations were not funded. More important reasons, to the extent that they were articulated, were lack of senior management interest or concerns about potential embarrassment. In some policy areas where evaluations were opposed on the latter grounds the Department could have set up internal monitoring systems to at least guide managers on how behaviours were changing. So far as I am aware there was no formal monitoring of any of the major organisational reforms up to 2002.

If there was no direct monitoring or evaluation of the reforms, can one take comfort from the results of similar reforms in other organisations? Some of the reforms were able to draw on evidence from the private sector. For example, those responsible for the reforms of the early 1990s had access to a review of BP's experience with implementing 'Project 1990'. This decentralised decision making, reduced bureaucracy and hierarchies throughout the BP Group, and aimed to develop flexible and responsive forms of behaviour.[15] Later the major reviews in 1994 were able to draw on a literature survey of 'The Effective Head Office'.[16] BP's experience was examined again when the Department Review was conducted in 2001. However, these attempts to learn from others were more the exception than the rule.

The problem of relying on experience elsewhere is that a hard evidence base on reforms to improve the effectiveness of the public sector is generally just not there. A recent major review of formal evaluations of the sources of public service improvement concluded that 'the existing evidence is meagre'.[17] This makes it even more disappointing that so little was learned from the organisational reforms in the Department of Health over the dozen or so years up to 2002.

If there was little systematic learning from the Department's own reforms and doubts about how much could be learned from reforms in other organisations, was there at least a careful attempt to assess in advance the likely costs and

---

*Neither the option appraisal nor the ex-post evaluation was able to assess the impact, if any, on the quality of Departmental advice and decision making.

benefits of each new set of reforms? Again, with the single exception of the relocation of staff to Leeds, the answer is no. The direct staff costs of the project teams leading the reform process were usually estimated. However, there was no attempt to assess the opportunity costs for the large numbers of staff who were diverted from their normal responsibilities to participate in the programmes. There were usually estimates of the financial costs of offering staff early retirement or making them redundant, but in general there were no ex-ante estimates of the transitional costs of winding up existing units or organisations or setting up new branches or offices. The short-term cost implications for 'the movement of the grand piano' (i.e. for the development or implementation of major new policies) was at times acknowledged, but it was never quantified. Nor were analysts (internal or external) asked to attempt quantification. Likewise, any impact of the changes on the Department's institutional memory or human capital was disregarded. With one exception the benefits were similarly unspe-cified and unquantified. The exception was the expected savings in staff costs. In some cases it may have been thought that these were so large that it was worth any conceivable cost to achieve them. In practice, many of these savings turned out to be short-lived as one Departmental reorganisation was rapidly overtaken by another.

Before embarking on any further major structural changes, the advice of the OECD should be heeded:

> Structural change can be a powerful lever for reform but it can also be risky. The political benefits of signalling change through reorganisation tend to come at the beginning, and the real costs later. Reorganisations distract staff attention, increase staff insecurity, and distract management attention from immediate challenges . . . there are also risks associated with the loss of institutional memory, networks and values.[18]

To increase the chances that future organisational changes will improve the efficiency of the Department and the effectiveness of the NHS, there should be a commitment to subject them to the same kind of rigorous appraisal and evaluation as is expected of any other intervention aimed at improving patient care and health outcomes. In terms of the current jargon, they should be subject to 'regulatory impact assessment' just like other policy initiatives. Assessing the cost-effectiveness of organisational reforms may raise particular methodological challenges, but it is no different in principle from other forms of cost-effectiveness assessment. With assessment of cost-effectiveness now being routine for new technologies and interventions, clinical guidance and National Service Frameworks, and increasingly common for service reorganisations, failure to apply the same test to major structural and management changes in the Department and the NHS is a growing anomaly. This failure provides an incentive to overinvest in such change and to inefficiently divert management and professional energy away from more direct ways of improving policies and service delivery.

What has been learned about managing organisational change?

If the benefits of many of the organisational changes of recent years are unclear, what has been learned about how better to manage the process of change? An internal Departmental review of the change processes adopted between 1990 and 2001 came up with the following guidance for future changes.

1   Recognise the legacy of previous change and the scepticism that it may have engendered.
2   Make a clear case for change – in particular why it is imperative and not just inevitable.
3   Set out both the longer-term mission and the short-term set of objectives to which the changes are expected to contribute.
4   Present reviews as a positive step, and not as an extension of a blame culture.
5   Invest heavily in communication, professional facilitation and training.
6   Properly assess the costs and benefits of proposed changes, including considering alternative options.
7   Plan for a long-term and sustained investment in change. Previous initiatives had put considerable effort into design (which is fine), less into testing (which is tiresome) and even less into building (which is a slog).
8   Avoid modernisation diffusion – too many strategies to be used at once.
9   Treat major reviews as exercises in modern policy making. This means that they should be forward looking, out looking, innovative, flexible and creative, evidence based, inclusive, joined up, reviewing, evaluating and lesson learning.

With the benefit of hindsight, from 2005 there is another lesson that should have been highlighted.

10 Avoid prolonged uncertainty. As Sir Robert Horton was reportedly fond of saying during BP's Project 1990: 'People can deal with virtually anything except uncertainty'.*

These lessons will change over time. It is to be hoped that in future the Department will carry out formal post-mortems on the change process accompanying major reforms with the aim of explicitly building on learning and adding to the guidance available to the next generation of reformers.

Role of analysts

Compared with most of the other issues discussed in this book, the role of internal analysts in relation to organisational change has been modest or even minor. This was not for lack of trying. The evidence on what works in terms of improved management and organisational arrangements may be much weaker than is normally true of the evidence on, say, new technologies, but as has been emphasised there is no reason to believe that the same analytical methodology cannot be applied to organisational change as has been increasingly applied to other interventions aimed at improving health outcomes. However, with a few notable exceptions, managers and policy leads responsible for taking forward the organisational changes discussed earlier have not generally been inclined to rigorously identify the nature of the problem, to specify clear objectives, to set out criteria to be used to assess options, to estimate and where possible to quantify

* Personal communications from several BP staff in 1991.

costs and benefits of options, and to make recommendations based on a full comparison of the alternatives.* Nor have they generally been interested either in monitoring the effects of the organisational and management changes or in carrying out more formal evaluations of their effectiveness. In these circumstances, analytical advice has tended to fall on stony ground.

Nevertheless, EOR advice was forthcoming and in some areas it was used. One theme running through EOR contributions over many years was the potential value of establishing yardsticks against which to judge administrative costs both in the Department and in the NHS. In relation to Departmental costs, various comparisons were proposed and explored, but the potentially most illuminating ones – with Health Ministries in other countries and with other Ministries in the UK – were never effectively studied. The EOR also initiated comparisons of administrative costs between NHS hospitals and health authorities, which generated further studies confirming the existence of large unexplained variations. A second theme was the importance of learning lessons from organisational changes elsewhere. In 1991, for example, when the Department was following through on the Gwynn and Malone–Lee Reports, an EOR attachment to BP led to attention being paid to experience with BP's 'Project 1990'. Small lessons were learned (e.g. about the potential role of staff surveys), but much of the BP experience was dismissed on the grounds that a public-sector organisation could not afford the scale of investment in change management found in the private sector. By comparison with best practice in the private sector, the management of change in the Department tended to suffer from under-resourcing throughout this period.

There were other suggestions from the EOR that initially received some support but were not followed through. These included proposals for assessing the value of different NHS Executive functions as a way of identifying those that should be built up and those that should be run down, as well as proposals for a systematic approach to prioritising options for reducing NHS Executive running costs, and proposals for evaluating related management and organisational reforms in other sectors. At a more pedestrian level, the EOR was able to contribute modelling and analysis for work-force planning, particularly in support of proposed reductions in staff. The division also played a part in developing the Department's thinking on 'better ways of working'. Although it was not politic to press the idea too hard, the EOR's characteristics of flexible and fast working, often in teams, and its use of project management skills exemplified many of the new behaviours that the Department was trying to encourage.

The modest use of internal analytical skills for assisting reorganisations would be easier to understand if the Department had made extensive use of external skills that were judged to be more relevant. There was some use of management consultants from time to time, particularly in the early to mid-1990s, and the work of external academics was also drawn on in the reviews of the NHS Executive and the wider Department in 1994. Through programs like 'Whitehall in Industry', individual members of the Department undertook a number of attachments to major private-sector organisations that were undergoing restructuring. Some of

---

* Justifications for adopting a non-rigorous approach varied from case to case. Common ones included the views that the change was a political requirement/imperative, that the need for change was self-evident, and that these kinds of judgements would not be improved by analysis or facts.

the lessons from these attachments were disseminated, but many were lost or ignored.* A further problem with organisational and management change is that many managers believe that they know how to do it, or should at least act as if they know how. In my experience this attitude was more prevalent in the Department than in the best private-sector organisations. However, organisational change is difficult at the best of times, and the evidence base of successful change in the public sector remains limited. The saddest feature of the Department's experience over these 20 years is that although it experienced huge changes, it contributed very little to expanding the evidence base and improving learning.

References

1 Nairne P (1983) Managing the DHSS elephant: reflections on a giant department. *Political Quarterly.* **62**(3): 243–56.
2 Schick A (2002) Opportunity, strategy and tactics in forming public management. *OECD J Budget.* **2**: 8–37.
3 Griffiths R (1983) *NHS Management Enquiry: report.* Department of Health and Social Security, London.
4 Jenkins K, Caines K and Jackson A (1988) *Improving Management in Government: the next steps.* HMSO, London.
5 Lyons M (2004) *Well Placed to Deliver? Shaping the pattern of government service.* HM Treasury, London.
6 HM Government (1999) *Modernising Government.* The Stationery Office, London.
7 Department of Health (1990) *Functions and Structure of the Department of Health (the Gwynn Report).* Department of Health, London.
8 Department of Health (1994) *Review of the Wider Department of Health (the Banks Report).* Department of Helath, London.
9 Klein R (2003) The new localism: once more through the revolving door? *J Health Serv Res Policy.* **8**: 195–6.
10 Department of Health (2004) *Reconfiguring the Department of Health's Arm's-Length Bodies.* Department of Health, London.
11 Dorsey L (1996) The productivity of healthcare systems. *McKinsey Q.* 1996: 3–11.
12 *See,* for example, Soderlund N (1999) Do managers pay their way? The impact of management input on hospital productivity in the NHS internal market. *J Health Serv Res Policy.* **4**(1): 6–15.
13 Gershon P (2004) *Releasing Resources for the Front-line: independent review of public service efficiency.* HM Treasury, London.
14 This is not a new plea. *See,* for example, Croxson B (1999) *Organizational Costs in the New NHS. An introduction to the transactions costs and internal costs of delivering health care.* Office of Health Economics, London.
15 Smee C (1991) *Management of Change: lessons from Project 1990. Report to Department of Health Management of Change Group.* (Unpublished)
16 Ferlie E and Pettigrew A (1993) *The Effective Head Office: a literature review and some implications for the NHS.* Warwick Business School, Warwick.
17 Boyne G (2003) Sources of public service improvement: a critical review and research agenda. *J Public Admin Res Theory.* **13**: 367–94.
18 OECD (2004) *Public Sector Modernisation: changing organisational structures. Policy Brief.* OECD, Paris.

---

* Until the late 1990s, comparisons that appeared to cast the Department in a bad light were commonly given a very limited circulation and therefore might not reach those responsible for managing the next set of Departmental changes.

Chapter 10

Learning from ourselves: policy and programme evaluation

Introduction

One of the key management insights that has been gained in the last 20 years is the importance of developing 'learning organisations'. A learning organisation has been defined in many ways. One of the more practical definitions is that 'a learning organisation is an organisation skilled at creating, acquiring and transferring knowledge, and modifying its behaviour to reflect new knowledge and insights'.[1]

The author of this definition went on to argue that learning organisations are skilled in five main activities:

1 systematic problem solving
2 experimentation with new approaches
3 learning from their own experience and past history
4 learning from the experience and best practice of others
5 transferring knowledge quickly and efficiently throughout the organisation.

This chapter and the next one look at how the Department has gone about developing its skills in the third and fourth of these areas, and sketch out the contribution of internal analysts. The present chapter considers how the Department has become more adept at learning from its own experiences, particularly through project, policy and programme evaluation. The next chapter looks at learning from overseas as perhaps the most important way in which the Department has learned from 'others'.

All functional organisations learn something from their past experience, even if the process is slow and the wrong conclusions are sometimes drawn. Monitoring, reviews and evaluation are about speeding up learning through careful planning. This chapter is about the planning of learning through evaluation, defined as rigorous, generally quantified analysis of whether and how far an existing management practice, policy measure or programme is obtaining the benefits for which it was designed (or which Ministers expected). The last 20 years have seen explicit evaluation in this sense change from being the exception to becoming close to the norm, at least for major health service policies. (As was noted in Chapter 9, it is still uncommon in relation to NHS and Departmental organisational changes and management practices.) This development was helped by the general trend (and not just in healthcare) towards evidence-based policy, and more recently by the government's increased emphasis on 'what works'. However, as will become clear later, the battle for planned learning is never won. There are always enthusiasts, advocates and believers who think they know what will work and see no reason to waste resources in finding out whether they are right. Such zealots can be found among Ministers, managers, clinicians and even analysts.

The chapter begins with a discussion of the background factors that promoted or retarded the development of formal evaluation within the Department. A short history of the stages in the mainstreaming of evaluation follows, and this leads into a discussion of some key themes to emerge during that evolutionary process. There is then a review of the Department's well-known failure to evaluate the reforms following on from the White Paper *Working for Patients*, and the less well-known reasons for this failure. The last section considers the role of analysts in championing evaluation.

Background

The development of a planned programme of work in the Department aimed at learning from the present and the past can be traced back to the Thatcher Government's establishment of the Financial Management Initiative in the mid-1980s. In 1985, a study from this initiative noted that across government there was frequently a lack of clarity in policy objectives and little evaluation of what was achieved. In the same year, Cabinet agreed that all new government policies should include evaluation arrangements from their introduction, and that those arrangements should be referred to in the relevant Cabinet papers. At the same time a central unit was established, first in the Cabinet Office and then in the Treasury, to promote policy evaluation across the public sector. The messages were reinforced in the next year when the Multi-Departmental Review of Budgeting recommended that one of four budgeting principles should be regular evaluation of what had been achieved compared with the objectives set. Departments, including the Department of Health and Social Security, found themselves bombarded with new guidelines[2] and with requests for case studies and plans for the organising of evaluation programmes. Strong pressure from the centre continued up until 1990, when the Treasury unit was disbanded on the assumption that evaluation activities were now well established in major government departments. However, well into the 1990s the Treasury would refer to the guidance on Cabinet papers if it thought that policies were particularly risky. Throughout the rest of the period under consideration it would periodically remind spending departments that evaluation of new policies was expected to be the norm.*

While the Financial Management Initiative and subsequent Treasury pressure were major stimulants for the adoption of an evaluation culture, there were a number of developments largely specific to the Department of Health that slowed down the process. The first of these was the unwillingness of some Ministers, most notably Kenneth Clarke, to see the radical reforms announced in *Working for Patients* delayed or undermined by carefully evaluated pilot projects. This attitude, which was shared by some junior ministers in later governments, gave encour-

---

* In recent years there has been a revived central interest in ex-post evaluation, this time coming from the Cabinet Office. New central guidance has been issued in the form of a Magenta Book; *see* http://policyhub.gov.uk/evalupolicy/index.asp

agement to officials and managers who were antagonistic or agnostic about evaluation for other reasons. Kenneth Clarke's opposition to pilot projects left a shadow over Departmental thinking about evaluation that extended on to 1997, if not later.

A second barrier to the mainstreaming of evaluation was the splitting of the Department between policy and operational arms. In the early and mid-1990s, as responsibility for policy development gradually shifted from the rest of the Department to the NHS Management Executive, attempts to develop evaluation programmes were sometimes victims of turf battles between Policy and Management Executive Directorates. In some cases it was simply not clear who should be responsible for policies or for their evaluation. In others, supposedly Department-wide working groups such as the Policy Evaluation Steering Group found that they had little or no influence over the activities of the Management Executive. A related challenge was the different culture brought into the Department by managers from the NHS. Although at an individual level there were notable exceptions, in general they were disinterested in analysis.

Later in the period under consideration, after policy responsibilities for health services had been moved into the NHS Executive, frequent organisational changes in the Department continued to weaken efforts at policy and programme evaluation. Rapid turnover both in organisational responsibilities and in staffing reduced interest in evaluations set up in the past by staff with different responsibilities. It also discouraged interest in the long view. Changes of government could have similar consequences. The resulting attenuation of the Department's institutional memory meant that the findings of past evaluations were less likely to have persistent effects in terms of future policy and programme behaviour. For these various reasons the advocates of policy evaluation within the Department, notably analysts in the EOR and the staff of the Research and Development Directorate, found that they had to work very hard both to promote the potential virtues of evaluation and to ensure that there was some learning when evaluation studies were completed.

A final important hurdle since around 2000 has been the sheer scale of the Government's ambition with regard to the modernisation and reform of health services. The pressure for rapid transformation of both access to and quality of health services has made it harder to argue for careful piloting. It has also given influence to those who claim to have new ideas offering major benefits which are so self-evident that they either need not or cannot be evaluated using normal evaluation methodologies. Although wiser councils have usually prevailed, by the time they have done so public expectations may have been raised too high or significant resources misallocated.

A short history

We have already referred to the Cabinet and Treasury initiatives that started active attempts to develop an evaluation culture in the Department. The Department's initial response to Treasury pressure was led and coordinated by finance divisions and the EOR. Each year the EOR would put forward a list of policies or programmes thought to be appropriate for evaluation, and would attempt to persuade policy divisions of the importance of formalised learning.

There were some 'successes' – for example, the evaluation of the Resource Management Initiative (RMI)[3] – but in general there was a limited buy-in from policy divisions. Nevertheless, in 1987 the Department decided against establishing a central policy evaluation unit, an approach used in some other departments, on the grounds that evaluation should be seen as a core responsibility of individual policy divisions.

Two years later the Treasury announced that it would be running down its central leadership role in relation to evaluation. This encouraged the Department to review the current organisational arrangements in order to develop an evaluation programme that served its own policy and management interests. A stock-take of existing evaluation activities revealed a disturbing picture. The Cabinet's 1985 requirements were not being met, and there was widespread uncertainty about the purposes of evaluation and scepticism about its value. There were also major variations in the use of systematic learning across the Department, with little or no evaluation of major hospital investments, major IT projects, NHS management reforms and quality-of-care initiatives. Work had not begun on the development of evaluation frameworks for the recent primary care reforms, the *Working for Patients* reforms, or the prospective community care reforms. These deficiencies persuaded the Department's senior committee, the Departmental Management and Policy Group (DMPG), to agree to establish a Policy Evaluation Steering Group (PESG) in order to promote 'a coordinated and targeted approach to policy evaluation' across all of the Department's businesses.

In the next four years the PESG met rarely and produced only two annual programmes of evaluation work. It commissioned a few studies in smaller areas, but saw its advice on major issues largely disregarded (e.g. the need to evaluate *Working for Patients* and major IT projects). A further review in 1993, initiated by the EOR and finance divisions, concluded that there had been 'a break-down' in arrangements for ensuring that the Department's policies, programmes and management practices were subject to well-targeted, timely and high-quality evaluation. It attributed this to limited progress in changing the Department's approach to evaluation. It was reported that a common cluster of views was:

> that evaluation should only be considered when other work pressures allow; that Ministers do not want evaluation studies because of the political trouble they might produce; that evaluation is only relevant if Ministers are willing to consider killing off a programme; and that in any event evaluation can be left to other bodies (e.g. universities or audit bodies).*

A paper to the Departmental Management Board (DMB), the successor to the DMPG, put forward a range of organisational options aimed at producing a better-targeted approach to evaluation. The DMB concluded that the PESG should remain but should be placed under a new chair.

Two years later, in 1995, the DMB again reviewed the position. This time it concluded that although it was important to continue to build evaluation into the policy culture, it was essential that individual business areas engage with the issue and work out their own approach and the application of policy evaluation to their

---

* In retrospect it is surprising how little value was attached to the help that Departmental conducted or commissioned evaluations might have been in handling National Audit Office and other external investigations. Such studies were not regarded as politically very threatening.

own programmes. The PESG was therefore wound up, and responsibility for taking forward evaluation was passed to the Department's four policy boards (for the NHS, social care, public health and central services). Each board was expected to consider its requirements in the context of its business plans, with the DMB undertaking an annual stock-take. The EOR was asked to continue to assist business areas in this process. For a couple of years the business area boards took this responsibility more or less seriously. Evaluation studies became more common, helped by the arrival of a Permanent Secretary (Chris Kelly) who took it for granted that evaluation proposals should be built into new policy initiatives. The last strategic discussion of evaluation activities by a senior departmental board took place in 1998.

The disappearance of formal evaluation stock-takes from senior management agendas after 1998 partly reflected management's focus on the huge reforming agenda of the Labour administration. However, it was also an acknowledgement of the extent to which monitoring and evaluation were now regarded as 'good practice' throughout much of the Department. Policy and management leads had come to accept that they should build evaluation into their day-to-day responsibilities, and many continue to do so. There has been some backsliding due to the huge organisational and staff changes that have taken place over the last two or three years. However, at the time of writing, the Department's analysts and Research and Development staff continue to act as prompters and prodders of the forgetful or less enthusiastic. Overall, the Department shows a level of commitment to planned learning that is much greater than it was 15 years ago, although there are still important shortcomings.

Common themes

The previous section reported on the history of formal evaluation in summary form. Reviewing papers and memories from the period, a number of perennial themes emerge. Three will be commented on below, namely local ownership versus central direction, maximising the benefits of evaluation activities, and persistent gaps in evaluation. These will each be discussed in turn.

Local ownership versus central direction

In some ways the struggle to promote an evaluative culture between 1985 and the present illustrates in microcosm the broader arguments about decentralised or centralised approaches to the management of change in the NHS. A central initiative by the Treasury was required to get the ball rolling. Having picked up the ball, the initial Departmental view was that responsibility should be decentralised to management and policy divisions. However, when it was found that this was a recipe for slow and varied progress, the centre attempted to stimulate behaviour in a non-directive way through a 'Steering Group' and the offer of technical assistance via the EOR. This process worked, but very slowly. Arguably the casualties included the failure to develop an evaluation framework for *Working for Patients* and the delayed development of rigorous evaluations of major IT projects. A more recent cost has been the slow application of rigorous methodologies to the innovative activities of the Modernisation Agency.

Maximising the benefits of evaluation activities

Long-standing scepticism in many parts of the Department about the value of evaluation led to several attempts to improve the targeting of the resources devoted to this activity. A simple rule of thumb was to concentrate resources on those areas where the value of lessons learned from evaluation was most likely to exceed the costs of the study. With this in mind, a series of criteria were developed for prioritising evaluation activities. For example, in 1994 the following criteria were used to assess the responsibilities of policy and management divisions:

- ignorance – is sufficient known about the objectives, implementation, results and adaptation of the policy?
- significance – how important is the policy/programme?
- timeliness – is it an opportune time for evaluation?
- interest – does it have a high (political/media) profile?
- likely benefits – is there scope for significant and cost-effective improvement?

Two years later the Department's analysts were arguing that better value might be obtained if a more strategic approach was taken by focusing the efforts of the ,major business groups both on periodic in-depth evaluations of performance in relation to the Department's key medium-term objectives and on evaluations of major common elements or functions that crossed the business group or were shared with other groups. More recently the focus has switched back towards ensuring that evaluation studies are sufficiently rigorous to allow confidence in the results that they produce.

One aspect of maximising benefits that continues to be underplayed is the importance of feeding learning from evaluations back into policy revision and improved management performance. Where the results of a policy evaluation have emerged at a time when the relevant policy area is under active consideration the feedback, has been fairly seamless. Examples include the evaluation of 'Health of the Nation', the results of which could be fed into the development of 'Our Healthier Nation'; and the evaluation of the total purchasing pilots, the results of which were fed into the Labour Government's new policies for primary care as they were developed in 1997 and 1998. However, in other circumstances arguably too little has been done to capture the learning in ways that could be transferred both through time and to different policy areas. As with health research in general,[4] the Department has devoted too few resources to developing easily accessible and user-friendly presentations of key findings. From time to time it would be salutary if the Department reviewed the following questions.

1 What have we learned from recent evaluations of health service policies, programmes and management practices?
2 How have our policies and practices changed as consequence?
3 How might more have been learned or have been changed?

Persistent gaps in evaluation

In retrospect there are a number of areas where the Department was (and in some cases still is) very slow to mount evaluations of major areas of expenditure or responsibility. Four that come to mind are information technology programmes, waiting-times initiatives, reforms of the organisation of the NHS and the Department, and hospital build projects. The arguments for evaluation in each of these areas have always been strong. They are all areas marked by considerable ignorance about what works (with the possible exception of hospital projects), they all claim to be of major significance for the effectiveness of health services, they are generally high-profile if things go wrong, there is thought to be scope for significant benefits if things are done well and, most importantly, their regular occurrence means that there is a continuing opportunity to learn from the past.

The reasons for the slow development of evaluation appear to vary from area to area. For information technology the root problem may have been asymmetry of knowledge. The Department's IT specialists convinced the non-technical managers to whom they were formally accountable that they knew what they were doing and that future benefits would be greater than hard-headed analysis suggested.* In the waiting-times area there was both an acceptance that waiting times were inevitable, and a belief that they could only be substantially reduced if the NHS was 'adequately' funded. In these circumstances evaluation of the Department's numerous small-scale initiatives appears to have been perceived as pointless. There were always good and 'uncontrollable' reasons for major geographical variations in waiting times (e.g. variations in resources or management skills and differences in clinican judgement (so called 'clinical signatures')).

The failure to evaluate NHS and Departmental organisational changes is easier to understand. The criteria for assessing improvements in organisational and management performance are contentious and imprecise, and measurement is difficult. Moreover, senior managers are understandably reluctant to assess changes for which they may have been responsible or that may have been imposed on them by political masters. The very slow development of post-project evaluations of capital projects is equally understandable. The benefits of such evaluations do not fall to those who are expected to bear their cost. Since 1994, responsibility for such evaluations has been placed on individual trusts, but because of the long time periods between major capital developments an individual trust is likely to gain little from studying its own experience. The beneficiaries of regular post-project evaluations are the next generation of capital projects. During the period under consideration in this book the Department was not willing to centrally fund the necessary evaluative work.

Evaluating Working for Patients

The failure of the Department to establish mechanisms for evaluating *Working for Patients* is widely seen as the biggest lost opportunity in health policy learning in the last 20 years. The loss is generally attributed to an embargo on piloting and

---

*This asymmetry (or possibly optimism bias?) appears to be continuing. At the time of writing (summer 2004) there is reportedly no Departmental evaluation programme for the huge National Programme for IT.

external research by Kenneth Clarke, the Secretary of State for Health, from July 1988 to November 1990. However, whilst Mr Clarke's views were one contributing factor, there were others. Overall, a failure of commitment and nerve by senior managers and officials in the Department was the main reason why the Department did not fund any significant evaluation of the major initiatives resulting from *Working for Patients* until 1994. This section sets out a chronology and argument to support this conclusion.

Chronology

The White Paper *Working for Patients* published in January 1989 proposed that the reforms would come into force in April 1991. The Secretary of State made it clear that he did not think formal piloting and academic study were necessary before the proposed reforms were rolled out. However, this was not interpreted by Departmental officials as ruling out looking for ways to learn from development projects and other initiatives in the period prior to April 1991. A survey of such opportunities was completed by October 1989. It showed that much monitoring was already under way or proposed, but that implementation of the White Paper could be facilitated if some gaps could be filled, notably with regard to early learning from the most advanced of the first wave of prospective NHS trusts, and from information systems to support the development and use of GP budgets. It was also suggested that where there already were development projects 'a more systematic approach to monitoring and evaluation could help to ensure that there is maximum learning and effective and timely dissemination of the results'. The Departmental analysts who initiated this work were asked to pursue their ideas with the units responsible for taking forward the 34 projects that constituted the *Working for Patients* agenda.

A year later the same analysts put forward proposals for monitoring the post-1991 impact and development of two of the key initiatives, namely NHS trusts and GP fundholders. In February 1991 these proposals were incorporated into a wider report on monitoring and evaluating *Working for Patients* that was forwarded to the DMPG by the PESG. It proposed that the initial emphasis of monitoring and evaluation activities should be on identifying 'examples of success and good practice which can then be more widely disseminated and applied', but it also recognised that there was a need 'to assess the extent to which the stated objectives for the new policies are being achieved'. In order to tackle both of these aims it was suggested that the reforms should be unbundled into their constituent parts and the individual components evaluated against their particular objectives. The report went on to note that a range of work was already in progress. The most relevant developments were seen to be the proposals referred to already to monitor the initial waves of NHS trusts and GP fundholders using a set of key indicators to throw light on the structure, conduct and performance of the new organisations. A second critical element was to be the close monitoring of six localities projects selected to 'go further, faster' on all aspects of the reforms, providing advance warning of the issues arising with more rapid implementation, and also highlighting good practice by assessing the impact of the reforms on the delivery of patient care and health outcomes. For this purpose, contracts were agreed with each locality setting out the requirements both for a common core of monitoring information and for disseminating results.

The same review also drew attention to the limited amount of external evaluation work in progress, and the willingness of external groups to undertake more work if Departmental funding was available. The report to the DMPG concluded that the main task of the NHS in 1991–92 would be to put in place the key organisational building blocks of the White Paper reforms, and that the corresponding role of central monitoring would be to ensure that this task was successfully carried out. However, it went on to note that the main gap in the arrangements for monitoring and evaluation was in specifying procedures and techniques for assessing progress against the long-term objectives of the reforms. It concluded that this and other outstanding issues in the Department's plans for monitoring and evaluating the reforms were being taken forward in a group known as the Critical Results Project Managers Group under the chairmanship of the Deputy Chief Executive of the NHS Management Executive.

It was another 10 months before the NHS Management Executive was formally asked to agree proposals for carrying work forward on evaluating the *Working for Patients* reforms. The delay in putting forward proposals was ascribed to:

> the former Secretary of State's known scepticism about academic evaluation in this area, the continuing intense controversy surrounding the reforms, the great difficulty of devising effective evaluations of such complex and wide-ranging reforms, and the pressures on the Management Executive in the run-up to implementation.

Another (unmentioned) contributing factor was a change in Deputy Chief Executive. The proposals to the Management Executive in November 1991 went little further than those that had been discussed with the DMPG and the Critical Results Project Managers Group nearly a year earlier. In important respects they went backwards. Rather than seeking agreement to the putting in place of particular monitoring and evaluation methodologies, they sought agreement to the drawing up of 'a framework document to be endorsed by the Management Executive which summarises the current position on evaluation arrangements and action planned in relation to all the main reform issues'.

The Management Executive agreed to this request, but further staff turnover ensured that it was not until June 1992 that an 'evaluation framework' was presented to senior management. It set out a proposed approach to evaluation and a short progress report on the development of evaluation arrangements. It noted that 'an extensive range of Regional networks, development projects, programmes of field visiting and other mechanisms [have] been instigated', although most of this work was qualitative. However, it went on to point out that there were weaknesses in the current arrangements, which needed to be tackled 'urgently' in order to sharpen up the effectiveness of evaluation. The weaknesses included major gaps in evaluation arrangements, particularly the absence of work to systematically assess the impact of *Working for Patients* both on quality and on access/choice issues. The development of evaluation measures was also impeded by 'a lack of clarity in many parts of the ME on how the success of particular aspects of the reform is to be evaluated'. A further problem was uncertainty about organisational issues and accountabilities. This was thought to partly explain why there was no coordinated plan to evaluate the impact of trusts. The report ended with a proposed timetable for deciding which gaps should be filled, who should be held responsible for filling them, and the establishment of agreed ongoing reporting and accountability arrangements for evaluation. The timetable stretched ahead to March 1993. It was not implemented. In August 1993 the new Deputy Chief Executive of the Management Executive asked for a report on earlier proposals to evaluate the healthcare reforms. He was informed that no significant action had been taken on the June 1992 proposals for an evaluation framework.

This was the end of the Department's attempts to develop an evaluation framework for *Working for Patients*. However, there was a postscript. In 1994 the NHS Executive announced a national total purchasing pilot initiative to build on bottom-up local initiatives by ambitious GP fundholders. There was a lively debate in the Department about how these pilots should be evaluated. The first proposal was that there should be heavy reliance on self-reporting by the individual pilot projects. The Department's analysts argued strongly that the importance of the innovation warranted a rigorous fully independent central evaluation. This view was backed up by pointing to the evidence of how little had emerged from the six localities projects referred to earlier.* To demonstrate the importance he attached to an independent evaluation, the Department's chief economist offered to contribute to its funding. The case for an independent evaluation was accepted, and the King's Fund coordinated a complex but remarkably speedy evaluation exercise. The interim results were presented to the Department in October 1997, in time to be taken into account in the preparation of the White Paper *The New NHS: modern, dependable*. Around the same time the Department finally felt able to fund a systematic review of evidence concerning the overall impact of the NHS internal market.[5]

Why did the Department fail to adopt and implement an evaluation framework for Working for Patients?

Kenneth Clarke's scepticism about academic research and his belief that pilot projects would simply encourage delay and continuing controversy have usually been seen as explaining why the Department did little to develop the information basis that could have been used to monitor progress with the reforms and to permit the before-and-after comparisons that could have contributed to more rigorous studies. However, it should be apparent from the above history that officials did not interpret the Secretary of State's views as preventing them from thinking about monitoring systems that would aid in the implementation of the reforms and the rapid learning of lessons. Moreover, by the end of 1990 Kenneth Clarke had been replaced by William Waldegrave.

A second possible reason why the Department might have chosen not to implement the evaluation framework on which it laboured for the best part of three years is because it concluded that all that should be done in terms of learning from experience was already in hand. However, this conclusion also

---

* Although these projects had agreed to standardise reporting arrangements, very little was reported and even less was written up. The Department's analysts drew the lessons that 'if you leave [local] managers to do their own evaluation, firstly it gets squeezed out by more pressing issues and secondly to the extent that it is done it is highly subjective and of very limited use to others'.

clearly does not stand up, given the consistent finding in internal reports from October 1989 onward that there were significant gaps in the Department's monitoring and evaluation activities.

If these were not the explanations, why did the Management Executive fail to take the lead in the development of adequate monitoring and evaluation procedures? A subjective and undoubtedly partial assessment, drawing on memories and papers from the time, points to the following factors.

- Fear that the findings from more probing monitoring or evaluation could embarrass or anger Ministers, particularly if they became publicly known. Even though Kenneth Clarke was moved to another Ministerial post in November 1990, his views on pilots and academic research continued to be quoted within the Department for much of the regimes of the next two Secretaries of State. It was not until 1995 that the ministerial waters were finally tested with proposals to evaluate both the total purchasing pilots and 'Health of the Nation'. In both cases Ministers readily agreed.
- An optimistic belief within the Management Executive about what could be learned from various trials and demonstrations launched in the wake of *Working for Patients* and from close liaison with NHS managers in regional offices, districts and trusts. The partiality and subjectivity of these sources of information were not always recognised.
- Scepticism among officials in both the Management Executive and the wider Department about the value of research and good information systems. In the early 1990s, many policy and managerial colleagues saw 'research' as something more likely to complicate their lives than to help them. Some may have remembered the words of a former Permanent Secretary, who said that he could not remember a single policy issue that had been informed by research!
- Changes in staffing and organisational responsibilities within the Department, particularly within the Management Executive. In the critical period when an evaluation framework was being considered there were three Deputy Chief Executives. There were also as many or more changes in the personnel charged with the front-line responsibility for this area.
- The absence from the Management Executive of anyone who believed sufficiently in the potential value of better monitoring and evaluation to champion it among their colleagues and, if necessary, to seek Ministers' views on the funding of external research in selected areas.
- The continuous pressure on policy analysts and managers to move on to 'the next new thing'.

It would be interesting to speculate about what would have been gained if an evaluation framework had been implemented along the lines developed between 1990 and 1992. However, this would take me too far from my agenda. Suffice it to say that one of the proposals in these documents was for the introduction of patient experience surveys, similar to those finally announced by the new Labour Government in December 1997. Another proposal was for data to be collected on the increases in minor surgery and the other new services (e.g. specialist clinics) that GP fundholders were expected to take on. The failure to collect this information bedevilled the Department's activity and efficiency indicators for the next dozen years – indeed up to their recent replacement.

Role of analysts

It should already be clear that the Department's analysts played a critical role in the promotion of project, policy and programme evaluation throughout this period. They were essentially the 'product champions' of policy evaluation in the critical period from 1986 to 1998 when formal evaluation of new initiatives moved from being the exception to the norm. The EOR provided the secretariat for the Policy Evaluation Steering Committee Group and wrote the great bulk of Departmental papers on the subject both before the PESG came into existence and after its demise. After 1995 the EOR also provided the main support to the Departmental Business Boards that were interested in taking a strategic approach to evaluation.

Another critical role for the internal analysts was the championing of evaluations of key policies. Although they failed to move the Department with regard to *Working for Patients*, they succeeded in relation to the Resource Management Initiative, the Community Care Strategy, Health of the Nation,* total purchasing and, later, NHS Direct, Walk-in Centres and digital TV, to mention some of the more important evaluations. In some cases they also contributed to the design of the evaluation proposals. In a few areas they both designed and implemented evaluations. Examples include studies of the Hospital Information Support System (HISS), the first ex-post evaluation of Private Finance Initiative (PFI) projects, and an evaluation of the process used to produce the 2000 NHS Plan.

Recently, with the greater mainstreaming of evaluation work, the EOR's contribution has focused mainly on encouraging management and policy divisions to sponsor evaluation where it is likely to be useful, on persuading new agencies, such as the Modernisation Agency, of the need to adopt rigorous approaches to assessing the effectiveness of their own programmes, and on supporting Research and Development staff in pushing out the frontiers and driving up the standards of evaluations. Hands-on evaluation still continues on a small scale where there is a requirement for something between an internal management assessment and an external academic study.

Where ministers and policy colleagues could be persuaded to support an evaluation, the Rearch and Development Directorate was usually very willing to find the funds. Most studies were (and are) undertaken by university researchers. Over the period under consideration there was an encouraging increase in the responsiveness of academics, particularly in the speed with which they were willing to complete formative evaluations. The Audit Commission and the National Audit Office were also increasingly important players in the evaluation market but, perhaps because of their statutory positions, potential synergies with the Department's evaluation activities were not exploited as much as would have been desirable.

After 2000 private sector consultancies (e.g. McKinseys) were also of growing importance. They can inject great speed into evaluations but in terms of wider learning a major weakness of their work is that they are often unwilling to see their reports published.

---

* Work on an evaluation framework was initiated by EOR. *See* Royston G (1993) A monitoring and evaluation framework for the implementation of the Health of the Nation. In: M Malek *et al.* (eds) *Managerial Issues in the Reformed NHS.* John Wiley & Sons, Chichester.

References

1 Garvin DA (1993) Building a learning organisation. *Harvard Business Rev.* **July-August**: 78–91.
2 HM Treasury (1988) *Policy Evaluation: a guide for managers.* HMSO, London.
3 Packwood T, Keen J and Buxton M (1991) *Hospitals in Transition: the resource management initiative.* Open University Press, Milton Keynes.
4 Dash P, Gowman N and Traynor M (2003) Increasing the impact of health services research. *BMJ.* **327**: 13339–41.
5 Le Grand J *et al.* (eds) (1998) *Learning From the NHS Internal Market: a review of the evidence.* The King's Fund, London.

Chapter 11

Learning from others: international comparisons

Introduction

Rudolf Klein has perceptively noted that 'learning about other countries is rather like breathing – only the brain dead are likely to avoid the experience'.[1] However, turning learning *about* other countries into learning *from* them requires incentives and hard work. Over the last 20 years or so the Department of Health has become much more willing to learn from others* – not only other countries, but also other Government departments and the private sector – and has devoted increasing resources to studying their experiences and identifying ideas or approaches that may be relevant to the NHS.

To keep this chapter manageable it focuses on the role of international comparisons in health policy making. There was a somewhat similar if more episodic growth in interest in learning from the experiences of other public-sector departments, particularly education, and in learning from the private sector, with BP being a favoured model. These experiences are not dealt with here. There has also, of course, been a huge amount of learning from other countries in relation to medical and clinical practice, pharmaceuticals and new health technologies of all kinds. Again this history is not our concern. Instead, the focus is on the contribution of international comparisons to health service policy making and to improvements in health service organisation and management.

The chapter begins with a discussion of the underlying influences that encouraged the Department to take a greater interest in learning from others. There is then a review of some of the areas in which international learning has been important, relatively unimportant, or misleading. The next section looks at the important role of analysts in promoting learning from other countries. The final section asks how our learning from international comparisons could be improved.

Underlying influences

Within the Department there has always been interest in the health policies of other countries. As noted elsewhere, at the beginning of the 1980s one member of the Department was funded to review the efficiency of the US and Canadian healthcare systems compared with England, and another visited European

---

* A simple indicator of the growth of interest in international learning is provided by comparing the number of references to international comparisons in the 1989 White Paper, *Working for Patients*, with the number in the 2000 White Paper, *The NHS Plan*.

countries to examine alternative methods of financing healthcare. Later in the 1980s, senior officials examined US health maintenance organisations and looked at the governance arrangements for Canadian hospitals, in both cases with a view to identifying lessons for England. The 1980s saw many other overseas visits with broader or narrower objectives. However, despite the interest in what other countries were doing, the learning was mainly negative. It was generally concluded that we were already on the right track and had little to learn from other countries, once allowance had been made for the difference in the levels of national funding. Throughout the 1980s and for much of the 1990s there was more consciousness both in the Department and in the NHS of England being a health ideas exporter rather than an ideas importer.

A major reason (perhaps *the* major reason) why an interest in other countries' experiences and thinking turned into a search for positive learning was increasing Ministerial, media and public discontent with the functioning of the NHS. This discontent occurred in two major waves associated with and stimulating the Conservative Government's *Working for Patients* reforms at the end of the 1980s and the Labour Government's reforms from 1997 onwards. Mrs Thatcher's unhappiness with the efficiency of the NHS provided fertile ground for US ideas of managed competition and their champion Alain Enthoven. The unhappiness of the 1997 Labour Government with the geographical inequities (e.g. 'postcode prescribing') and poor outcomes of the service inherited from the Conservatives provided similar fertile ground for American ideas on performance management, patient feedback, quality improvement and self-care. It also opened the door to Australian ideas on technology appraisal and Scandinavian approaches to hastening hospital discharges and using health funds to reduce long-term disability-benefit claims.

The discontent was further fuelled by the growing proportion of the population who had direct or indirect experience of the health services of other countries as a consequence of the increasing ease of international travel and the reduction of barriers to accessing health services in European countries. This experience showed the public and the media that there were alternatives to the NHS, and that in terms of responsiveness those alternatives were sometimes superior.

Somewhere around the turn of the century these various sources of discontent prompted what can only be described as a strategic shift in the way in which government used international comparisons.* Up until then, foreign experience had been a source of ideas on *how* to improve efficiency or effectiveness by doing things differently (e.g. by introducing an internal market or strengthening performance management). After 1999, there was an increasing interest in *what* was being achieved elsewhere as well as in how it was achieved. The discontent was combined with an ambition to emulate the standards of expenditure and care in other countries. The first and critical manifestation of this ambition was Tony Blair's statement in January 2000 about matching average European Union (EU) health service spending levels. A further indication was the commitment in the 2000 NHS Plan to bring hospital waiting times down to levels comparable with those in the rest of Europe. The new commitment to international standards of care reached its fullest flowering (so far) in the government's acceptance of the first Wanless Report.

---

*I am grateful to Richard Murray for articulating this idea of a 'strategic shift'.

Discontent with the NHS and even fears about its future have not been the only factors stimulating demand for international learning. The price of learning has fallen. First, there has been a huge improvement in the quality and coverage of international databases. The work of the OECD and other international collaborations has extended the areas in which comparisons are possible beyond healthcare costs and activities and increasingly into quality and outcomes, and from national systems to major disease areas. Secondly, the improved databases have stimulated, and been stimulated by, a major growth in research on international comparisons. The OECD has continued to maintain a leading role in this work, but it has been joined by growing research programmes in other inter-governmental organisations, notably the World Health Organization and the EU. There has also been a significant increase in the international comparative work of private foundations, most notably the New York Commonwealth Fund and the UK Nuffield Trust. These organisations have not only increased knowledge of the healthcare policies and systems in other countries, but have also used face-to-face meetings to create new networks between policy makers from different countries. As studies of technology transfer repeatedly show, conferences and demonstrations remain the most potent vehicles for the transfer of ideas.[2]

The growth of these more formal networks has been both stimulated and complemented by the growth of informal networks between the increasing number of analysts, particularly economists and operational researchers, working in the health departments of OECD countries. Apart from its value in their day-to-day work, these analysts see the understanding of other countries' healthcare policies as a significant tool in the fight for influence in their national or regional bureaucracies. Certainly in the Department of Health it was analysts' knowledge of other countries' policies that was sometimes as important as or more important than their analytical skills in eliciting invitations to Ministerial tables.

A further factor facilitating the supply of information on international comparisons was the 'death of distance' brought about by the Internet. Given the importance of face-to-face contacts for policy learning, the reduction in air-travel costs has also made a major contribution to the development of what has been termed 'the global commons'.*

The effect of these developments is that UK governments can no longer afford to see international comparisons as an optional extra, 'nice to know' but not critical to domestic decision making. The growth of comparative information on healthcare quality, responsiveness, access and other aspects of outcomes means that standards of healthcare are increasingly set internationally. International benchmarks rapidly become national standards. Unless a government unilaterally withdraws from the collection and publication of outcome data, it will find that disease area by disease area the success of national policies is judged against international benchmarks. Tony Blair's commitment in 2000 to match the average healthcare expenditure levels of the EU is confirmation that international benchmarking already extends to health service resourcing. As international data become available on treatment survival rates and other indicators of quality of care, the pressure on governments to aspire to the standards of the best is likely to

---

* In 2004 two people could be sent on a study tour to New Zealand for the same real air-travel costs as were required for one person in 1988.

prove irresistible. A new mechanism for the upward ratcheting of health expenditure has been born.*

Where has learning been important?

Over the last 20 years, ideas from other countries have come to the fore both during major reform periods and as contributions towards the perennial health-care debates that continue within health ministries even when governments are not in reforming mode. We shall discuss examples of both uses.

The contribution of US ideas of managed competition to the 'Working for Patients' reforms has already been referred to and is too well known to require expansion. However, apart from advocating the separation of purchasers and providers and the promotion of provider competition, Enthoven also argued that England (along with the rest of Europe) needed major improvements in its healthcare management information systems.[3] The improvements that he proposed included the adoption of diagnostic related groups (DRGs) for costing purposes, the analysis of practice variations, risk-adjusting outcome measures, outcomes management, the setting of service and access standards, measuring patient satisfaction, publication of information on service providers, utilisation reviews and the development of longitudinal patient records. Within the NHS the last 15 years have seen major progress in all of these areas except perhaps for the last two. The causes have been multiple, and certainly cannot all be traced to Enthoven's advice. However, knowledge of the more innovative and effective management information systems available in some parts of the USA has provided a constant reminder that the Department and/or the NHS could be doing better.

The contribution of foreign ideas to the Labour Government's healthcare reforms is less well documented but it has been more pervasive. Few domestic policies have one source, and the civil servants and ministers involved in a policy debate may trace their favourite ideas back to very different origins. However, there can be no doubt that the initial designers of the Performance Assessment Framework drew very heavily on the attempts of US employers to systematically compare the performance of American health plans (the Health Plan Employer Data and Information Set – HEDIS), and to a lesser extent on the work of the Australian Commonwealth Government to compare the performance of Australian states. Similarly, the proposal to extend the role of the National Institute for Clinical Excellence (NICE) to include the economic appraisal of new technologies was strongly informed by the Australian experience with the use of economic analysis in the Pharmaceutical Benefits Scheme. Several other initiatives that were announced in *A New NHS: Modern, Dependable* also either had foreign origins, or knowledge of foreign experience that accelerated their development. For example, NHS Direct learned from American nurse helplines, and the introduction of systematic patient surveys drew on a review of

* The appeal to international standards to lever up the scale or effectiveness of health expenditure is not, of course, new. An earlier example was the World Health Organization's 'Health for All' programme. What is new is the strength of the appeal now that there is reliable information on the comparative quality and outcomes of health services as distinct from the broader effects of social and economic environments.

experience with eliciting patient feedback in the USA, Canada, Australia and New Zealand.

A raft of more recent reforms has also either been sparked by, or drawn heavily on, overseas experience. Examples include attaching penalties to late hospital discharges (from Scandinavia), Foundation Hospitals (Spain and Sweden and not-for-profits in the USA), and offering a choice of hospital for elective care (Denmark and Sweden, as well as European countries funding health care through social insurance). The new system of hospital financing, 'payment by results,' also draws heavily on international experience. As was noted in the June 2004 NHS Improvement Plan, 'Similar schemes are already operating or are being developed in the United States, Australia, Norway, the Netherlands, Germany and other countries.'[4]

The Department has also increasingly drawn on international experience in its more bread-and-butter policy-making work. Examples of areas where there have been regular or continuous scrutinies of international experience include the preparation of public expenditure bids, alternative financing, improving quality, strengthening incentives (for organisations and staff), resource allocation mechanisms and prioritisation.

The preparation of annual (now biennial) public expenditure bids

This is probably the activity for which international comparisons have been used for longest and most continuously. From the 1980s the OECD's database was regularly mined by the Department to see whether it would support arguments for increased public funding. However, although the comparisons always showed that England was lagging behind its peers in terms of healthcare expenditure and, more particularly, doctor numbers, it was not until the middle of the 1990s that they began to signal that health outcomes were slipping below the OECD average. Arguably the absence of good measures of health outcomes and the reliance instead on measures of population status led Departmental analysts and the Department itself to exaggerate the effectiveness of the NHS.

The most important example of the value of international benchmarks for decisions on public expenditure was, of course, the Prime Minister's commitment in early 2000 that the UK would catch up with the EU average level of healthcare expenditure of 8% of GDP by 2005. Interestingly, it was Treasury officials who provided the initial briefing for this calculation. Departmental analysts were only too pleased to confirm the assumptions on which it was based (*see* Chapter 2).

Alternative financing

The regular reviews of the pros and cons of alternative methods of financing the NHS have always drawn heavily on experience in other countries (*see* Chapter 3). One of the strongest arguments for believing that there are no panaceas is that virtually all countries are looking for ways of improving on their current mix of funding methods regardless of what that mix may be.

Improving quality

International research projects on treatment outcomes for particular diseases, such as cancer, helped to stimulate domestic interest in improving quality. An additional spur was provided by the findings of a growing body of US research which showed that there were important variations between providers and patient groups in terms of clinical quality and patient experience, and that there were also major safety concerns with regard to hospital activity. In addition to contributing to the pressures leading to a series of English strategies to promote quality and improve safety, these findings also helped to encourage a search for international collaborations at Government level. Perhaps the most important of these has been the UK/USA collaboration on quality brokered by the Commonwealth Fund of New York and aided by the Nuffield Trust. Box 11.1 illustrates how this collaboration developed.

Box 11.1 From small acorns . . . the USA/UK collaboration on quality

It started with a phone call from the USA some time in 1998. Brian Biles, a Vice-President of the Commonwealth Fund of New York (whom I had met two or three years earlier when the Harkness Fellowship Programme was being reviewed), told me that for 1999 the Fund was thinking about an English location for one of its annual meetings of US health policy experts, the Margaret E Mahoney Symposium. He wanted to know whether I thought this would be welcomed by the Department, and if so, what subject would be of most interest to us. Two possibilities were discussed, namely primary care and healthcare quality. We also discussed possible locations for the conference, and Ditchley Park was identified as perhaps the most distinguished venue for Anglo-American meetings.

The first symposium focusing on quality of care duly took place in May 1999 at Ditchley Park. The Nuffield Trust took responsibility for organising the external UK participants and the EOR coordinated the Department's representation. The USA and the UK both fielded distinguished teams led, respectively, by Donna Shalala, Secretary for Health and Human Services and Frank Dobson, Secretary of State for Health. Although few conclusions were reached, John Eisenberg, the energetic director of the US Agency for Health Research and Quality, immediately sought opportunities for extending the cooperation.

John Eisenberg's enthusiasm helped to ensure that the Commonwealth Fund and the Nuffield Trust supported a second conference at Ditchley in June 2000 under the title 'Improving Quality of Healthcare in the US and UK: Strategies for Change and Action'. The EOR again organised the Departmental contribution to this meeting and helped to focus it on two issues of current interest to the Department, namely improving quality of care for coronary heart disease and cancer. John Eisenberg once more pressed strongly for a longer-term agenda of collaboration. Working with the Department's Chief Medical Officer, Sir Liam Donaldson, it was agreed that future collaboration should initially focus on three areas, namely medical error, information technology and national reporting on quality.

A third meeting (under the same heading 'Improving the Quality of Healthcare in the US and UK: Strategies for Change and Action') was held at Penny Hill Park in June 2001. In addition to following up on the agenda items agreed at the previous meeting, the consultative agenda was expanded to include primary care, health system disparities, quality monitoring of targeted conditions, cost-effectiveness and healthcare workforce issues. Reflecting the importance he attached to it, John Eisenberg pressed for the collaboration to be placed on a more formal basis through a written Ministerial agreement.

In Washington DC in October 2001 the US Secretary for Health and Human Resources, Tommy Thompson, and the UK Secretary of State for Health, Alan Milburn, formally signed a joint statement of intent to collaborate on improving the quality of healthcare and to work together on bioterrorism. This committed both countries to continuing the international programme of policy exchange and co-operation.

The collaboration has now grown into a programme of meetings, research projects and joint working organised in and from both sides of the Atlantic. Further meetings at Penny Hill Park in July 2002 and July 2003 were used to report back on progress. The EOR and the Department's Strategy Unit provided the secretariat from the UK, and the Agency for Health Research and Quality fulfilled a similar role in the USA. Help and enthusiasm came from the Modernisation Board, Don Berwick at the Institute for Healthcare Improvement, and others. In 2004, for the first time, the annual meeting was held in New York.

From the UK perspective, the imagination and generosity of the Commonwealth Fund and the Nuffield Trust have given the Department and the NHS extraordinary access to the thinking, experience and research of senior US policy makers and leading US experts on the quality of healthcare. This has both broadened and enriched UK policy thinking.

Prioritisation

Most developed countries have from time to time considered whether public expectations of healthcare systems could be brought more in line with the resources to pay for such systems through the development of some form of explicit prioritisation or rationing. In the late 1980s and early 1990s there were major studies of health service prioritisation in the Netherlands, Sweden and New Zealand. All of these reviews were considered by a succession of working groups in the Department. The main conclusions drawn were as follows. First, the categories of care that did not provide important benefits to some people were few in number and small in size. Secondly, as a consequence of this the withdrawal of public funding from whole categories of care that were largely ineffective or cosmetic would save very little money. Thirdly, there were more obvious opportunities to improve value for money by prioritising new and existing technologies on the basis of cost-effectiveness. Fourthly, this might often mean identifying the types of patients for whom particular treatments were likely to be cost-effective, and discouraging the public funding of those that were likely to be cost-ineffective. Finally, the mechanisms for deciding priorities needed to be seen as fair and transparent.

The ways of working of the NHS Screening Committee and more recently of NICE have both benefited from these conclusions. The emphasis in National Service Frameworks on prioritising by cost-effectiveness can also be seen as building on this earlier work. Work on the systematic prioritising of patients on waiting lists, which was also encouraged by these and other international studies, has largely been overtaken by the Government's determination to reduce waiting times. It is likely that interest in fairer prioritisation will resurface as it is discovered that there are limits to how far waiting times can be reduced.

Where has learning been unimportant?

In contrast to the areas where the Department has identified foreign ideas that appear to be relevant, there have been other problem areas where the search has either yielded very little, or there has been very little searching. Four examples are: hospital waiting times, health system management costs, the measuring of health service efficiency, and the effective use of information technology.

Hospital waiting times

In view of the dominant position of waiting times in healthcare policy debates, it might be expected that this would be an early area for international comparison. In fact, there was surprisingly little attention to overseas experience with waiting times until around 1990. Although there were desk reviews and comparisons and ad-hoc visits to individual countries (e.g. Sweden) to discuss innovative waiting-times initiatives, the Department did not actively support a major international research project on this subject until 2001. The slowness in attempting to systematically learn from other countries may have been partly due to a widely held view (propounded, it has to be said, by economists) that waiting times were inevitable and probably desirable in a system in which care was free at the point of use. The low levels of health expenditure were seen as another easy excuse for England's outlier position. It was some time before it was noted that nearly all European countries provided hospital care free at the point of use, and most of them had shorter waiting times than in England. In some cases shorter waiting times were combined with activity rates that apparently differed little from those in the NHS. With hindsight, the delay in pushing hard for a major international research programme in this area was an unfortunate example of policy myopia. Ironically, by the time the research programme launched by the OECD in 2001 had reported, the Department thought that it knew the solution to waiting times – a massive injection of additional resources, and changes in hospital and clinician incentives.

Health system management costs

Claims of the scope for reducing health service management costs are seen by politicians of all parties as an easy way to gain political popularity. Although all bureaucracies have a tendency to generate unnecessary fat (like others, civil servants prefer to be responsible for growing rather than declining empires), it is very difficult to judge whether a system is over- or under-managed. Many of the beneficial organisational reforms of the last 20 years have required more 'management'. Examples include the setting of care standards, closer monitoring of progress and the related development of better information on the quality and effectiveness of interventions, mechanisms for incentivising performance improvements, the appraisal of new technologies and dissemination of results, and the introduction of new hospital payment systems and of patient choice.

Little progress has been made in developing objective indicators for judging whether the Department and the NHS are under- or over-managed, given these and other new responsibilities. As many of the evolving functions and management approaches adopted in England are also being implemented elsewhere, one might expect international comparisons to be useful for judging whether those functions are being efficiently or inefficiently staffed. However, over the last 20 years there has been no serious attempt to compare Health Department and NHS management costs with those in other systems. This is partly because the problems are very great. Henry Aaron has recently written:

> *an economist is struck by how hard it is to identify and estimate administrative costs accurately at a single point in time in a single nation, how doubly hard it is to compare costs at a single point in time among nations, and how triply hard it is to make meaningful international comparisons of trends in administrative costs over time.*[5]

It is harder still to identify what levels and types of management costs pay for themselves through improvements in technical or allocative efficiency. For over 15 years when Ministers have sought comparative data it has been explained that available analyses such as the data put together by the OECD are 'generally unreliable'.* Departmental promises to address this issue have never been followed up.†

The shyness about developing research projects in this area is not unique to England. The only serious attempts at comparing management costs have been between the USA and Canada. Personal experience from attachments to health departments in the USA, Canada, Australia and New Zealand suggests that the UK Department of Health was relatively lightly staffed by international standards after downsizing in the mid-1990s. Whatever the arguments for the '38%' reduction in Departmental staff announced in 2003, they were not based on international benchmarking. This may be one area where prejudices (of all political parties and of many managers) are so entrenched that there is little interest in being better informed. A more charitable explanation is that the functions of central health departments are so different that comparisons are not helpful. However, to make this case also requires new empirical work.

---

* As was noted in Chapter 9, the OECD's implementation of System of Health Accounts-based National Health Accounts should greatly improve the position.

† For example, in December 1996 the then Secretary of State for Health wrote to the Deputy Prime Minister: 'we will continue to look for opportunities for making more accurate comparisons with other countries'.

Measuring health service efficiency

On this issue there has been no lack of interest or support from UK health ministers and senior managers, but it has proved very difficult to find countries willing to co-operate in comparative studies of aggregate efficiency. There is plenty of international evidence on partial measures of efficiency, such as hospital length of stay, day-case rates, staffing ratios, etc., although definitional differences can make comparisons difficult to interpret. However, judging by the reports of the OECD, few countries appear to have made serious attempts to develop time series of trends in overall efficiency either for the hospital sector or for all healthcare. In thinking about this subject, and more particularly in grappling with the challenge of incorporating quality improvements into the measurement of efficiency, the UK, Sweden and the USA look to be out on their own.

Effective use of information technology

A particularly challenging area for the NHS has been the effective use of IT. A series of ambitious projects has failed to deliver the claimed benefits. With hindsight, these projects were frequently poorly planned, costed and managed, they exaggerated the likely benefits, and they made too little attempt to involve clinicians. These problems have not been unique to the UK, but until the late 1990s there was little attempt to learn from the (admittedly limited number of) successful health IT projects in the USA. Thankfully the position has now changed. In the last four or five years, with the assistance of the Commonwealth Fund and the Nuffield Trust there have been sustained attempts to learn from successful American experiences.

Two other areas in which international experience might have been exploited to a greater extent are health system decentralisation and the development of clinicians as managers. Swings between centralism and decentralism in the governance arrangements for health services have been commonplace in many countries (e.g. Canada and New Zealand). To increase the chances that the move to decentralising health services announced in 'Shifting the Balance'[6] in 2001 will improve the performance of the NHS it will be important to draw on the lessons learned from these countries. Similarly, the fluctuations in Departmental interest in encouraging clinicians to become health service managers suggests that too little has been learned from the experiences of countries where clinician managers are more commonplace, such as the USA.[7]

Where has 'learning' been misleading?

Learning from comparisons is often not straightforward. In looking to learn from other countries' ideas there is general recognition of the importance of taking account of context. The Department's experience suggests that the wrong lessons can also be learned if the comparability of data is not carefully checked.

Hospital admissions provide an example of the difficulties that are caused when definitions vary across countries. In the middle years of the 1990s, analysts in the Department (including myself) used OECD tabulations to claim that NHS hospital admission rates were catching up with those in other countries – offering prospects of falling waiting times – and that lengths of stay were declining exceptionally sharply – providing further evidence of the efficiency of the NHS. Both claims turned out to be exaggerated. The English data were based on a statistical construct unique to the UK, namely the 'finished consultant episode' (FCE), while the rest of the OECD was reporting actual hospital admissions or discharges and the time between admission and discharge. Moreover, at times the rate of increase in FCEs was inflated above that of hospital admissions because of changes in internal hospital practices. England is almost certainly not the only country whose performance in international league tables has been distorted by definitional differences. For example, the New Zealand method of measuring hospital lengths of stay for acute care also appears to be out of line with general international practice.*

Incomplete data can also lead to misleading conclusions. As noted earlier, one of the reasons why the Department (and its analysts) was slow to recognise that the NHS was performing less effectively than other healthcare systems in the 1990s was the absence of good data on healthcare outcomes and the reliance instead on measures of health status.

What has been the role of analysts in promoting learning?

The Department's analysts have made three main contributions to promoting international learning. First, they have acted as identifiers or early importers of new ideas, and in some cases have become their champions. An example is the balanced scorecard or systematic approach to performance measurement, which was developed into the Performance Assessment Framework. The transfer of the Performance Assessment Framework from health to personal social services was also initiated by an analyst. Another Departmental analyst helped to introduce the idea of such a framework to the Department of Education. Departmental analysts also championed the introduction of nurse telephone helplines and Walk-in Centres, and organised the initial piloting of both under the title of NHS Direct.

Other ideas had been around for some time in the academic literature, but the Department's analysts acted as brokers for their adoption by the Department. Examples include expanding the role of NICE to include assessing the cost-effectiveness of new and existing technologies, and systematising and universalising patient experience surveys. Two smaller examples are the introduction of incentives for hospitals to avoid delayed discharges, and the use of health service funds to accelerate the return to work of recipients of long-term disability benefit. In this last case it took analysts more than a decade to persuade Ministers of the value of piloting models that were first trialled in Sweden in the 1980s. Another example of a large time gap between the international evidence emerging and UK action is the recent ban on cigarette advertising. The effect of bans in other countries was reviewed in 1993.[8]

The second way in which Departmental analysts have helped to promote learning from overseas is by strengthening the mechanisms and networks used for the international transfer of health service ideas. Over many years analysts

---

* As in England, a downward bias in reported average lengths of stay has encouraged over-optimism about local hospital efficiency.

consistently supported the development of comparative measures of health system performance through data sets such as OECD Health Data. They took the lead in pressing for broadening of the measures to include information on the technical quality of care. They also encouraged the Department and Ministers to support the important OECD health research agenda while using membership of the OECD Social Policy Committee to influence that agenda in directions that would be useful to the Department and the NHS. More recently, they organised the Department's contribution to the first two or three of the annual US/UK conferences on quality organised by the Commonwealth Fund and the Nuffield Trust (*see* Box 11.1 on page 180).

The international attachments and research interests of the Department's analysts have also contributed to the build-up of bilateral networks. These have invariably been used for the two-way exchange of ideas. An example is the almost continuous exchange of ideas with New Zealand, the country with a health system that perhaps most closely resembles that of the UK (*see* Box 11.2).

Box 11.2 Exchanging healthcare ideas with New Zealand

The Department of Health is continually exchanging policy ideas with officials and Ministers in other countries. In the period 1988–97 there was a particularly large number of exchanges with New Zealand, the country with a health system that perhaps most closely resembles the NHS. A sample of the exchanges involving Departmental analysts is given below.

1988. The DHSS Chief Economist advised the secretariat for the Gibbs Report, *Unshackling the Hospitals*. The report was sent to Number 10 Downing Street and was taken into account in thinking about NHS trusts.

1989

1 The New Zealand Finance Minister had discussions on 'Working for Patients' while visiting England.
2 The UK Department of Health considered New Zealand Treasury thinking on relationships between the Ministry of Health and Area Health Boards as part of the review of the relationship between the Department and the NHS Executive.

1990. The New Zealand Ministry of Health report *Health Goals and Targets* was drawn to the attention of UK health ministers. It was seen as indicating the political and policy attractions of health targets and the value of complementing reform of health service 'means' with a clear view of health 'ends'. In 1992 the Department published *Health of the Nation*.

1991. The Department of Health Chief Economist was invited to New Zealand to advise on the draft report of the Health Service Taskforce. His advice was credited with discouraging the Taskforce from committing to a social insurance funding model.[9]

1992. The New Zealand Treasury sought advice from the Department of Health on lessons from UK health reforms for implementing the new New Zealand Green and White Papers.

1996

1 The Departmental Chief Economist reviewed lessons that the UK might learn from PHARMAC, the agency responsible for the public purchase of pharmaceuticals in New Zealand.
2 Later that year he was commissioned by the New Zealand Ministry of Health to produce a report on the organisation of central agency responsibilities for health-sector performance.

1997. The Department of Health sought advice from New Zealand on the performance agreements between New Zealand ministers and the Ministry of Health Chief Executive.

The exchanges have continued up to the present, aided by the transfer of key staff between the UK and New Zealand public services.

The third way in which analysts have contributed is by bringing work on international comparisons within the mainstream of the Department. The regular importing of overseas ideas and the demonstration that international experiences could make a critical contribution to improved policy making* convinced Ministers of the need to build up the Department's capacity for international learning. Work that was initially thought by senior policy colleagues to be so marginal that the time allocated to it had to be 'hidden' in the EOR work programme is now seen as warranting full-time posts in the Department's Strategy Unit and International Branch.

Why have analysts played such a prominent role in identifying and championing relevant international ideas within the Department of Health? One reason is that they have access to disciplines, economics and systems thinking, which are particularly dominant in the present diffusion of ideas around the world. Belief in the value of searching out alternatives and in measuring and comparing are part of the core toolkit of most analysts. A second reason is that the Department's economists and operational researchers have their own international professional networks from which they can receive early warning of new health service ideas. A third reason, referred to earlier, is that they had an incentive to move into the field of international comparisons as a way of extending their influence.

---

* One example is: Department of Health (2001) *National Beds Inquiry: long-term planning for hospitals and related services*. Department of Health, London. A more recent case is the learning from Kaiser Permanente. *See* Ham C *et al.* (2003) Hospital bed utilisation in the NHS, Kaiser Permanente and the US Medicare Programme: analysis of routine data. *BMJ.* 327: 1257–60.

How could our learning improve?

With the growth of comparable quality and outcomes data, standards and expectations for healthcare will increasingly be set internationally. In order to meet these standards and keep up with public expectations, learning from other countries will have to become a routine part of healthcare policy making. Over the last 20 years the Department has moved some way in this direction, but there is still further to go. Our proposals fall into two categories – first, those aimed at strengthening the Department's demand for and use of international learning, and secondly, those aimed at strengthening the networks for sharing and disseminating international learning.

On the demand side, ideas that might be considered include the following.

1 Maintain and strengthen the Department's existing mechanisms for scanning international healthcare developments. For instance, the monthly internal *International Health Care News* is a useful overview of the main health news stories in comparator countries, but it is restricted to returns from UK embassies. It might be improved first, by the addition of a front piece drawing attention to developments that are directly relevant to current UK policy concerns, and secondly, by incorporating pertinent material from other health news reviews, such as *Euro Observer*, and abstracts of new international research in the areas of current policy interest.

2 Develop a set of national benchmarks of the effectiveness and efficiency of healthcare policy to be used to publicly compare England with its main comparators on a regular (possibly annual) basis. (This would be somewhat similar in purpose to the benchmarks of national productivity performance recently developed by the Department of Trade and Industry.) Over the years there have been many 'one-off' attempts to compare England or the UK with other countries on the dimensions of healthcare services monitored by the OECD. With the development of the first set of internationally comparable quality indicators, and with work continuing to extend their coverage, it may be time to identify a more 'ideal' set of indicators on which to benchmark and monitor the performance of the NHS. This could draw on the work of the Healthcare Commission, the new health accounts and the requirements of the National Service Frameworks, and it could be used to help to influence international debates on the development of new quality and outcome indicators. The benchmark international comparisons could be presented in the Department's annual report.

3 Require a review of overseas ideas and experience to be incorporated in all *major* policy development processes. To the extent that the Department has built up its knowledge base on overseas policies by means of some of the mechanisms identified above, this should be much easier to achieve. A range of evidence is also now readily available from sources such as the Cochrane Collaboration and WHO Europe.* The objective would be to reach a stage where no new policy proposals went to Ministers without indicating how current English performance standards compared with those of our normal peers. In areas where the NHS lagged, an explanation would be expected of the likely reason(s) for the greater success of the leading countries.

* On the latter, *see* www.euro.who.int/HEN

Turning to the supply side in order to build up the networks for international learning, the Department should consider the following.

1 Adopting a strategic approach to influencing the research agendas of the major international organisations with significant comparative research programmes. In the past the Department's analysts attempted to develop such an approach towards the work of the OECD, but found it difficult because of the limited interest of policy colleagues. A strategic approach is also required to influence the analytical and research agendas of the EU and the World Health Organization. There are many possible ways into this. One of the most promising is disease-based comparisons along the lines pioneered by McKinsey[10] and recently developed by the OECD.[11] This would tie in with the Department's National Service Frameworks and the introduction of disease-based programme budgets.

2 Similarly, adopting a strategic approach to the international collaborations supported by foundations such as the Commonwealth Fund of New York and the Nuffield Trust. The Department has benefited enormously from the comparative work of the Commonwealth Fund and the Nuffield Trust, but it has had difficulty in developing a strategic approach to their activities. Because the Department has not had a clear view of where it would like to go with international learning, liaison with these outside initiatives has fallen disproportionately on departmental analysts, rather than being mainstreamed.

3 Promoting the development of international clearing houses for evidence relating to health service processes and policies that are replicated widely across developed countries. Obvious candidates include health technology assessment, National Service Frameworks, clinical pathways, and cost-effectiveness registers. Greater international collaboration should result in efficiencies in the national production of these tools.

4 Improving the scale of its contribution to the data collection and research work of the OECD. One priority should be building on the innovative work of the OECD (and the Commonwealth Fund) in developing comparable measures of the technical quality of care. Despite the difficulties, cross-country data on quality are essential in order to assess the cost-effectiveness of different approaches to healthcare delivery.[12] A second priority should be the judicious deployment of research funds to give the UK more leverage over international research agendas. It is worth remembering that international research programmes offer major leverage benefits. A UK contribution of one-tenth of the cost of a major international research programme may yield benefits that are up to 10 times as large as the UK contribution.

5 Systematic briefing and debriefing of UK personnel who engage in international exchanges. The Department directly funds a number of its staff to undertake attachments in other countries, and it participates in the selection of UK Harkness Fellows. In the past, too little attention has been given to the briefing and more particularly the debriefing of these important carriers of overseas learning. Departmental scholars/secondees and Harkness Fellows should all automatically be invited to give seminars to the Department on their return.

References

1 Klein R (1995) *Learning from others: shall the last be the first?* Paper for Four Country Conference on Health Care Reforms and Health Care Policies in United States, Canada, Germany and the Netherlands. February 1995, Amsterdam.

2 Mulgan G (2001) International comparisons in policy making: the view from the centre. Talk to Institute of Public Administration, New South Wales. *See* www.nsw. ipaa.org.au/07publication

3 Enthoven A (1989) What can Europeans learn from America? *Health Care Finance Rev.* 1989 Supplement: 49–63.

4 Department of Health (2004) *The NHS Improvement Plan. Putting people at the heart of public services.* The Stationery Office, London.

5 Aaron H (2003) The costs of health care administration in the United States and Canada – questionable answers to a questionable question. *NEJM.* **349**: 801–3.

6 Department of Health (2001) *Shifting the Balance of Power Within the NHS. Securing delivery.* Department of Health, London.

7 *See,* for example, Crosson F (2003) Kaiser Permanente: a propensity for partnership. *BMJ.* **326**: 654.

8 Smee C, Anderson R and Parsonage M (1992) *Effect of Tobacco Advertising on Tobacco Consumption: a discussion document reviewing the evidence.* Economics and Operational Research Division, Department of Health, London.

9 Jacobs K and Barnett. P (2000) Policy transfer and policy learning: a study of the 1991 New Zealand Health Services Taskforce. *Govern Int J Policy Admin.* **13**: 185–213.

10 Dorsey L *et al.* (1996) The productivity of healthcare systems. *McKinsey Q.* 1996 **4**: 3–11.

11 Organisation for Economic Co-operation and Development (OECD) (2003) *A Disease-Based Comparison of Health Systems. What is best and at what cost?* OECD, Paris.

12 Ad Hoc Group on the OECD Health Project (2004) *Towards a High-Performing Health System. Final report on the OECD Health Project.* OECD, Paris.

Chapter 12

Concluding reflections

Introduction

Earlier chapters have focused heavily on history. This final chapter attempts to identify lessons that may be of interest and relevance to current and future decision makers and analysts. The prime focus is future generations working in health policy analysis and particularly the Department of Health (or any successor), but some of the points about maximising the contribution of policy analysis may well be relevant to economists, operational researchers and statisticians working anywhere in the public sector.

The general reflections are grouped under the following three headings:

1 improving policy making
2 optimising the contribution of policy analysts
3 the future.

Each of these will be discussed in turn.

Improving policy making

If the NHS in 2005 is compared with the NHS in the early 1980s, one cannot help but be impressed by the scale and radicalism of the policy changes. For example, resourcing has doubled in real terms and risen by over one-third in terms of the share of an increasing national income. Likewise, patient responsiveness has moved from being something that was given lip-service but little else to become a central focus of the NHS which should have real bite with the expansion of patient choice. Similarly, performance measurement has expanded beyond inputs and activities to include outputs and, increasingly, clinical and patient service outcomes. Through the introduction of targets, standards and a host of new incentives, performance improvement has been transformed from a responsibility that was left largely to clinicians and relatively passive regional health authorities to one that is pursued actively at every level of health service management. And for all the talk of decentralisation, the setting of policy priorities and the degree of stretch required of service providers remain concentrated in the hands of the Department to a far greater extent than would have been thought conceivable in the early 1980s.

For analysts working on these changes at the time, their speed and radicalism often appeared much less impressive. Indeed, as is illustrated by previous chapters, a common reflection is to ask why change was so slow with regard, for example, to introducing systematic assessments of patient experiences, to moving beyond narrow measures of efficiency to measures of outcomes and a 'balanced scorecard', to extending rigorous approaches to the (ex-ante) appraisal of value for money across the bulk of healthcare policies, to adopting (ex-post) policy evaluation as the norm rather than the exception when new policies were being trialled, and to exposing to public scrutiny the Department's models assessing the demands for services and for additional public expenditure. Unsurprisingly, the reasons for this slowness varied from area to area. In some cases, for instance, it was primarily a question of the time it takes to develop and test new databases or analytical techniques, in others it reflected a need to change public and/or clinician attitudes, and in yet others it was a cost of frequent organisational and staff turnover both in the Department and in the NHS. Undoubtedly where the natural lead lay with the Department's analysts, I and my colleagues were also not always as persuasive as we might have been. However, looking back I am also struck by the ingrained conservatism of many Civil Service colleagues (perhaps a consequence of the emphasis in their training on protecting Ministers from short-term risk), and the preference of NHS managers for a quiet life. These added to the factors that dampened the pace at which new ideas were picked up, and led to most major changes during this period being initiated by Ministers.

Nevertheless, over the last 20 years healthcare policy making has generally become more evidence based and rigorous. This is a sweeping assertion but, given the large increase in national and international evidence and the growth of analytical resources within the Department of Health, it would point to gross inefficiencies if it was not true. However, if the average policy initiative is more likely to be adequately appraised for its costs, benefits and cost-effectiveness in 2005 than it was in 1985, there are still too many exceptions. In recent years the exceptions have partly reflected a failure to expand analytical capability in line with the number of new policy initiatives. However, they also reflect a steady raising of the bar used to define an 'adequate' appraisal. Most obviously there is now far more attention to implementation issues than was the case in the 1980s. Others have rightly pointed to the 'implementation gaps' that were a major feature of healthcare reforms (by both political parties) before 2000 – that is, the formally announced policy was not the same as the policy that was actually put into action.[1] The lessons from the 'implementation gap' and other disappointments in the 1980s and 1990s may seem commonplace, but they can still easily be overlooked, particularly with very rapid changes in staffing and organisational responsibilities within the Department.

Identifying important lessons from the last 20 years that may still not have been fully learned inevitably involves judgement. My personal list of the issues that should continue to be at the forefront of the Department's thinking includes the following.

1 Continually scrutinise the incentives for the public sector to improve efficiency and to focus on the patient.
2 Devote as much or more attention to changing NHS behaviours as to changing organisational structures and processes.
3 The direct and indirect costs of governance reforms should be assessed and quantified alongside their potential benefits.
4 Greater attention should be given to the skills, capabilities, incentives and time constraints of staff charged with the front-line management and delivery of new services or policies.

5 In particular, clinician incentives and objectives are nearly always critical to the success of reforms aimed at changing health service behaviours.

6 Policy makers at the centre should give more attention to human resource planning (and to other issues that require long-term planning).

7 The rapid dissemination of 'best practice' requires special transfer mechanisms.

8 Performance management should focus on rewarding success, not failure.

9 The power of hospitals to hold on to resources and patients should never be underestimated.

10 Developing smart purchasers or commissioners of care remains an aspiration rather than an achievement.

11 The policy and resource balance between prevention and health promotion on the one hand and treatment and care on the other should be regularly and rigorously reviewed.

12 Information systems should more actively support policy development and monitoring, and must be adequately resourced for this purpose.

13 Effective evidence-based policy making and implementation requires policy makers/managers to have some understanding of the contribution of analytical skills.

14 To speed up Departmental learning, recurrent policy-making and implementation processes should be captured in guidelines or templates that are actively promoted and monitored.

15 To further speed up Departmental learning, evaluation of significant policy and management initiatives should be made more automatic and supported by greater investment in disseminating findings.

Each of these issues will be discussed in turn.

Continually scrutinise the incentives for the public sector to improve efficiency and to focus on the patient

Critics of the public sector often claim that it is inefficient because it has no inherent incentives either to improve efficiency or to serve the public. Defendants of the sector argue that professional ethics and democratic participation will ensure that there is pressure to improve. The experience of the last 20 years suggests that in the health field this pressure will not be sufficient to generate improvements that keep up with public expectations.

Professional ethics might have been expected to generate pressures for change in the public provision of health services from three main groups, namely the medical profession, NHS managers, and Health Department civil servants. However, the major policy innovations of the last 20 years have not been advocated by any of these parties. The search for policies that offer greater patient responsiveness and choice – the key theme of the last 20 years – has been driven by politicians (of both parties). Similarly, politicians have led in recognising the need for strengthened incentives for clinicians and managers and for greater public accountability and transparency (e.g. through disclosure of quality indicators). In all of these areas old-style civil servants usually responded quite quickly and the medical professions more cautiously to the policy windows opened by politicians. The response of newer-style civil servant managers from the NHS often reflected a strong belief that the NHS should be protected from 'political interference'. In none of these areas can it be claimed that officials, the professions or NHS managers were actively pressing for political action.

Recognising that professional ethics places insufficient pressure on public-sector providers to improve their performance (particularly where there are conflicts of interest), the governments of the last two decades have sought ways to strengthen such incentives. A range of mechanisms has been tried, including greater voice for patients, public disclosure, performance monitoring, benchmarking, targets and standards, and financial incentives. Two of the most recent innovations (or re-inventions), namely choice and competition, clearly borrow directly from the 'inherent incentives' of well-functioning private markets. The jury is still out on which of these mechanisms, or more accurately what mix of them, will prove most effective in motivating publicly funded services to continually search for ways of improving both responsiveness and efficiency. However, what has been clearly demonstrated is that governments can no longer look to professional ethics together with a limited role for public voice as sufficient drivers for keeping the NHS in pace with public expectations.

Devote as much or more attention to changing NHS behaviours as to changing organisational structures and processes

Unless there are very sharp incentives, changing behaviours invariably takes much longer than changing organisational structures, and usually much longer than politicians expect. The internal market was a prime illustration of this. NHS trusts and GP fundholders were set up rapidly, but the majority of the new organisations were very slow to exercise their new freedoms.[2] Primary care trusts and practice-based commissioning are illustrating the point again. Implementation plans need to allow for these delays and to give as much or more attention to the training, mentoring and incentives needed to change behaviours as to the requirements for changing organisational structures.

Where sharp incentives are introduced (e.g. with the 'payment by results', the opening of healthcare markets to independent providers and the offering of choice to patients), the implications of those incentives, particularly the potential perverse effects, need to be very carefully thought through. Ideally, methods of minimising or regulating expected perverse effects should be developed before the new incentives come into play.

The direct and indirect costs of governance reforms should be assessed and quantified alongside their potential benefits

This applies to reforms proposed for the Department as well as for the NHS. Because of the relative ease of changing governance structures and processes, there is a tendency to see such reforms as a solution to any problem. The absence of a good evidence base for the relationship between organisational structures and public-sector performance appears not to discourage change but to make it all the more tempting to try something different or new. However, the setting up of new organisations or agencies, sometimes quickly followed by merger or replacement, has substantial costs both to the taxpayer and to the staff involved. Most importantly, there are costs to patients if the energies of healthcare managers and professionals are diverted to worrying about their jobs, seeking new ones, or setting up new organisations.

A favourite maxim of Len Peach, the second Chief Executive of the NHS Management Board, was that it was inadvisable to change the removal men when in the middle of moving house. He would probably have been the first to agree that there were exceptions – for example, if the furniture was not being moved! However, in recent years the proliferation of new health service agencies and the alacrity with which they have been built up, downsized and merged has sometimes suggested that changing the agents of change in the middle of the change process has become the norm rather than the exception. Careful attention to the costs of organisational change in terms of delays to service improvements – and sometimes even the worsening of services – would encourage greater attention to 'getting it right first time'. Sad to say, I cannot think of a single major reform of Departmental and NHS governance arrangements where the costs have been properly assessed before the decision was made to proceed.*

Like the adoption of new technologies or the introduction of new care standards, changes in governance are aimed at improving the effectiveness and efficiency of health services. They should be subject to the same expectations of an evidence base and rigorous appraisal as are other investments aimed at improving the public's health. To assist learning they should also be subject to the same regime of monitoring and ex-post evaluation.

Greater attention needs to be paid to the skills, capabilities, incentives and time constraints of staff charged with the front-line management and delivery of new services or policies

Most of the major organisational reforms of the last two decades have initially underestimated the front-line management skills required to implement them (and/or overestimated the current availability of those skills). One major reason has been the wish to keep administrative costs down. A second reason has been the chronic conservatism (until the last five years) of longer-term human resource planning for the NHS. A third reason has been the lack of any such planning for NHS management skills.† Over-optimism about local skill availabilities has delayed the realisation of benefits from many reforms, and lies behind some of the recent worries of the Audit Commission and the Commission for Health Improvement.[3,4] Improved systems are required for assessing the skills and capabilities of front-line staff in NHS trusts, primary care trusts and strategic health authorities if a more informed balance is to be struck between the number and complexity of central policy initiatives and the size and capability of local delivery staff.

Clinician incentives and objectives are nearly always critical to the success of reforms aimed at changing health service behaviours

This issue has long been given lip-service in the Department (as in the academic literature), but many policy initiatives have ignored it in practice. Examples include waiting-time initiatives and IT projects. The former often ignored the perverse incentives to co-operate faced by clinicians whose incomes were heavily

---

* One partial exception (partial because it was not strictly a governance reform) was the option appraisal of the 1990 decision to move the NHS Management Executive staff out of London.
† Before 2000 there was no attempt to relate the number of NHS management trainees to any formal estimates of the likely future demand for management skills in the NHS.

dependent on private practice generated by long waiting times. Similarly, IT projects were surprised by the unwillingness of hospital clinicians to co-operate with new systems where the costs in terms of the demands on their time exceeded their assessment of the likely benefits. There is more to be learned about the design of optimal incentive packages for clinicians, but a starting point should be recognition that most hospital doctors and GPs are already dependent on remuneration systems that are partly performance related. If governments wish the performance of doctors to change, they must be willing to reward the new forms of performance sufficiently to compensate for both the loss of freedom and the income forgone as a result of squeezing out old types of behaviour. The new GP and consultant contracts recognise this reality, although arguably the consultant contract does not give it enough weight.

Policy makers at the centre should give more attention to human resource planning (and to other issues that require long-term planning)

This follows on from the previous two points. It covers forecasting the demand for and supply of professional and management staff under various scenarios, assessing training and remuneration implications and identifying the most cost-effective ways of bridging gaps between supply and demand. The preparation of the NHS Plan revealed the extent to which the Department's capacity in these areas had been allowed to wither away. It also showed the limitations of decentralising responsibilities for human resource planning. Most disturbing was how few of the Departmental staff responsible for developing service policies had the skills necessary to estimate the human resource implications of the policies that they were putting to Ministers. The need to radically improve the Department's human resource planning skills was one of the key lessons to emerge from the process of putting together the NHS Plan in 2000.

The need to give greater attention to longer-term planning also applies to other issues, notably capital investment and research. In the past the absence of longer-term plans in these areas and of senior officials committed to championing the plans has encouraged the tendency of politicians – of all parties – to see cutting back capital spending (and research) as the easy option when resources are tight.

The rapid dissemination of 'best practice' requires special transfer mechanisms

The fragmented ways of working in healthcare (with clinicians in one primary care practice or hospital often unaware of how their behaviours and performance compare with those of colleagues in another) and the strength of the 'not invented here' syndrome in the NHS have both long been recognised. However, the development of what might be called 'best practice transfer mechanisms' is almost entirely a creation of the last 20 years. Favoured transfer mechanisms have moved through comparative data, publicity and guidebooks to centrally funded and led 'collaboratives', and on to the establishment of the Modernisation Agency and the new NHS Institute for Learning, Skills and Innovation and the host of technical assistance and self-help mechanisms that they currently deploy. Although the benefits of these approaches have sometimes been over-sold, there is now little doubt that they meet a real need, particularly in the absence of competitive markets (and indeed even if they existed). The issue is not whether mechanisms specifically aimed at the transfer of best practices are needed, but what mechanisms will achieve the transfer most efficiently.

Performance management (whether by the Department, the Regulator or the Healthcare Commission) should focus on rewarding success, not failure

Too many of the waiting-time initiatives of the 1980s and 1990s followed the opposite approach and allocated additional resources in line either with failure or with the promise of future good performance. In doing so they rewarded poor management and created perverse incentives. Laggards should, of course, continue to be assisted in improving their performance, but the assistance should be time limited, tied to changes in performance and backed up by commitments to change management or switch services if improvement is not forthcoming. The introduction of choice and payment by results, makes a hard headed approach all the more important.

The power of hospitals to hold on to resources and patients should never be underestimated

A common thread linking the development of GP fundholders, primary care groups, primary care trusts and now practice-based commissioning has been recognition by governments of both major parties that more services should be moved out of hospital and 'closer to home'. Given the limited knowledge of patients and the public and the limited information available to them, GPs and other primary care workers have been seen as best placed to act as their agents in commissioning and coordinating healthcare services. In practice, effective commissioning has been slow to develop. The size of many hospitals, their information and status advantages, the immobility of their clinicians and their importance to local communities have ensured that they have generally proved more than a match for the small and frequently reorganised primary care groups.

If primary care trusts and practice-based commissioning are to have a real influence on local health services, particularly secondary and tertiary care, it will be necessary to make continuing large investments in their skills and capabilities, to identify ways of re-engaging GP practices in service decisions,* and to allow practices and primary care trusts freedom to move resources away from traditional suppliers on the grounds of quality, cost-effectiveness or patient responsiveness. In broad terms these challenges have been recognised since the evaluations of the total purchasing pilots in the mid-1990s. However, effective action has lagged behind. Offering choice to patients and opening up hospital services to competition from both the public and private sectors should help to redress the balance. Encouraging clinicians to move between hospitals and to work outside them would also help.

Developing smart purchasers or commissioners of care remains an aspiration rather than an achievement

This issue is related to the previous point. Early in the 1990s the Department recognised that a market-like approach to the delivery of healthcare required an effective purchasing function that was able to reflect and respond to local

---

*The recent (October 2004) reintroduction of budgets for GPs should be helpful here.

population needs and to make difficult prioritisation decisions in the face of providers who had long enjoyed a large measure of monopoly power. Two models of purchasing were trialled, namely district health authorities and GP fundholding. By 1997 the second model was generally regarded as the more effective in terms of meeting patient needs, although it covered only half of the population, and its performance was patchy and was achieved at relatively high administrative cost. The new primary care groups and trusts were seen as a way of reducing administrative costs and expanding the benefits of fundholding to the whole population. To ensure continuing GP 'buy-in', the commissioning function was meant to be shared between the new primary care trusts and individual GP practices.[5] Unfortunately, between 1998 and 2004 the Department effectively lost sight of the role expected of GP practices.

The recent (2004) reassertion of the importance of devolving healthcare budgets to individual GP practices reflects a re-found belief that for many decisions the GP is more likely to have (or be able to develop) the specialised knowledge and incentives necessary to act as an efficient or smart agent for the patient (in other words, to exert real bargaining power) than is any other organisational unit yet devised.* I share this belief, but the hard evidence for it both nationally and internationally remains weak. The national evidence is unlikely to be accumulated until there is a degree of stability in commissioning structures.

The current emphasis on expanding patient choice and developing a 'patient-led service' implies placing less reliance on an agent for the patient, a GP or a health authority, and instead giving more power to the patient to directly determine what services are purchased and used. How many patients will be able and willing to exercise their new choices, and whether they will have access to information on provider quality that enables them to make well-informed choices remains to be seen. Some present plans for patient information point to long delays and a possible worsening of health inequalities – *see* Box 12.1.

Box 12.1 When will adequate information be available for patient choice? The example of colorectal cancer.

- Colorectal cancer is the second most common cause of cancer in the UK and over 30 000 new cases are reported each year. Survival rates are poor compared with other European countries and the USA. Surgery is the principle first line treatment.
- Research evidence suggests that there is 'wide variability in outcomes achieved by individual surgeons, with large differences in both perioperative and long term survival rates'.[6]
- However the public currently (summer 2005) has no access to any quantitative information on the comparative performance of either particular hospitals or individual consultants.
- Since 1999 the National Bowel Cancer Audit Project has been attempting to collect information on risk adjusted comparative performance. The latest information on the project's web site:

---

* I am grateful to Ray Robinson for pointing out that no other major country has so far accepted this idea, although several have toyed with it from time to time.

- covers only one third of colorectal cases in the UK
- relates to 2001–2
- and is not disaggregated by hospital, clinical unit or surgeon.[7]
- The project organisers hope some of the disaggregated data may be sufficiently robust to be accessed by the general public in 2006. But access will require patients to contact the local trust through the Chief Executive and Clinical Audit Committee. The information provided will relate to clinical units not individual surgeons, will initially probably cover only one aspect of performance and will be confined to indicating whether the unit's performance falls below agreed national standards. Initially, data will also be confined to units that have voluntarily cooperated in the audit. But, in time, cruder data on outcomes covering all units should be accessible via linking DH Hospital Episode Statistics (HES) and mortality data.
- There is no reason to believe that the position on colorectal cancer is worse than for other major cancers. On present plans all cancer patients are clearly going to have to wait some time before their choice of hospital, let alone of consultant, can be said to be well informed. And the proposed hurdles surrounding access to information could worsen health inequalities.

The policy and resource balance between prevention and health promotion on the one hand and treatment and care on the other should be regularly and rigorously reviewed

There are strong political, information and incentive arguments for expecting governments to under-invest in prevention and health promotion relative to treatment and care. These help to explain why the second Wanless Report[8] represents the first attempt in at least the last 20 years to address the issue of balance head on. Major shifts in resources will (probably) need to await the results of research that is only now being set in hand into the effectiveness and cost-effectiveness of new types of assistance to prevention and health promotion. In future the balance should be regularly reviewed – risk factor by risk factor and disease area by disease area – to take account of the findings of emerging research, both domestic and international.

Information systems should more actively support policy development and monitoring, and must be adequately resourced for this purpose

Departmental and NHS information systems have too often been 'off the pace', reporting on yesterday's concerns rather than today's. One contributing factor has undoubtedly been the isolation of the Department's statisticians from mainstream policy making. Although there were many attempts to develop new information strategies, usually by employing outside consultants, limited direct exposure to the policy thinking of senior managers and Ministers meant that statisticians were sometimes slow to pick up warning signs of changing needs. Continuing battles over statistical probity – with Ministers from both parties – also distracted attention from emerging needs. Where new needs were recognised, the costs of reform might be seen as too high, either by the statisticians or by their policy colleagues. Whatever the precise cause, recognised major information gaps, such as quantifying shifts of traditional hospital-based services to primary care settings, went unmet for years.

A second major weakness of the NHS information systems managed by the Department has been the very limited attention given to simple analysis and user-friendly presentations. Up until 2002 the Department never published regular commentaries on the statistical series that it produced, and internal analyses were intermittent at best. As a consequence, it has sometimes been slow to recognise new developments and changes in trend. In the mid-1990s, for example, inflation of the number of 'finished consultant episodes' (caused by changes in hospital or consultant practice) was for some years misinterpreted as a real acceleration in hospital emergency admissions. There was similar late recognition of the slowing down in the reduction of the average length of hospital stay. More recently there has been under-investment in the development of user-friendly presentations of service performance that would aid patients and the public in holding local providers to account (and latterly in choosing between them).

Looking ahead, the solution is probably twofold – first, to integrate statisticians more closely with policy divisions (as is now in hand), and secondly, to devote greater resources to producing regular analysis of and commentaries on the Department's major information series. Given the low level of public confidence in government statistics, the latter functions should probably be given to an independent body somewhat akin to the Canadian Institute for Health Information. From this perspective it looks sensible to establish the new Health Information Centre as a special health authority outside the Department.

Effective evidence-based policy making and implementation requires policy makers/managers to have some understanding of the contribution of analytical skills

A review of analysis and modelling set up in the light of experience writing the NHS Plan in 2000 drew particular attention to the need for analytically aware customers in policy and management divisions. Within these divisions, pressure of work, restructuring, rapid staff turnover and accompanying loss of institutional memory were found to have hindered joint working between analysts and policy colleagues. In some cases, by impeding recognition of the need for analytical support and/or research evidence, these problems led to delays or substantial weaknesses either in submissions to Ministers or in published reports. The review recommended that basic analytical training should be introduced for non-analysts in policy and management divisions, and that the ability to commission and use appropriate analysis should be a minimum requirement for promotion to all posts at junior management level and above. At the time of writing it is not clear whether this recommendation has been implemented.

Analytical literacy should now also be seen as a basic skill requirement of the most senior posts in the Department. Complexity, evidence and analysis are so central to the policy and management issues facing the Department that in a sense they have become too important to be left to a relatively small group of professional analysts. The Department's most senior managers need the skills and the mindsets to be able to grapple with these issues themselves.

To speed up Departmental learning, recurrent policy-making and implementation processes should be captured in guidelines or templates that are actively promoted and monitored

An implicit emphasis on 'learning by doing' may just about have been defensible when most managers served long apprenticeships in the Department and often worked in the same policy or management areas for many years. It became a sure recipe for reinventing wheels once the pace of organisational change picked up and there was increasing reliance on recruits from the NHS and outside the Department. In recognition of these changed circumstances, the 2000 review of analysis and modelling recommended that the Department should capture its policy and analytical learning through the development and regular updating of sets of guidelines or templates. These could be in either electronic or hard-copy form. National Service Frameworks (NSFs) are a good example of a repetitive activity where enshrining experience in guidelines would be helpful to future policy makers. The potential value of such guidance was recognised early in the development of NSFs, and was reportedly endorsed by a review of policy making in 2003. Other areas identified as suitable for templates or guidelines by the 2000 review included policy appraisals, assessing human resource implications, identifying appropriate methods for obtaining information, and the use of spreadsheets.

In 2004 the Department established a Policy Hub with the aim, inter alia, of promoting good policy making. It is encouraging that it has developed a Policy Tool Kit, has expanded the formal coverage of Regulatory Impact Assessments to cover all major policy initiatives (not just those with an impact on the private sector) and has reissued a revised version of the guidance on 'Policy Appraisal and Health' originally developed by the Department's economists and published in 1996. The earlier experience with 'Policy Appraisal and Health' (it was arguably more influential in other departments than in the Department of Health) highlights how important it will be for the Policy Hub to actively promote and monitor the use of its new tools.

To further speed up Departmental learning, evaluation of significant policy and management initiatives should be made more automatic and supported by greater investment in disseminating findings

Although the use of formative and ex-post evaluation to accelerate learning from experience has grown enormously in the last 20 years, the coverage of significant management and policy changes is still not as routine as it should be, and the planning of studies often starts too late to facilitate early learning. There is still under-investment in disseminating the lessons both within the Department and in the NHS. Rapid changes in staff and organisational responsibilities – and the consequent loss of institutional memory – make investment in the dissemination function all the more necessary.

Optimising the contribution of policy analysts

Over the last 20 years the Department's analysts can reasonably claim to have made a significant contribution to health service policy making. The contribution can be illustrated in summary form in terms of the stages of the policy cycle (*see* Box 12.2).

Box 12.2 The contribution of Economics and Operational Research Division (EOR) to the policy cycle: an illustrative summary

It is common to identify five stages in the policy cycle:[9]

1 agenda setting
2 policy formulation
3 decision making
4 policy implementation
5 policy evaluation.

Over the period under consideration the EOR has contributed to all five stages. The contribution was probably most significant for agenda setting, decision making and policy evaluation.

- *Agenda setting (problem recognition).* Areas where the Department was helped to recognise emerging problems or opportunities included the ageing population, patient feedback, improved access to services, hospital capacity constraints, self-care, perverse consultant incentives, and the inefficiency of national pay levels. In all of these areas pressure from analysts speeded up the adoption of new ideas and policies.
- *Policy formulation (identification of solutions).* The EOR's key contribution in this area was one of challenge – to suggest that there *are* alternative solutions and to assist in identifying them. For the alternatives it drew on knowledge of international health systems and of practice in the private sector, and on systems thinking. One example is the promotion of NHS Direct (and later digital TV) as new solutions to the issue of healthcare access. Another example is the National Beds Inquiry, where international experience was used to argue that there were three feasible scenarios, namely maintaining current direction, building up numbers of hospital beds, and building up intermediate care services to promote care closer to home.
- *Decision making (choice of solution).* The EOR has been a strong advocate of the rational or optimising model of decision making. Arguably its greatest achievement was to expand the use of systematic methods of appraisal, and particularly of cost-effectiveness, across most areas of central decision making. It also made major contributions to the more equitable allocation of resources and to the development of systems thinking. To support rational decision-making it initiated or supported major research programmes on, for example, QALYs.
- *Policy implementation (putting policies into effect).* The EOR led major piloting exercises in relation to NHS Direct and digital TV. However, its more common role was to push for attention to critical components of policy

---

implementation, notably proper costing, human resource assessment and monitoring. It was also a major supplier of project planning skills.

- *Policy evaluation (assessing how the policy is working)*. Over many years the EOR was the 'product champion' of policy evaluation within the Department. It also played a leadership role in developing a balanced-scorecard approach to monitoring the performance of health authorities, NHS trusts and primary care organisations.

How was this contribution achieved? The purpose of this section is to highlight some of the key lessons that I have drawn from 20 years of trying to optimise the contribution of analysis to policy making and policy. Many of the lessons were learned from my analytical colleagues. Others were learned from policy customers or senior managers and mentors. Some were learned far too late, and not all were practised as regularly as they should have been. Nevertheless, on reflection I think that they all helped to improve the EOR's influence. Hopefully, some will strike chords with analysts wishing to increase their influence in the health field in the future.

The lessons are organised under three headings, namely attitudes, skills and organisational arrangements.

Attitudes

Like other people, analysts want to do a good job. Given the demanding selection criteria of the Government Economic Service, Operational Research Service and Statistical Service, successful candidates can normally be assumed to have the required technical skills in their disciplinary areas. However, a range of other attitudes and skills are necessary in order to be effective as analysts in the Department of Health (and in other public-sector organisations). In my view, six attitudes are particularly important determinants of the influence both of individual analysts and of an internal analytical unit. These will each be discussed in turn.

Customer focus

Analysts are employed by government departments to improve the quality of public decision making. The key criteria for judging the success of an internal analytical unit should therefore be first the proportion of major departmental policy and management issues to which it is contributing, and secondly the value that it is adding or the difference it is making to decisions on those issues. These criteria require analysts to focus on the concerns of departmental decision makers – the officials who act as policy leads and Ministers. They are the analysts' customers, and their confidence must be gained if analysts are to be invited to the party.

Analysts are no different from other professionals in being inclined to give preference to the tools and techniques in which they are skilled rather than to focus on the problems and perceptions of their customers. However, a sure way of being sidelined in a public department is to be seen as the advocate of a particular analytical technique or tool regardless of the nature of the problem. Effective analysts get close to their customers, attempt to understand and empathise with their views of the world and work to gain their confidence. Without customer confidence, internal analysts are powerless. This is an obvious truism, but one that is surprisingly easily forgotten by some analysts who, when their advice is ignored, conclude that it is the customers, not they, who need to adjust or adapt.

Building up knowledge of customers and gaining their trust requires an investment of time and thought. It may also require an initial willingness to say 'yes' to even the most trivial request. The EOR followed a conscious policy of agreeing to requests for simple pieces of analytical work (often of a kind that the customers should have been able to do for themselves) in order to open doors for commissions on more central issues. Gaining customer confidence also requires an ability to communicate – both orally and in writing – in the customer's language. More ideas for good analysis have probably been lost because they were expressed in language that turned off the customer than for any other reason.

Analysts who want to gain and retain influence must always be aware that customers can walk away. In government departments it can be hard to remain conscious of this and to avoid complacency, especially in periods when contracting out or staff cuts are not on the agenda. Regular customer surveys are one way of creating internal pressures to do better. Another is for senior analysts to continually remind colleagues that they should emulate competitive markets in the time and effort that they devote to customer relations.

Anticipation and flexibility

Good policy analysis often takes time, and many policy leads in the Department still have little understanding of what policy analysts can contribute. For both of these reasons a key responsibility of analysts is to proactively look for policy issues coming over the horizon and to volunteer assistance rather than waiting to be asked. A reactive approach leads to the loss of many opportunities to influence policies. Responses that are slow in the sense of missing deadlines are even more likely to be ineffectual. An effective analyst needs to balance her current work programme with keeping an eye on emerging issues. She must also be willing to reprioritise very rapidly, sometimes literally overnight, if analytical windows open up that are more central to key Ministerial goals than current work activities. This can be stressful, particularly for analysts who have become heavily committed to their current work.

In major Government departments there are always policies under active review. In periods of radical reform the agenda can change extraordinarily rapidly. To keep up with Ministerial ambitions and to be seen to be helpful rather than 'part of the problem', analysts must be willing to reprioritise their work programmes at very short notice. Effective internal analysts do not in general have the luxury of academics in being able to follow a particular line of work for many years. Given the pervasive interest in 'make-or-buy' choices, internal analysts who attempt to hang on to yesterday's areas of policy or political interest will rapidly find themselves bypassed, if not redundant. The advice of management gurus is often clichéd and obvious, but there were two phrases that were taken to heart by EOR managers during this period and were used as guides to action. These were the importance of the division being 'chunkable' (or capable of rapid redeployment) and of analysts collectively and individually being seen as 'fast, friendly, flexible and focused'.[10]

Patience and persistence

In the words of one of the Department's senior policy analysts, 'in analysis all things come to pass, given sufficient time'. Just as policy windows need to open for issues to come on to the policy agenda,[11] so analytical windows need to open for new forms of analysis to be seen as relevant. By being close to customers and demonstrating the attitudes and skills discussed in this section, analysts can do much to influence the opening of these windows. However, there is sometimes no alternative to patience and persistence (*see* Box 12.3 on coordinating healthcare and social security expenditures). The persistent advocating of ideas may be necessary in order to wear down resistance or to build up a critical mass of supporters. Patience is often necessary until problems come to be seen as compelling, or until the arrival of a new Chief Executive or Minister provides a more receptive environment. Given the range of other actors wanting a share in health service policy making, and the speed with which many of them change, it is not surprising that patience and persistence proved to be two of the most important determinants of the EOR's analytical contribution to the Department.

Box 12.3 Patience and persistence: coordinating healthcare and social security expenditure

1 In the mid-1980s, DHSS economists drew attention to the faster growth in social security expenditure on sickness and disability benefits than in health service expenditure. They asked whether the right balance was being struck between spending on palliative cash benefits and the treatment or rehabilitation of incapacitated people. Senior management decided not to pursue the issue, in part because social security expenditure was demand led and there was no great pressure to cap it.

2 At the beginning of the 1990s, after the split with the DHSS, Department of Health economists raised the issue again. Once more no action was taken, perhaps because the Department of Social Security now saw little virtue in redirecting social security funds to support the actions of another department.

3 In 1998, Department of Health economists returned to the charge. This time they were armed with the encouraging results of a 5-year Swedish experiment with shifting resources from social security to healthcare (the FINSAM project). The experiment found that total public expenditure and sickness-benefit days could be reduced if a proportion of sickness-benefit monies was used to buy healthcare and rehabilitation for social-security recipients. Against a background of rapidly rising UK expenditure on short- and long-term sickness benefits, Health Ministers were persuaded to pay a visit to Sweden to study the local experience in more detail.

4 In 2002, the Department of Health and the Department for Work and Pensions (the successor to the Department of Social Security) launched a collaborative initiative, the Job Rehabilitation and Retention Pilots (JRRP). Employed people who are in danger of becoming long-term sickness or disability recipients are being assigned extra rehabilitative

> healthcare services and advice. The Department's economists have contributed to the design and evaluation of the pilots. An evaluation report is expected in autumn 2005.

Realism about problem solving

Analysts who believe that all problems should be solved by using optimising methodologies and that the solution should be fully supported by the evidence can quickly become disillusioned when faced with the reality of public-sector decision making. Ministers and senior managers take a range of approaches to policy making and naturally adjust their approach to the political, time and resource constraints facing them. Although economists and operational researchers should always push for quantification of the appropriate range of costs and benefits for different options, they need to recognise that the rigour of 'quantification' and the meaning of 'appropriate' will depend on the circumstances facing decision makers. Realism should also extend to acknowledging that evidence and analysis never make decisions, they only inform them. Analysts should always try to improve the quality of decision making, but realism about the process is essential if personal motivation and work satisfaction are to be maintained.

Appropriate level of sophistication

Sophisticated techniques may impress academic colleagues, but they can lose the support of policy customers. Internal analysts often add most value by providing relatively simple analytical frameworks, such as the explicit specification of objectives, the identification, quantification and appraisal of costs and benefits, and the use of clear criteria for decision making. Because they are more readily understood by policy leads and managers, in many circumstances such simple tools can have more impact than, for example, stochastic frontier estimation of hospital cost functions. This is not an argument for avoiding sophisticated techniques where they can add value. It is an argument for matching the techniques with the analytical understanding and confidence of customers who are expected to act on them. The level of understanding of analytical techniques among public service customers is rising, but much more slowly than I had anticipated 20 years ago. It has taken roughly that period for the QALY (quality-adjusted life year) to become broadly acceptable to most health service policy makers. Using monetary valuations of life to compare policy options may now be strongly favoured by economists,[12] but it is still not acceptable to many health policy makers and politicians.

Corporate spirit

The size of major government departments, the frequency with which they are reorganised and the rapidity of policy changes all mean that small support units need sensitive antennae, good information-sharing mechanisms and flexible working practices if they are to stay focused on the key concerns of Ministers. Information sharing and co-operative work practices are encouraged by a strong corporate spirit with everybody committed to working towards the same goals.

Over the period under consideration a major source of the EOR's strength was its corporate spirit.* This was in part encouraged by adversity. The physical split between London and Leeds and the reporting split between the NHS Management Executive and the rest of the Department threatened the unit's continued existence. The threats were overcome by the development of formal and informal arrangements for collaboration and communication across the division, and particularly between Leeds and London. These arrangements included away-days, joint working parties and staff exchanges. Such was their success that the EOR reasonably claimed to be part of the 'glue' that held the Department together during the years in the 1990s when relationships between the NHS Executive and the rest of the Department were particularly poor.

A corporate spirit was also engendered by a general belief that there was huge scope to improve the quality of Departmental decision making and that, given the small number of analysts and the size of the Department, success required all analysts to support each other. A third element was the initiative of individual members of the EOR in developing a range of social programmes that rapidly became annual fixtures, including annual cycle rides around London and annual weekend walks in the Yorkshire Dales. Through their contribution to internal trust, communication and flexibility, these activities all assisted the EOR to add value to the Department out of proportion to the Division's numerical size.

Skills

In addition to sound technical skills and knowledge in their respective disciplines, there are a number of other skills that are either essential or desirable if analysts are to maximise their contribution to policy and management decisions. Four skill sets are in my view particularly important. These will each be discussed in turn.

Policy knowledge

Effective analysis usually requires a good understanding of the policy area. Without understanding of the perceived policy problem, the political imperatives and constraints, the main actors and the relevant evidence base, an analyst is unlikely to command the confidence of policy leads. In some areas these requirements are more demanding than others. For example, if the challenge is to identify cost-effective interventions for a National Service Framework, it will also be necessary to have a good grasp of the main clinical interventions and to be able to discuss the evidence base for them with clinicians. The requirement can also change over time. For example, in recent years in parts of the Department rapid staff turnover (a product of constant organisational change and downsizing) meant that analysts developed greater knowledge of particular policy areas than the policy leads they were meant to advise.

---

* 'The one thing I found amazing when I joined EOR from an academic background was its corporate nature – it was such a pleasant surprise to be part of an organisation where everyone was working towards the same goals, was so willing to help each other out and interested in what their colleagues were doing.' Personal communication from Maria Goddard, Deputy Director, York Centre for Health Economics, June 2004.

Confidence building

In Whitehall, analysts generally act as advisers. Outside any personnel management roles they will only rarely (arguably too rarely) have executive responsibilities. This means that their power depends on their ability to influence first their civil servant colleagues with policy lead responsibilities, and secondly the Ministers who take the final decisions. Influence depends on gaining the confidence of the officials and Ministers who have decision-making powers. In my experience perhaps the commonest touchstone used by policy colleagues on selection panels in judging the quality of analysts was the question 'Would I have confidence in the advice offered by this person?'.

Gaining the confidence of official and Ministerial colleagues requires analytical skills and policy knowledge, but it also requires ability to communicate, interpersonal skills and political sensitivity. Such skills are necessary for all analysts, but they are most important for senior analysts whose responsibilities include opening doors for analysis into areas where it has previously not been seen. They are critical skills for chief analysts.

At the end of the day the contribution and influence of an analytical unit will depend on whose confidence it has been able to gain. All analytical units need to maintain the confidence of their line manager and (usually) of the departmental chief executive/permanent secretary. However, their influence is likely to be greatest when they have the ear of Ministers, particularly Secretaries of State. In the 20 years up to 2002 the EOR enjoyed the particular trust of three of the seven Secretaries of State, namely Norman Fowler, Virginia Bottomley and Alan Milburn. From time to time they also had very close relationships with a number of political advisers and more junior ministers. These relationships enabled the EOR to get a seat at the decision-making table (which was usually in a Minister's office). Analytical advice could then be fed in directly without filtering by the officials with formal policy lead responsibilities.

Senior civil servants and NHS managers are jealous of their hierarchical positions, and the less confident among them tend to want to keep meetings with Ministers as their own preserve. However, so long as many policy issues remain poorly analysed and proposed solutions are not rigorously appraised, internal analysts should strive for a place at the decision-making table. This requires gaining the confidence of Ministers and their political advisers.

Market research/problem seeking

To be in a position to anticipate policy or management problems, analysts need to actively look for weaknesses and emerging problems in the policy area for which they have responsibility. This process is helped by building up awareness of (and contact with) the work of academics and think tanks in the relevant subject area. The scanning should extend to the international scene. Analysis of recent trends can also often assist in the early identification of problems.

Marketing

The effective analyst must be willing and able to market himself to those he is expected to influence. Decision makers who do not understand what is meant by 'operational research' or who have made decisions or offered advice for many years without using economists will invariably need some persuading that these disciplines have relevance to their day-to-day responsibilities. Careful thought should be given to how best to present what analysts can 'bring to the party'. This contribution will need to be actively communicated, usually most effectively through face-to-face (and often one-to-one) meetings. As in other fields, the effective marketeer will seek out his customers and attempt to understand their likes and dislikes.

In addition to the skills that are 'essential' for all effective analysts, there are others that I came to see as highly desirable, particularly for more senior analysts. Three that are especially valuable are lateral knowledge, networking and the challenge role.

Lateral knowledge

Analysts can often widen the range of options and deepen the evidence base by knowledge of relevant experience in other countries or other sectors, including the private sector. Comparisons of these kinds – a type of benchmarking – are one of the most potent ways of challenging incrementalism and conservative thinking. Building lateral knowledge should be seen as a critical skill for senior analysts with management and leadership roles.

Networking

There are a large number of powerful 'agents' seeking active involvement in policy making in the healthcare field. In addition to Ministers and the formal Departmental policy leads, it is usually necessary to engage clinicians and NHS managers. In recent years the growing influence of political advisers and the proliferation of special agencies has added to the complexity of what is sometimes called the 'policy sub-system'. For analysts, the proliferation of policy stakeholders can make influencing decisions more complicated and time consuming. However, it also generates more potential allies who may be open to new analytical ideas.

Over most of the period under consideration the Treasury was a particularly supportive 'lever' for opening up issues to more rigorous analysis. Treasury officials (and sometimes their Ministers) were important allies to internal analysts both by promoting analytical and evaluative frameworks across the public sector[13] and by highlighting specific health service issues that required more detailed analysis. In some cases support of the latter kind was ventriloquised by Departmental analysts. Later in the period, special advisers became powerful allies of internal analysts because of a common interest in identifying radical solutions and improving the analytical rigour of Departmental decision making.* As actors change and organisational responsibilities are redefined, the sources of support and partnership will also evolve. A critical task for analytical leaders in the Department is to identify and network with the key policy entrepreneurs and policy actors with an interest in improving decision making.

Clinicians both inside and outside the Department are central to effective health service decision making. Earlier chapters have referred to particular Departmental doctors who were important allies in the search for ways of

---

* Simon Stevens was a particularly influential and helpful ally both as adviser to Alan Milburn and subsequently as health adviser to Tony Blair.

improving the prioritisation, appraisal and evaluation of health service policies. The growth in the number of distinguished doctors who have been brought in to act as 'czars' or leaders in key areas, such as cancer and emergency care, suggests that working with medical leaders will be even more important in the future than it has been in the past.

The challenge role

In the past, one justification for having a significant group of analysts within the Department was that they could draw on their analytical disciplines and specific knowledge to challenge and broaden the range of policy options put before Ministers. In the 1990s, at least one Permanent Secretary (Sir Graham Hart) saw this challenge role as the EOR's most important contribution to the Department. The move towards more open and consultative government may reduce the value of the internal challenge function. However, so long as Ministers wish to initiate consideration of policy agendas and identification of policy options in conditions of confidence there will be a role for internal analysts to challenge Departmental conventional thinking, to question assertions that 'there is no alternative', and to dispute the inclination of policy leads to foretell what options will be acceptable to Ministers and choke off alternatives at too early a stage.

For the challenge role to be given full reign requires one or more senior analysts to develop a close and trusting relationship with the Secretary of State. Three of the Secretaries of State with whom we worked during this period actively encouraged alternative views and would look to the EOR to supply them. This could be an uncomfortable experience for senior officials whose views might be disputed. However, wise colleagues accepted the value of the challenge function so long as Ministers found it helpful. Some Permanent Secretaries and Chief Executives also found it helpful to have an alternative perspective, and on occasion asked for the EOR's views alongside those of the formal policy leads. Such high-level support naturally gave analysts more freedom to exercise the challenge function at lower levels in the Department.

Examples of areas in which analysts successfully took the lead in championing alternative policies include the following:

- the introduction of a system of Payment by Results for hospitals
- the introduction of regular patient experience surveys
- the development of self-care initiatives. including the NHS Direct Digital TV Service
- delayed hospital discharge reimbursement system based on the Scandinavian model
- formal evaluations of total purchasing pilots and of the Health of the Nation.

These alternative options may not always have given Ministers better answers, but they certainly helped to provide them with a richer menu from which to choose.

There are a series of small but important steps that should be taken by officials in the Department of Health (and in other Civil Service departments) to ensure that in future Ministers continue to be presented with a wide range of well thought out options. These include the following.

- Use the most knowledgeable officials to provide oral (and written) briefing, not the most senior ones. This will usually give greater exposure to analysts.
- Present Ministers with alternative options, not a 'single departmental view' (Ministers who insist on a single view should recognise that they are putting public funds – and their reputations – at unnecessarily high risk).
- Allow contestability in advice until Ministerial views are clear.
- In briefing and presentations, attribute analyses to their authors so that the analysts are recognised (by Ministers) and can be held to account.
- Reward rigour and objectivity in advice above 'what Ministers want to hear'.
- Reward innovative ideas and forward thinking.

Many Civil Service managers and policy leads recognise the importance of these steps and practise them. Others see them as threatening to their position and particularly to their relationships with Ministers. All should be encouraged and incentivised to implement them as necessary steps towards improved policy making.

Organisational arrangements

In addition to attitudes and skills, a third major set of factors affecting the influence of analysts concerns organisational arrangements. This term is used to cover both administrative procedures or formal ways of working and the organisation of analysts within the Departmental structure. In terms of administrative procedures, a particularly powerful way of ensuring a role for analysis is the institutionalising of that role.

Institutionalising the role of analysis and/or analysts

Enshrining economics or operational research methodologies as formal procedures for assessing new health technologies or policies is an obvious way of strengthening the role of analysis. For capital projects, the building of option appraisal into a capital projects manual and the linked Treasury requirement that Departmental economists should contribute to the sign-off of large new capital projects was a good way of institutionalising the role of economics. Establishment of the National Institute for Clinical Excellence with a mandate to assess clinical guidelines and new technologies from an economics perspective, is another illustration of how this role can be institutionalised, although in this case it was moved out of the Department into an agency. Treasury insistence that National Service Frameworks (NSFs) incorporate assessments of the cost-effectiveness of proposed policies is a further example of the scope for institutionalising the analytical role. (Given the sometimes cavalier way in which this requirement for NSFs has been met, it also illustrates the limitations of such formal requirements. If officials or Ministers are determined to ignore them, any set of formal procedures can be honoured in the letter but not the spirit.)

In some cases, Departmental procedures may not require the involvement of a particular analytical discipline, but they may call for the participation of particular Departmental analysts. For example, Departmental working parties on resource allocation and on forecasting and modelling usually require the participation, sometimes in a chairing role, of one or more of the Department's analysts. Recent work on identifying a new approach to the measurement of productivity in the health sector provides a further illustration – it has been chaired by the Chief Economic Adviser.

Organisation of analysts

Joint working between specialists and policy leads is essential to ensure the integration of anlysis with policy making and to ensure that policy making is evidence based.[13] Virtuous circles arise from joint working. The provision of data and analysis leads to more policy questions being asked, and this in turn leads to a demand for further data and more informed analysis. These virtuous circles can be encouraged by organising analysts in various ways. Two common models have been used in the Department (and the rest of Whitehall). First, analysts can be 'bedded out' within policy branches, with budgets for analytical resources and line-management responsibility resting with senior policy colleagues. Secondly, analysts can be physically co-located with other professional colleagues with budgets and line management in the hands of senior analysts, but working day to day with policy teams. In the 20 years up to 2003, both models were used, although the second one was more common.

The first model has the highest degree of integration with policy advice (because of the day-to-day contact), and can transfer analytical skills to colleagues from different backgrounds. However, it can be inflexible (it is administratively difficult to take analysts out of a policy team to service a different policy need as priorities change) and it may also compromise quality in the long term (because analysts are not directly managed by professionals who can monitor the quality of the advice provided and share ideas). It has also been found that analysts tend to be assimilated into policy work and can lose their capacity to question and challenge the mainstream thinking of senior colleagues and Ministers.

The second model provides a good compromise between integration and quality control, although it is imperative that the senior analysts keep in close touch with the latest policy thinking in order to remain influential and avoid gaining an 'ivory-tower' reputation. Analysts working under this model can learn from one another and be managed by one another, while still working for 90% of the time with policy teams.

The balance that is struck between these two models may partly depend on the number of analysts. Over most of the 20 years under consideration there were far more policy areas requiring the continuing or occasional use of analysts than there were analysts employed by the Department. It was therefore physically impossible for most policy branches to have their own dedicated analyst. Brigading the analysts into central teams and being willing and able to flex analytical resources between policy areas as priorities changed therefore represented an appropriate and efficient model of deployment. For most of the 1980s and 1990s the EOR was probably the most 'chunkable' or flexible part of the whole Department. One consequence was that it was able to find staff to contribute to new reviews, such as *Working for Patients* and the NHS Plan, faster than any other part of the organisation. This organisational flexibility was a main reason why the EOR was able to contribute to such a high proportion of the major policy reviews over this period.

After the end of the period covered in this book, senior management decided to make the bedding out of analysts within policy branches the predominant organisational model. The downsizing of the Department relative to the number of analysts makes this option more feasible. However, care will need to be taken to ensure that it does not lead to loss of analytical flexibility and failures to switch the focus of analytical effort as policy imperatives change. There will also need to be adequate arrangements for continuing professional development and peer support if analytical standards and the challenge function are to be maintained.

A third model for providing analytical input to policy decisions involves commissioning work from academic departments and private consultants. In this period, considerable use was made of both sources of external expertise. Academic units that kept up with the ever-changing policy context and were willing to respond to requests for rapid research, analysis and advice proved an increasingly valuable source of input to Departmental decision making. The Centre for Health Economics at York was an outstanding example of this. Unfortunately, in health economics only a minority of academic units showed an interest in getting close enough to policy thinking and being willing to respond with sufficient speed to serve as useful sources of advice and analysis on the majority of national issues with short time horizons. This lack of responsiveness left the door open for consultancy firms. Their use has reportedly grown greatly since 2000.*

The future

The literature on public policy argues that the appropriateness and rationality of public decision-making styles depend on the nature of the environment.[14] Similarly, the form, style and role of analysis will also have to change as the policy environment changes.

Over the 20 years considered in this book the Department's economists and operational researchers showed great flexibility in responding to radical environmental changes, both in the content of policy and in the organisation of the Department. The environment for analysis can be expected to continue to evolve. One change that is already under way is the shift from co-locating analysts with their fellow professionals to bedding them out with customers. Another is the declared intention to shift NHS decision making away from the centre. A third change is the greater use of arm's-length agencies within the centre, even though their numbers are now being rationalised. A fourth change is the increasingly dominant role of recruits from the NHS and the private sector at the top of the Department. These and other changes pose different challenges to the analytical services – for example, to remain flexible and rigorous while bedded out, to develop analytical tools to assist local decision makers, to network with the key arm's-length agencies so that analytical wheels are not reinvented, and to convince managers who may not be used to working with analysts that decision making will be improved by understanding the problem, identifying alternative solutions, rigorously assessing both costs and benefits, and monitoring and evaluating the results.

Alongside the organisational changes is a continually evolving analytical

---

*In the past, concern about the cost and cost-effectiveness of consultancies led to a requirement that EOR should consider plans for all major new analytical studies to assess whether they could cost-effectively be done in-house. This requirement appears to have lapsed.

agenda. For example, on the *resourcing* of the NHS there is the issue of what rate of expenditure increase can be warranted and justified (given the opportunity costs) once current commitments come to an end in 2008. There will also be the challenge of how to bring public (and NHS) expectations and service expansion in line with the slower growth in health expenditure that is almost inevitable well before the end of this decade. Part of this challenge may be to identify mechanisms for ensuring that the payment-by-results system does not overinflate hospital activity. Another part may be to develop commissioners of care who have the knowledge and bargaining power necessary to manage demand and to switch it towards more cost-effective care settings outside hospitals, a task that has been on the Department's agenda for 15 years but which has so far seen only limited progress.

There is an equally challenging agenda in relation to *effectiveness*. One issue that is gaining new prominence is how far and how fast to shift resources from treatment to prevention and public health. Another is how to identify ineffective practices and treatments, and more particularly how to develop arguments that will convince Ministers and the public that NHS funding for them should be phased out. A third issue should be learning lessons about the effectiveness and efficiency of NSFs as instruments for improving treatment and outcomes in key disease areas.

In relation to *equity*, some of the issues are hardy perennials, such as how best to reduce avoidable health inequalities. However, others are relatively new, such as how choice can be used to narrow inequalities rather than to widen them.

Responsiveness raises questions about what level and types of choice can be afforded in a publicly funded health system, and what will be the cost of the degree of choice already proposed. It also raises questions about what new information will need to be developed and how it should be presented in order to optimise patient choice. There are further major issues concerning the acceptable trade-off between individual choice and system efficiency. Patient choice also raises questions about the future role of service commissioners.

Finally, under the heading of *efficiency* there are questions about how to improve measurement, particularly by incorporating changes in the quality and safety of care. There are also continuing uncertainties about how best to promote it, particularly when resources are increasing rapidly. If competition is to be the major mechanism in the future, how will anti-competitive behaviours be regulated and by whom? And how can the adverse political and social effects of competition be instigated?

These brief thoughts on the challenges ahead may or may not turn out to be good predictions. What is certain is that the analytical agenda for economists and operational researchers in the Department of Health over the next 20 years will be at least as exciting as that over the last two decades. In one critical way it will be much more important. In 1984 the EOR was advising on a health budget that accounted for barely one-twentieth of national income. On the Wanless scenarios by 2024 it (or its analytical successor) is likely to be advising on a public budget that takes at least one-tenth of national income.

References

1 Boyne GA *et al.* (2003) *Evaluating Public Management Reform.* Open University Press, Buckingham.

2 *See*, for example Audit Commission (1996) *What the Doctor Ordered: a study of GP fundholding in England and Wales.* Audit Commission, London.

3 Audit Commission (2002) *Data Remember: improving the quality of patient-based information.* Audit commission, London.

4 Commission for Health Improvement (2004) *What CHI has Found in Acute Services.* Commission for Health Improvement, London.

5 Department of Health (1997) *The New NHS: modern, dependable.* The Stationery Office, London.

6 National Institute for Clinical Excellence (2004) *Improving Outcomes in Colorectal Cancer: Manual Update.* National Institute for Clinical Excellence, London.

7 *See*: www.nbocap.org.uk/docs/report2004.pdf Accessed 21 June 2005.

8 Wanless D (2004) *Securing Good Health for the Whole Population. Final report.* The Stationery Office, London.

9 Howlett M and Ramesh M (1995) *Studying Public Policy: policy cycles and policy sub-systems.* Oxford University Press, Oxford.

10 This thinking drew heavily on Kantor R (1989) *When Giants First Learn to Dance: mastering the challenge of strategy, management and careers in the 1990s.* Simon and Schuster, New York.

11 Kingdon JW (1984) *Agenda, Alternatives and Public Policies.* Harper College, Boston, MA.

12 HM Treasury (2003) *The Green Book. Appraisal and evaluation in central government.* HM Treasury, London.

13 Productivity and Innovation Unit, Cabinet Office (2000) *Adding It Up: analysis and modelling in central government.* Cabinet Office, London.

14 *See*, for example, Forester J (1984) Bounded rationality and the politics of muddling through. *Public Admin Rev.* **44**: 28–31.

Index